'This man has, I repeat, no place in a community whose basic principles he flouts without compunction . . .'. I tried to explain that it was because of the sun, but I was only too conscious that it sounded nonsensical . . . I explained that I didn't believe in God . . . I told him that I wasn't conscious of any 'sin'; all I knew was that I'd been guilty of a criminal offence . . .

In Camus's *The Outsider,* Meursault's struggle with authenticity leads to his being judged more than just a criminal. Other fictional heroes, or anti-heroes, have been created by philosophers to explore certain ideas or theories: like Meursault, Kierkegaard's Abraham, Nietzsche's Zarathustra and Sartre's Mathieu all embody the contradictions of trying to live outside society's accepted norms.

Jacob Golomb's *In Search of Authenticity* examines these characters in his analysis of the ethics of authenticity. His own passionate commitment to the quest for such an ideal is clearly evident in his writing. Golomb is particularly concerned that postmodernism devalues the subjectivity and pathos that inextricably link an individual's search for authenticity. He argues that this search is now all the more pertinent and relevant when set against the general disillusionment characterizing the mood of the late twentieth century.

In Search of Authenticity provides invaluable insight into the heroes and anti-heroes of the great Continental philosophers. Like them it marries philosophy and literature by looking at the rational model of ethics compared with the romantic ideal of authenticity. Consequently, it will prove vital reading for students of both philosophy and literature.

Jacob Golomb is Senior Lecturer in Philosophy at The Hebrew University of Jerusalem. He is author of *Nietzsche's Enticing Philosophy of Power* (1989) and *Introduction to the Philosophies of Existence* (1990)

**PROBLEMS OF
MODERN EUROPEAN THOUGHT**

Series Editors
Alan Montefiore
Jonathan Rée
Jean-Jacques Lecercle

Also published in the series:

Situation and Human Existence
Freedom, Subjectivity and Society
Sonia Kruks

Philosophy at the Limit
David Wood

Poetics of Imagining
Richard Kearney

IN SEARCH OF AUTHENTICITY

From Kierkegaard to Camus

JACOB GOLOMB

London and New York

1 1995
ge
ndon EC4P 4EE

the USA and Canada
by Routledge
29 West 35th Street, New York, NY 10001

© 1995 Jacob Golomb

Phototypeset in Garamond by Intype, London
Printed and bound in Great Britain by
T J Press Ltd, Padstow, Cornwall

British Library Cataloguing in Publication Data
A catalogue record for this book is available from the British Library

Library of Congress Cataloging in Publication Data
Golomb, Jacob
In search of authenticity / Jacob Golomb.
p.   cm.—(Problems of modern European thought)
Includes bibliographical references (p.   ) and index.
ISBN 0–415–11946–4—ISBN 0–415–11947–2 (pbk.)
1. Authenticity (Philosophy)   2. Existential ethics.   I. Title.
II. Series.
B105.A8G65   1995
179′.9–dc20   94–43130
CIP

ISBN 0–415–11946–4 (hbk)
ISBN 0–415–11947–2 (pbk)

This book is dedicated to my daughter Orianne, in the hope that, having been born an individual, she will not turn into a copy.

Contents

Editors' foreword

During most of the twentieth century, philosophers in the English-speaking world have had only partial and fleeting glimpses of the work of their counterparts in continental Europe. In the main, English-language philosophy has been dominated by the exacting ideals of conceptual analysis and even of formal logic, while 'Continental philosophy' has ventured into extensive substantive discussions of literary, historical, psychoanalytic and political themes. With relatively few exceptions, the relations between the two traditions have been largely uncomprehending and hostile.

In recent years, however, Continental writers such as Heidegger, Adorno, Sartre, de Beauvoir, Habermas, Foucault, Althusser, Lacan and Derrida have been widely read in English translation, setting the terms of theoretical debate in such fields as literature, social theory, cultural studies, Marxism and feminism. The suspicions of the analytical philosophers have not, however, been pacified; and the import of such Continental philosophy has mostly been isolated from original philosophical work in English.

The PROBLEMS OF MODERN EUROPEAN THOUGHT series is intended to help break down this isolation. The books in the series will be original philosophical essays in their own right, from authors familiar with the procedures of analytical philosophy. Each book will present a well-defined range of themes from Continental philosophy, and will presuppose little, if any, formal philosophical training of its readers.

Alan Montefiore
Jonathan Rée
Jean-Jacques Lecercle

Acknowledgements

As in other matters that concern authenticity, this book is a product of personal pathos as well as fruitful interaction with others. The space is insufficient to mention all those who contributed, but the most significant assistance was generously provided me by the following: Alan Montefiore, who trusted me to do the job; Jonathan Rée, whose patience, encouragement and many helpful suggestions made his maieutic role invaluable; and Eva Shorr, who read some chapters. Special thanks to Nessa Olshansky-Asthar, whose meticulous linguistic editing has made this book readable.

I also wish to express my gratitude to the S. H. Bergman Center for Philosophical Studies of the Hebrew University of Jerusalem, for its financial support, and to the *Thyssen Stiftung* for enabling me to visit the Nietzsche and Heidegger archives. Finally, I wish to thank the editors of *Philosophy Today* and *The International Journal for the Philosophy of Religion*, where earlier versions of the chapters on Nietzsche and Kierkegaard were published.

To them, and to the many others who were part of this journey, I can only say that I have tried my best to be worthy of the trust placed in me.

Introduction

> I have not found any reliable example of the knight of faith. . . . Here he is. . . . I clasp my hands and say half aloud, 'Good Lord, is this the man? . . . Why he looks like a tax-collector!' . . . He tends to his work. . . . Toward evening he walks home, his gait is as indefatigable as that of the postman. On his way he reflects that his wife has surely a special little warm dish prepared for him. . . . He lives as carefree as a ne'er-do-well, and yet . . . he does not do the least thing except by virtue of the absurd. . . . what a tremendous paradox faith is, a paradox which is capable of transforming a murder into a holy act well-pleasing to God, a paradox which gives Isaac back to Abraham, which no thought can master, because faith begins precisely there where thinking leaves off . . . The ethical expression for what Abraham did is, that he would murder Isaac; the religious expression is, that he would sacrifice Isaac . . . This contradiction consists the dread which can well make a man sleepless, and yet Abraham is not what he is without this dread.[1]

This is the first fictional description in modern philosophical literature of an authentic hero and the problematics such a hero entails. Unable to point to any historical figure who could be objectively judged an authentic individual, Kierkegaard used the Biblical (or mythological) figure of Abraham to exemplify authentic faith.

Nietzsche, too, unable to come up with any historical example of an authentic hero, or *Übermensch*, instead portrays the fictional figure of Zarathustra:

> When Zarathustra was thirty years old he left his home and the lake of his home and went into the mountains. Here he enjoyed his spirit and his solitude, and for ten years did not tire of it. But at last a change came over his heart, and one morning he rose with the dawn, stepped before the sun, and spoke to it thus:
> 'You great star, what would your happiness be had you not those

1

for whom you shine? . . . I must descend to the depths, as you do in the evening' . . .

Human existence is uncanny and still without meaning. . . . I will teach men the meaning of their existence – the overman. . . .

Like the sun, Zarathustra too wants to go under; now he sits and waits, surrounded by broken old tablets and new tablets half covered with writing. Behold, here is a new tablet. . . . Man is something that must be overcome. . . . God died: now we want the overman to live.[2]

More recent work by existentialist philosophers also makes much use of fictive portraits, biographies and diaries of heroes of authenticity. Sartre's hero in *Road to Freedom* is depicted as follows:

Mathieu stiffened, and threw an agonised look at the driver's back: all his freedom had come back on him once more. 'No', he thought, 'no, it isn't heads and tails. Whatever happens, it is by *my agency* that everything must happen.' . . . Even if he let himself be carried off like an old sack of coal, he would have chosen his own damnation: he was free, free in every way, free to behave like a fool or a machine, free to accept, free to refuse, free to equivocate: to marry, to give up the game, to drag this dead weight about with him for years to come. He could do what he liked, no one had the right to advise him, there would be for him no Good nor Evil unless he brought them into being. . . . He was alone, enveloped in this monstrous silence, free and alone, without assistance and without excuse, condemned to decide without support from any quarter, condemned for ever to be free.[3]

In Sartre's play *The Flies*, which is in large part a debate between God (Jupiter) and Man (Orestes), the latter proclaims defiantly:

Alien to myself, I know it. Outside of nature, against nature, without excuse, without recourse save myself. But I shall not return under your law; I'm condemned to have no other law but my own. Nor shall I return to nature, where a thousand paths are marked out, all leading up to you. I can only follow my own path. For I'm a man . . . and each man must find his own way.[4]

Sartre's fellow-thinker, and later his ideological antagonist, Camus, presents his own hero of authenticity in *The Outsider*:

Every nerve in my body was a steel spring, and my grip closed on the revolver. The trigger gave, and the smooth underbelly of the butt jogged my palm. . . . I fired four shots more into the inert body, on which they left no visible trace. And each successive shot was another loud, fateful rap on the door of my undoing. . . . The prosecutor paused again, to wipe the sweat off his face: 'This man has, I repeat, no place in a community whose basic principles he flouts without compunction. . . .' I tried to explain that it was because of the sun, but I was only too conscious that it sounded nonsensical. . . . I explained that I didn't believe in God. . . . I told him that I wasn't conscious of any 'sin'; all I knew was that I'd been guilty of a criminal offence. . . . I laid my heart open to the benign indifference of the universe. To feel it so like myself, indeed so brotherly, made me realize that I'd been happy, and that I was happy still.[5]

The thematic connection between these heroes is their wish to transcend their social and ethical predicaments and achieve authentic modes of living. Not content with being the heroes and heroines of their life-stories, they strive to write these stories themselves. They want to attain authenticity by being faithful to scripts they have written for themselves.

But even the concept of 'heroes of authenticity' is problematic, since a hero is one admired for outstanding achievements and noble qualities which reflect the prevalent values of his community, or what I shall call the prevailing 'ethos'. Yet one of the main characteristics of these 'heroes' is their desperate attempt to transcend this ethos and attain a personal and subjective pathos (in terms of a particular experience, feeling or sentiment) which expresses their individuality as human beings who become what they singularly are. 'Anti-heroes' may be a better term for these characters.

The quest for authenticity becomes especially pronounced in extreme situations. These include not only personal and external crises, but also significant social and historical crises such as that arising from the decline of the powerful and long-enduring ethos of objectivity, rationality and enlightenment. Using Nietzsche's terms, this era of the 'twilight of the idols' and the 'death of God' reopens the issues of personal identity and meaning frequently referred to as central dilemmas of the postmodern world. However, the 'sun' which inspires Zarathustra to 'descend to the depths' in order to entice people into becoming authentic, is the same sun that blinds Meursault and provokes him to commit murder. Thus the crucial question is whether

Dostoevsky's dictum 'were there no God, everything would be permitted' is relevant in the context of authenticity.

Our story of these unusual heroes will start with Abraham, the authentic 'knight of faith' who lives 'within the religious sphere'. It is God who prevents him from becoming a criminal, from murdering his son Isaac. By virtue of his passionate and absurd belief, Abraham becomes the first modern hero of authenticity. Our story ends, however, with another kind of hero – almost the antithesis of Abraham – Meursault, the non-believer in Camus's *Outsider*, who is 'guilty of a criminal offence'. He is, indeed, a murderer, whose attempt to live authentically leads to the guillotine. In Meursault's strictly immanent world there is no God, no supernatural agency, no universal reason to keep one from becoming a criminal, a moral 'outsider'. These heroes illustrate the dilemmas and critical questions I grapple with here: is there no middle ground between the 'inhuman monster wholly without moral sense', as the prosecutor calls Meursault,[6] and the religious knight of faith? Can authenticity be a viable ethical norm? Can its 'heroes' find a place in a community? Or is it a romantic ideal, an immature protest against the levelling processes of the unidimensional objectivity that dominates our modern, excessively technological civilization? If the latter is indeed the case, why bother at all? What is the point of the enormous effort made by so many serious European thinkers to provoke us into embracing authenticity, if there seems to be little chance that it can be realized? Must we be content with postulating authenticity as an ideal to aspire to rather than a viable social norm – an ideal that is nevertheless necessary if we are to become what we are given a cultural and social context that undermines this authentic selfhood?

Before reaching any conclusions about authenticity and ethics, I use the first two chapters of this book to point to certain motifs and problems inherent in any attempt to analyse authenticity; then, in the remaining chapters, I explore in chronological order the most important of these attempts, by way of examining their philosophical and literary manifestations.

Yet the question 'Why bother at all?' can also be posed regarding this study, and may well concern its potential readers, given that today the ideal of existential authenticity is out of fashion not only among analytic philosophers (who have, of course, never been keen on it) but also in other traditions. I witnessed this disparagement of authenticity at first hand in 1987, while attending a lecture on 'False Emotions' by a well-known philosopher in Oxford. After the lecture, I questioned the legitimacy of the distinction between authentic and inauthentic emotions; to which he replied that he had no interest in the 'crazy notions of Continental philosophy'. It is hardly surprising that it is unfashionable to speak of authenticity today. It is nonetheless surprising that this notion was so fashionable in the 1950s, for fashion and authenticity are virtually antithetical: the former by definition an expression of the current ethos; the latter the rallying-cry of those who would overcome it. But is authenticity really such a 'crazy' notion? Is the century-long European involvement with it merely an obsession with a vague Romantic ideal? Has it nothing important and relevant to teach us? This book attempts to provide some answers, or at least call into question the view that authenticity is a 'crazy' notion best set aside by responsible philosophers. If authenticity is madness, we should all be a little crazy in order to become what we cherish most: our own true selves.

There is no difficulty in understanding the terms 'authentic' and 'authenticity' as they are used in everyday language. Those unsure as to their precise meanings can consult any dictionary. In the *OED*, for example, 'authentic' is defined as something 'first-hand, original as opposed to copied', something 'real, actual, genuine as opposed to imaginary, pretended'. Examples usually refer to genuine documents and works of art 'as opposed to counterfeit [items]' or those of disputed origin.

Indeed, with regard to works of art, documents and archaeological finds, this is the principal use of the term. It presupposes the existence of a genuine and original product, to be contrasted with potential copies and forgeries. But is it wise to adopt a model from art and apply it to human life and human selves? Who is the legitimate prototype, the paradigm of authenticity? The eighteenth-century poet Edward Young provided one paradoxical answer: 'Born originals, how comes it to pass that we die copies?' Yet surely babies are hardly models of authenticity. The philosophical understanding of 'authenticity' is far more complex than its everyday use suggests.

Notes

1 Søren Kierkegaard, *Fear and Trembling*, trans. W. Lowrie (Princeton, NJ: Princeton University Press, 1941), pp. 41, 49, 50–1, 64.

2 'Thus Spoke Zarathustra', in *The Portable Nietzsche*, ed. and trans. W. Kaufmann (New York: Viking, 1954), pp. 121–2, 132, 310–11, 399.

3 J.-P. Sartre, *The Age of Reason*, trans. E. Sutton (Harmondsworth: Penguin, 1986), pp. 242–3.

4 As cited in *The Philosophy of Jean-Paul Sartre*, ed. R. D. Cummings (New York: Vintage, 1965), p. 240.

5 Albert Camus, *The Outsider*, trans. S. Gilbert (Harmondsworth: Penguin, 1961), pp. 64, 102–3, 114, 116, 120.

6 Ibid., p. 97.

1

Authenticity, sincerity and honesty

The term 'authenticity' is used in so many different contexts that it may very well resist definition. Yet the most significant difficulty that arises in attempting to define it lies in the philosophical nature of its meaning. Even to speak of 'the nature of its meaning' is misleading, since it implies a kind of essentialism, a perspective of objectivity which is foreign to authenticity. As Sartre pointed out, authenticity does not denote 'objective qualities' such as those associated with the notions of sincerity and honesty, qualities one predicates of 'the person' in the same way one asserts, for instance, that 'the table is round or square'.[1] The notion of authenticity, it seems, signifies something beyond the domain of objective language, while the notions of sincerity and honesty have to do with attributes to which language can refer directly.

This feeling is strengthened by reading *Being and Nothingness*, where Sartre describes 'human reality' as 'being which is what it is not and which is not what it is'.[2] This idea, and his insistence that authenticity is something we are aware of when 'we flee it',[3] suggest that authenticity is a negative term. Its presence is discerned in its absence, in the passionate search for it, in inauthenticity and in various acts of 'bad faith' (*mauvaise foi*). The latter are described far more extensively in Sartre's writings than are the authentic modes.

The works of other existentialist writers manifest a similar disproportion between those that directly address authenticity itself and those that critique societal values and inauthentic modes of living. Nietzsche, for example, devotes relatively little space to describing his ideal *Übermensch* and never points to a concrete historical figure who exemplifies it. The same is true of Kierkegaard and Camus. All agree in principle that any positive definition of authenticity would be self-nullifying.

7

The existentialist writers hope to shatter our dogmatic beliefs and lure us into giving up blindly accepted ethical norms and ideologies. Only when we successfully shed these values that we have been conditioned to uphold by various institutions – our families, schools and universities – will we be able to reach beyond them to the genuine roots of our selves and ultimately attain authenticity. The unnecessary information we have collected during our lifetimes, the 'facts' postulated as an integral part of the ethos of objectivity fostered by society and its institutions, are inapplicable to the sphere of human existence in which one struggles for one's self. There, in their stead, the notion of authenticity emerges.

The indirect approach to understanding the notion of authenticity, akin to the theological *via negativa*, is also reflected in the *OED*, where the term 'authentic' is defined largely by its antonyms. Given this elusive nature, we may be better off approaching the notion of authenticity by attempting to distinguish it from the kindred terms of sincerity and honesty.

I

In *Sincerity and Authenticity*, Lionel Trilling defines sincerity as 'the state or quality of the self which refers primarily to a congruence between avowal and actual feeling'. He goes on to claim that one of the main criteria of sincerity is 'the degree of correspondence between the principle avowed by a society and its actual conduct'.[4] Thus for Trilling the term 'sincerity' is used for the self as manifested in the social domain. Sincerity can be objectively tested – for example, by checking whether outward behaviour is consistent with public declarations. 'Sincere' in this sense is synonymous with 'true' and 'honest'. All three of these concepts are foreign to the idea of authentic life as understood by the existentialist writers. For them, the notion of authenticity expresses, among other things, revolt against the traditional conception of truth and the ideal of sincerity derived from it.[5] Authenticity resides neither in the external correspondence of sentences to what they refer to, nor in the internal coherence of various statements. This, in fact, is the heart of the existentialist revolution: the eclipse of 'truth' by 'truthfulness', the transition from objective sincerity to personal authenticity.

The terms 'sincerity' and 'honesty' are applicable to an individual whose inner convictions and commitments are congruent with that individual's behaviour. As such, they differ from 'authenticity', which cannot be said to apply to any such correspondence, since correspondence presumes a static subject, while authenticity requires an incessant movement of becoming, self-transcendence and self-creation. It calls for no particular contents or consequences but, rather, focuses on the origins and the intensity of one's emotional–existential commitments, on what Kierkegaard calls 'subjective inwardness' and Sartre 'engagement'.

However, the existentialists' reservations about sincerity and honesty are in no way similar to Hegel's[6] and stem from different considerations. In *Phenomenology of Spirit*, Hegel criticizes the 'honest individual'. The notions of honesty and sincerity in a given historical period, he argues, exemplify submission to the prevailing morality and nullify the urge of the Spirit to escape the conditions which circumscribe it and to assume an existence of complete freedom determined by itself alone. Since the Spirit is always undergoing the dialectical movement of unfolding itself in history, there is an inherent tension between the agent, as the vehicle of this development, and 'the honest individual' who 'takes each moment to be an abiding essentiality'[7] and derives his or her identity from the prevailing *Sittlichkeit* – the ethos based on current social, legal and cultural institutions. The rational essence of any individual, according to Hegel, can be adequately actualized only within the framework of a state organized so that its citizens and its social and cultural institutions coexist harmoniously. Since such a state is as yet just an unactualized idea in the practical realm of Spirit, those who conform to society by internalizing the prevailing ethic are actually subjecting themselves to a framework devoid of comprehensive rationality. And since social conformity is inconsistent with disbelief in the rationality and moral validity of society, such 'honest individuals' suffer from self-alienation, a state characterized by double standards and conflicting norms.

On Hegel's analysis, the 'honest individual' is actually a hypocrite lacking real freedom. For Hegel, the absolute rationality which will be fully realized with the end of history will bring with it total freedom, but this freedom is far removed from that aspired to by the thinkers on authenticity. For them, freedom consists in negating the current ethic, in overcoming the demands of one's personal history by not defining oneself according to present or future historical predicaments. Rejec-

9

tion of the ethos of 'the honest individual' makes way for the pathos of authenticity.

Authenticity and sincerity are thus fundamentally opposed and should not be regarded as equivalent or synonymous.[8] Trilling maintains that authenticity is 'a more strenuous moral experience than "sincerity", a more exigent conception of the self and of what being true to it consists in, a wider reference to the universe and man's place in it, and a less acceptant and genial view of the social circumstances of life'. The distinction, however, is not merely a quantitative one. As Trilling notes, 'much that culture traditionally condemned and sought to exclude is accorded a considerable moral authority by reason of the authenticity claimed for it, e.g., disorder, violence, unreason'.[9] But authenticity is not a 'moral authority', for it is contrary to the nature of authenticity to tell others what to do. Though the term is indeed derived from *auctoritas*, the authority in question is self-directed – it is the mastery of one who freely creates the pathos of authenticity and strives to express and live it in the everyday.

II

David Hume is one of those who use the term 'authenticity' in the sense of genuineness, of things being what they profess in origin or authorship.[10] But Hume did not apply this notion to the concept of the self, arguing that the term 'self' is a meaningless metaphysical obfuscation denoting an allegedly permanent entity that is in fact no more than a bundle of impressions and ideas to which we mistakenly ascribe an identity.

In reaction to Hume, certain German philosophers sought to restore the metaphysical validity of the self. Kant introduces the 'transcendental Ego' to shift the focus away from the individual or 'empirical Ego'. He transfers God's creative functions to human beings, who, as transcendental Egos, create the whole knowable world, including their empirical Egos, around themselves. This move cleared the way for the self-creation of one's selfhood – for authenticity. Nietzsche, Sartre and Camus soon follow with their claims of the death of God and their demands that all individuals adopt for themselves the God-like role of being the originator of their own selves. As the theory of the 'pre-established harmony' between our thoughts and reality, guaranteed by God, fell into disfavour, that of the self-creation of the self gained popularity. The proponents of authenticity took the opportunity to have us become God.

Like Kant's transcendental Ego, the notion of authenticity is formal: it too focuses on the origin of creativity and spontaneity, on 'how' rather than 'what'. It is also formal in the sense of the categorical imperative. No less than the Kantian conception of the morally autonomous human agent, the concept of authenticity is a protest against the blind, mechanical acceptance of an externally imposed code of values. The existentialist thinkers' preoccupation with origin and genealogy, then, is largely a product of the Kantian outlook. Yet the Kantian perspective evokes a kind of 'transcendental pretence'.[11] The transcendental Ego, construed as supra-personal, leads ultimately to a destructive collapse of all individual selves into an abstract universal Self.[12] The existentialist revolt should thus be seen as an attempt to counteract this tendency, to call us back to our all-too-human but none the less authentic sense of self.

The concept of 'self' denotes that which one intrinsically is. However, this being, according to thinkers on authenticity, is not a fixed entity or abstract essence, but an existence that precedes any essence and determination. Thus, existentialism rejects the traditional ontological notion of the subject, the grandiose metaphysical idea of the Absolute or Universal Self. Hume himself encouraged this rejection by fostering a profound confidence in human emotions. In contradistinction to Kant's rational ethics and unqualified faith in reason, Hume argued: 'Reason is and ought to be the slave of the passions',[13] thereby strengthening the claim of pathos to be a legitimate constitutive element of the self.

Further, Hume's notion of the self as a 'bundle of impressions' conceived of the individual as chaotic raw material which one's creativity could organize and mould without any ontological constraints. The Humean individual lacks the ontological rigidity and fixedness of an a priori essence and is therefore more amenable to self-creation, providing one is in control of these impressions. Once ordered, they become a set of expressions which transform the self into an aggregate of sentiments and life-pathos, of 'true pathos of every period of our life'.[14] This conception of pathos as an experience, feeling or sentiment of a particular individual, as a sensual feeling of one's own authentic self in its emotional richness, requires no definite ontological status or metaphysical aggrandizement.

The Continental existentialists' revolt against Western metaphysics, however, does not deny its history. To invert values, to revise, one must have a good command of the original versions and dogmas against which one is reacting. The thinkers of authenticity, though seeking to replace conventional concepts of truth, retain certain traditional motifs. Thus, for example, when Sartre succumbs to the temptation to define authenticity despite the essential impossibility of such a definition, he is simply regressing to the traditional concept of truth as correspondence:

> Authenticity consists in having a true and lucid consciousness of the situation, in assuming the responsibilities and risks that it involves, in accepting it in pride or humiliation, sometimes in horror and hate.[15]

Another example is the ideal of coherence, which reappears as a whole, congruent and harmonious personality in the existentialist quest for *individuum*, which rejects any symptom of *dividuum* within one's authentic self. They thus oppose those components of the prevailing social ethos that, when internalized, prevent one from attaining this ideal inner harmony and simplicity.

III

The notions of honesty and sincerity can be defined as congruence between one's inclinations and the prevailing ethos, or as congruence between one's behaviour and one's innermost essence.[16] Authenticity, however, is not in keeping with such a definition. Not only does it deny any rigid a priori essence, but it also rejects any intrinsic value in compliance with a given set of standards. It regards any such compliance as flight from one's responsibility for freely forming one's selfhood. Authenticity defines itself as lacking any definition. It is a pathos of incessant change, as opposed to a passive subordination to one particular ethic.

This explains why the rise of philosophies of authenticity took place during a period when the prevailing ethos was a target of scepticism and ceased to function as an unchallenged authority. The birth of authenticity is rooted in revolution, or at least in the transfiguration of all prevailing social values and institutions, including those of Judaeo-Christian culture. Congruence – the essence of sincerity – is not viable at such a time. One is left to one's own devices, to one's lonely self, and this selfhood must suffice to provide everything previously supplied by various cultural and social institutions. One is now obliged to create values and patterns of behaviour from one's own mental resources. Here I am not just speaking of the disruption of a given ethos and the disintegration of society and authority, but of something far more traumatic: the death of the highest sanction and the absolute guarantee of our values – the death of God. The almost universal belief in God, which has in the West for two millennia sustained a single dominant ethic with minor variations, is now badly shaken. It is a time when, in Nietzsche's words, one 'would sooner have the void for his purpose than be void of purpose'. This vacuum, where humanity is left without any 'pillars of fire' to guide its way, is the cultural and intellectual background for the emergence of the search for authenticity.

The failure of congruence is a condition for the emergence of authenticity in another sense as well. Ethical 'oughts' are never fully actualized: there is always a gap between the declared ideals and values of a society and its actual conduct. The question is how to respond to this unbridgeable gap between theory and practice? Several responses are possible. There is the response of the honest individual who, despite his awareness of this gap, complacently conforms to the 'ought' of the prevalent ethic. There is the opportunistic reaction of conforming to the 'is', and the nihilistic rejection of both 'ought' and 'is' hinted at in Nietzsche's above-quoted statement. There is the Romantic search for another 'ought' and, finally, the authentic response of being true to the project of forming one's own self, which entails reluctance to conform to any external 'is' or 'ought' or to seek some transcendental 'ought'.

To heighten the differences between authenticity, honesty and opportunism I want to have a brief look at the hero of Denis Diderot's *Rameau's Nephew*, a literary figure wrongly regarded by some, under the influence of Hegel, as exemplifying authenticity. Moreover, though I said that a climate of revolution is most conducive to the emergence of the cry for authenticity, not all historical revolutions did give rise to this ideal. The French Revolution is a case in point.

IV

Written in 1762, *Rameau's Nephew* is a bitter satire in which Diderot describes an imaginary dialogue between two characters. The first is Diderot himself, depicted as an honest soul who believes in bourgeois virtues: 'we ought all to behave like decent people . . . fill a position in society and carry out its duties'.[17] The second is a fictional nephew of the French composer Rameau. They discuss, among other things, the dilemmas of an immoral society, in which sincerity is not necessarily the best policy, and honesty is not thought worthy of respect.

In contrast to the honest philosopher, who sticks to certain humanistic values like 'the good, the true, the beautiful', Diderot presents the bohemian 'parasite and buffoon' who, aware of society's deceitfulness and hypocrisy, adopts an opportunistic attitude. The decent philosopher is 'completely bewildered by this alliance of so much cleverness and so much baseness, by this torrent of alternately true and false ideas, by such a total perversion of right feeling, by such utter turpitude and so rare a candour' (p. 125). However, he is strongly attracted to this 'eccentric' character, who 'provides such a contrast to the normal run of people', because he makes 'a change from the tedious uniformity that our upbringing, our social conventions and our habitual propriety have imposed on us', and because he 'brings out the truth; he makes you see who the decent people are; he unmasks the rogues' (p. 115).

This outsider 'unmasks' the double standards of bourgeois society and sets out to live in accordance with its operative norms, as expressed in such maxims as 'Gold is everything' and 'you can't dishonour yourself if you're rich, whatever you do' (p. 134). Rameau's nephew turns these implicit norms into explicit rules of everyday conduct, and proclaims:

It would be very eccentric and stupid of me if I refused to conform. Oh, I know perfectly well that if you go and apply certain general principles to these things, dragged in from this morality they all talk about and never practise, well of course everything that's black turns out to be white and everything white becomes black.

(p. 130)

This candid beggar unmasks the comedy of a social order which has lost all moral validity and legitimacy in the daily lives of people who 'are all extremely honest . . . yet there is not one of them whose conduct does not depart in some particulars from the general principles of morality and is not full of moral idioms' (ibid.). By this candour, this courageous exposure of what society does but never speaks of, Rameau's nephew acquires uprightness and dignity. Proud of his intellectual integrity, he is aware that by unmasking hypocrisy and corruption he can escape it. His consciousness, in Hegel's words, 'derides existence and the universal confusion, and derides its own self as well',[18] yet in this world of pretence, the one who is not pretending – Rameau's nephew – is the genuine 'honest individual'. By pointing to the negative and calling black things 'black', he is acting positively, and hence is more deserving of our esteem than Diderot the *philosophe*, with his obsolete ethic of honesty which affords unambiguous self-definition but only within an existential void. Rameau's nephew has no definite self to be true to, but only a disintegrated and confused consciousness; yet he represents the sincere individual who is 'not a hypocrite', and therefore commands respect: 'He was merely being more honest, more willing to face facts, and occasionally profound in his depravity' (p. 139). Hegel concurs, describing the 'disrupted consciousness' as manifesting 'the greatest truth'.[19] Rameau's nephew has a disintegrated self because he has consciously internalized society's double standard – the disparity between the practical 'is' and the theoretical 'ought' – but feels alienated from this divided ethic, whose division is its 'greatest truth'. We have to ask ourselves, however, whether the opportunistic and estranged character of Rameau's nephew exemplifies authenticity.

The opportunism of Rameau's nephew lies in the fact that he reacts to the double standards by adopting the prevailing 'is' as his declared 'ought' and living accordingly. In so doing he is merely responding to circumstances and is thus no less dependent upon them than the 'honest individual' who tries to live according to the public ethos. He even attempts to find his place 'among wealthy robbers' (p. 137) and conforms to their unwritten standards by deliberately manipulating the gap between 'is' and 'ought' to his own advantage. This conformity engenders a degree of coherence since it minimizes the conflict between one's inner convictions and the public ethic.

Thus if honesty indeed consists in correspondence to a prevailing ethic, Diderot is right to judge Rameau's nephew as 'more honest' than his seemingly upright contemporaries. But he is not yet an authentic hero, for the authentic hero is active rather than reactive, wielding, as we shall see in the next chapter, constructive and creative irony rather than destructive and opportunistic cynicism.

Notes

1 J.-P. Sartre, *Being and Nothingness*, trans. H. E. Barnes (London: Methuen, 1957), p. 55. Sartre would regard the attempt to construe authenticity as an objective quality as a clear example of 'the spirit of seriousness' and 'bad faith'.
2 Ibid., p. 58.
3 From Sartre's preface to N. Sarraute, *Portrait of a Man Unknown*, trans. Maria Jolas (New York: George Braziller, 1958).
4 Lionel Trilling, *Sincerity and Authenticity* (London: Oxford University Press, 1972), pp. 2, 27.
5 Before this revolt in Western philosophy, there was a tendency to confuse authenticity with sincerity:

> This above all - to thine own self be true,
> And it must follow, as the night the day,
> Thou canst not then be false to any man.
> (*Hamlet*, II.iii.77-9)

Later writers, however, imply that authenticity at times may encompass insincere behaviour, lies and dishonesty - witness Mathieu's relations with his girlfriend Marcelle in Sartre's *The Age of Reason* after she tells him of her pregnancy.
6 As Trilling, *Sincerity and Authenticity*, believes.
7 G. W. F. Hegel, *Phenomenology of Spirit*, trans. A. V. Miller (Oxford: Clarendon Press, 1979), p. 317.
8 R. G. Olson, e.g., fails to distinguish between Sartre's notion of inauthenticity and the concept of insincerity, in his 'Sincerity and the moral life', *Ethics*, 68 (1957/8), pp. 260-80. He disregards Sartre's assertion in *Being and Nothingness* (p. 63) that 'sincerity' is 'precisely a phenomenon of bad faith' and as such cannot be identical with authenticity.
9 Trilling, *Sincerity and Authenticity*, p. 10.
10 'I am not surprised to find ... that Mr. Gray should have entertained suspicions with regard to the authenticity of these fragments of our Highland poetry', *The Letters of David Hume*, ed. J. Y. T. Greig (Oxford: Clarendon Press, 1932), p. 328 (letter 176, dated 16 August 1760).
11 Cf. R. C. Solomon, *Continental Philosophy since 1750* (London: Oxford University Press, 1988), pp. 1-15.
12 Thus, e.g., against Fichte's world-encompassing Self, Heine remarked: 'Himself as everything! How does Mrs. Fichte put up with it?!', *Religion and Philosophy in Germany*, trans. J. Snodgrass (London: K. Paul, Trench and Trübner, 1981) p. 137.

13 *A Treatise of Human Nature* (Oxford University Press, 1951), p. 451.
14 Nietzsche, *The Gay Science*, para. 317; and cf. its poetic definition in the introduction to Sarraute's *L'Etre du soupon: Essais sur le roman* (Paris: Gallimard, 1956).
15 Sartre, *Anti-Semite and Jew*, trans. G. J. Becker (New York: Schocken, 1965), p. 90.
16 Cf. D. Wood, 'Honesty', in *Philosophy and Personal Relations*, ed. A. Montefiore (London: Routledge, 1973), pp. 191–223.
17 *Diderot's Selected Writings*, ed. L. G. Crocker, trans. D. Coltman (London: Collier-Macmillan, 1966), pp. 136, 134.
18 Hegel, *Phenomenology of Spirit*, p. 319.
19 Ibid., p. 317.

2

Authenticity, literature and irony

Arguing for authenticity is self-defeating in that it presupposes the authority of rationality and objectivity, which is called into question by this ideal. Since one cannot argue rationally for adopting authentic life, one must be satisfied with the subtle enticement of the reader. But how can someone be enticed into authenticity? Through descriptions of authentic lives? But how can an authentic subject or self be depicted? Indeed, the traditional ontological meanings of 'subject' and 'self' must themselves be rejected. And how is one to identify authentic patterns of living without appealing to normative criteria? Part of the solution lies in the use of literature as a medium for indirectly communicating about authenticity. Various literary styles are exploited to this didactic end, notably irony.

Almost half the writing of the most influential philosophers of authenticity take some form other than straight exposition. Even Heidegger, who did not write any literary fiction, made use of a variety of different literary genres, such as the lecture, the essay, the dialogue and poetry. Other proponents of authenticity experimented with such literary styles as short stories, novels, plays, poems, aphoristic essays, fictitious diaries, biographies and even autobiographies.

This is by no means a coincidence. Nor does it originate solely in the existentialists' dislike of systematic philosophy or disbelief in its 'scientific' status. It is true that Kierkegaard, Nietzsche, Heidegger, Sartre and Camus constantly changed their styles in an attempt to avoid any appearance of building a system. Most would endorse Nietzsche's confession: 'I mistrust all systematizers and I avoid them. The will to a system is a lack of integrity'.[1] It is also, one might add, a betrayal of personal authenticity, which eschews the protective ethos of objectivity. However, there are further and more profound reasons for the variety of literary forms used to promote authenticity. These reasons can be divided into two main groups: some have to do with the problems arising from the very attempt to explicate the notion of authenticity, while others have to do with the desire to achieve certain effects by writing indirectly.

I

The principal aim of writers on authenticity was to evoke in their readers the pathos of authenticity. They hoped to restore a personal mental power and sense of selfhood that modernity had diminished. Since they could not argue, they had to be satisfied with portraying the sublime and heroic patterns of authentic life. These portraits are intended to provoke us into creating genuine selves. Since, in matters of authenticity, the 'how' is more crucial than the 'what', literature is particularly helpful in engaging the reader's attention and provoking her to action, since it tempts the reader to follow the path of authenticity without making this aim explicit, and, more importantly, without defining authenticity.

The variety of literary styles that can be utilized indicates that there is no one exclusive and definitive path to authenticity – to be authentic means to invent one's *own* way and pattern of life. Here the concept of originality does not refer so much to the idea of *origin* as to undogmatic openness – or, to use Nietzsche's terminology, a 'horizon of infinite perspectives' from which the individual can survey his or her own life and mould it accordingly. Open-ended experiments with possible world-perspectives and literary styles are intended to serve as a firsthand example. The construction of possible worlds (and this does not refer solely to science fiction) frees literature, especially that of the narrative variety, from strictly realistic or referential constraints. This freedom allows for experimentation with notions, such as that of authenticity, that go beyond the conventional dichotomies of true/false, sincere/insincere, honest/dishonest, good/evil. It even permits, as the case of Heidegger shows, the coinage of new expressions and usages which undermine rigidly traditional modes of living and thinking. Only literature can produce and diffuse new senses so effectively. The literary pluralism of the writers of authenticity is, among other things, a solution to the problem of enticement via the perlocutionary effects of speech acts without relapsing into limited ontological and epistemological paradigms of communication. The existential predicaments and the pathos of authenticity that cannot be propositionally expressed still leave room for indirect communication: not of a 'what' but of a 'how'. By varying styles and rhetoric, we are invited to embrace authenticity, though not any particular content, for authentic expressions of self are in principle indefinite and infinite. Moreover, the writers of authenticity change their genres and styles to stress the fact that certain kinds of pathos originate *within themselves*. The variety of their styles is yet another expression of the revolt against the tradition of impersonal and detached objectivity, a constant reminder that we are reading *their* writings, the personal products of their own values and goals.

II

One can portray authentic forms of life, but one cannot justify them rationally. This is especially true of narrative fiction, where the texts do not assert the existence of authenticity but, rather, presuppose and reproduce it. Corresponding to these indirect means of communication are parallel means of undermining the literary portraits of authenticity. How does one refute or object to that which was never directly asserted or argued for? By the very means employed to introduce it – literature and irony. An illuminating example is John Barth's parody of Sartre's notion of authenticity, in which Barth uses narrative fiction, irony and satire to provoke us into rejecting the whole ideal as sheer nonsense. In particular, he juxtaposes caricatures of 'authentic' and 'inauthentic' characters, so grotesquely misrepresenting each mode that both are reduced to absurdity.[2]

In any case, the reader must rely solely on the narrator's descriptions in deciding whether or not the characters are authentic. Here lies another reason for the wide use of literature in dealing with authentic life; this has less to do with the intention to allure the reader and more with the external observer's inability to judge whether acts are genuine expressions of authenticity. As a writer of literary fiction, the philosopher is omnipresent and omniscient like the creating God. Through such writing, the reader can, as it were, enter the characters' innermost selves: the reader can participate in their intimate intentions, share their feelings and think their thoughts. Since authenticity and its various kinds of pathos belong, in principle, to the private domain of the individual, who alone can experience them, others can judge her only by some sort of 'privileged' access to her consciousness. Such privileged access can be gained through the creation of 'transparent' fictional characters.[3]

This accounts for the fact that many of the works in question use first-person narration and the present tense. Notable examples are Sartre's *Nausea* and Camus's *The Outsider*. Another example, Nietzsche's *On the Future of Our Cultural Institutions*, is less familiar. An exercise in story-telling, it uses first-person narrative technique at two levels: at one level, Nietzsche addresses an audience at the University of Basel; at another, Nietzsche is a high-school student describing events and conversations from his youth.

What is often referred to in literary theory as the author's point of view, namely, the specific mode in which the author or narrator presents the fictional world, is useful in discussing literary works on authenticity. The more information the author discloses about private events, such as his characters' feelings and thoughts, the more the author asserts himself as the omnipotent controller of the narration. Where the knower is also the creator, to know all is to be responsible for everything. To accept such responsibility without excuses, as creators should do, is to be authentic. This sense of responsibility is conveyed to us by the deliberate choice, on the part of the author, of the most intimate point of view. This is vividly expressed in attempts to write 'autobiographical' accounts of the search for true self. Thus, for example, the pivotal claim of Sartre's celebrated autobiography is 'Je n'avais pas de verité'; his story reveals his personal difficulties in attaining authenticity and living up to his 'verité solitaire'.[4] This gives him the credibility to urge us to keep trying ourselves.

Becoming what one is involves an incessant yet indefinite process which cannot be univocally characterized. It is an ever-present happening without any causally determining past or rationally defined future. The literature attempts to capture this process, as, for example, when the diary novels of Kierkegaard's 'Seducer' or Sartre's Roquentin or Camus's heroes provide us with this ever-presentness of the spontaneously lived life whose only passionate commitment is to the formation of its own unique authenticity. To write about this a-rational enterprise in a systematic manner – say, by using logic and the traditional expository style – would be self-defeating.

The problems associated with the evaluation of the authenticity of others also account for the interest in the biographies of literary or historical/intellectual figures. Nietzsche's 'Schopenhauer as Educator'

21

and Sartre's numerous biographies are intended, among other things, to assess the authenticity of these figures, our knowledge of whom came to us in the form of secondhand information: theoretical or literary studies, 'common-knowledge' facts about their lives, their own diaries, etc. All these attempts at evaluation end in a kind of Socratic *aporia*: no definite verdict can be reached. The futility of these biographical ventures motivated Kierkegaard, Nietzsche, Sartre and others to concentrate on fictional characters of authenticity, such as Abraham, the knight of faith, Zarathustra, etc. Only within the realm of fiction can we gain access to the elusive realm of the pathos of authenticity.

III

Narrative fiction is 'the narration of a succession of fictional events'.[5] The narrator can be inside the story as one of the characters, as in Camus's *The Outsider*, or outside it as anonymous observer, like Sartre in his trilogy. Narratives, and for that matter plays (e.g. those of Camus and Sartre), have plots made up of strings of actions, and hence are suitable for presenting the extreme situations Jaspers referred to as *Grenzsituationen* (boundary or limit situations).[6] Since authentic life is impossible without significant actions, literary forms that focus on actions are the best media for presenting authentic life. The extreme situations and events so abundant in this literature also serve as a magnifying lens through which it is easier to see the almost invisible details of authenticity and its inner pathos.

Yet even assuming that fiction can portray extreme situations, the following question remains: why are the philosophers of authenticity so eager to resort to literary descriptions of these events? Indeed, they are frequently accused by critics of dealing with situations which most of us would never experience. Consider Kierkegaard on Abraham's attempt to sacrifice his son Isaac, or his account of the uncommon seduction of an innocent girl by the sophistic 'Seducer' in *Either/Or*; Nietzsche's portrait of Zarathustra's esoteric modes of living, and his insistence on the existential import of sickness, under the slogan 'What does not destroy me makes me stronger'; the existential nausea and anxieties of freedom and war suffered by Sartre's literary heroes; and the experiences of Meursault in Camus's *The Outsider* and of Dr Rieux in *The Plague*. What accounts for this almost obsessive preoccupation with, and glorification of, extreme situations?

A clue is provided by Joseph Conrad, who specialized in the presentation of extreme situations, and used his works to explore the following question: 'Can you pull your authentic self together when you lose all support? Will you survive or go under?' In a paradigmatic literary expression of contemporary interest in authenticity, Conrad's *Heart of Darkness* (1902) sets out the challenge starkly:

> Mr Kurtz lacked restraint in the gratification of his various lusts. . . . But the wilderness had found him out early, and . . . had whispered to him things about himself which he did not know, things of which he had no conception till he took counsel with this great solitude – and the whisper had proved irresistibly fascinating. It echoed loudly within him because he was hollow at the core.[7]

Unlike Rousseau, Conrad viewed the wilderness not as the biological paradigm of authentic life but, rather, as the perfect chance to test for its existence. In *Heart of Darkness*, the jungle provides the opportunity for the novel's characters to experience extreme situations to which conventional Western values are inapplicable. The individual's behaviour in such an ethical 'darkness' illuminates his innermost self: he may be swept away by the bestiality and inhumanity of the jungle and turn into a bloodthirsty monster like Kurtz; or he may, like Marlow, stand fast against the terrible temptation to succumb to the jungle. Marlow's humanistic values do not disappear in this existential purgatory and he manages to leave the jungle with authenticated honesty.

At the outset, the ethic of honesty and sincerity is an externally imposed constraint. One is born to it and formed by the conditioning mechanisms of its educational institutions. Success in conforming to the letter of this ethos is amply rewarded. But the outward or behavioural honesty of those who are successful, and their verbal sincerity, tell us nothing about their authenticity. How can we know that behind compliance with that ethic lies an authentically honest and sincere person?

We are unable to answer this question, not only with reference to others, but also with respect to ourselves. Introspection into the inner layers of one's self is of no avail, since, as Nietzsche warns us, the individual is 'a thing dark and veiled; and if the hare has seven skins, man can slough off seventy times seven and still not be able to say: "this is really you, this is no longer outer shell" '.[8] Here Nietzsche identifies an acute problem that arises both from the lack of objective criteria for authenticity and from the psychological make-up of those who attempt to make such judgements. How can one reach the inner core of the self or become conscious of its 'hollowness' if it is covered by so many defensive layers, especially if the one who is searching and the self being searched are one and the same? Nietzsche, Sartre and others reject the viability of the Delphic injunction 'Know thyself'. Not because, like Nietzsche (who anticipated Freud in this respect), they believed in an unconscious mental life, but because, notwithstanding their belief in the transparency of our consciousness, they perceived the individual as *homo ludens*, as playing at being a particular artificial self. On this existentialist perception, one tends to mask one's own genuine self with different masks (*personae*) and to play various roles and personalities until the mask and one's self become inseparable. Hence the philosophers of authenticity used indirect means of testing authenticity – particularly, literary descriptions of extreme situations.

In these situations one can no longer be governed by internalized norms. Without this ethical safety net, one is wholly responsible, and thus free to invent oneself. Without this freedom and personal responsibility – thrown into sharp relief by the dramatic presentation of extreme situations – authenticity cannot be attained. Under the stress of these circumstances, one's behaviour reveals the inner genuine self behind the masks and disguises that no longer function. One must find one's way without recourse to the guiding systems of social institutions. By acting in circumstances that are beyond the 'good and honest' ethic, the world of shallow appearances and pious ethical codes – namely, in the real jungle and in traumatic moments of personal truth – we can arrive at some conclusion as to whether genuine selfhood or a hollow core lies behind one's cultural shell. In *Heart of Darkness*, for example, Conrad shows Kurtz's ethic of honesty crumbling, while Marlow's, which is more than a conditioned semblance and 'outer shell', remains firm.

Another assumption underlying the extensive use of extreme situations is expressed by Sartre's slogan: 'Man is nothing else but that which he makes of himself . . . he is the sum of his actions'.[9] There is no vague, elusive emotion called 'love', there are only concrete deeds and acts of love. The same applies to any other feeling. How can we judge the existence or sincerity of feelings if not by way of judging acts? We can know about our love by examining how our acts express this love. In the context of our everyday humdrum lives, it is hard to know what we feel genuinely and what we really are, since most of our acts are expressions and consequences of conditioning, imitation and convenient conformity. But in the crucial moments that require definite and significant decisions and action, we are more capable of discerning who we genuinely are. There is no one but ourselves to condemn or appreciate our behaviour. There was nobody left in the hopeless situation of *The Plague* to reward Dr Rieux for the brave humanitarian services he rendered to the victims; nevertheless, he rendered them to the end. This, perhaps, explains the existentialists', notably Heidegger's, intense interest in death. Our deaths and, especially, our ways of dying are touchstones for our authenticity. For many of us, death is the most individual, genuinely true – and surely the only radical – action performed in our entire lives. Thus, for example, an atheist's death without rites in a Christian society is revealing, since he is not acting for the sake of adjustment or reward. We cannot but admire Meursault's consistency in rejecting the chaplain's insistence that he confess and thereby be 'absolved' of his 'sin'. His response seems authentic:

> I didn't believe in God. . . . I wasn't conscious of any 'sin'; all I knew was that I'd been guilty of a criminal offence. Well, I was paying the penalty of that offence, and no one had the right to expect anything more of me.[10]

Extreme situations reveal that accepted social values often conflict. We are unwilling to take up these contradictions directly, and prefer to ignore them. Only if it becomes necessary do we beat around the bush in an attempt to straighten things out, usually arriving at an artificial compromise. We constantly avert our eyes from the dilemmas of our working values, and avoid definite engagements one way or the other. These conflicts come to the surface when an existential emergency calls for immediate action.

We create our authenticity; it is not delivered to us by higher authorities. As human beings, however, we are often morally compromised by escaping our responsibility for ourselves. To block off certain avenues of escape and bring about fundamental changes in our lives, the philosophers of authenticity use fictional portraits and dramatic descriptions of extreme situations that make us realize how, even in everyday situations, it is up to us to create our own selves.

The link between the form and the content of literary-philosophical writings on authenticity is significant. In fact, here the medium is a substantial part of the message. In writing, an author is taking action; indeed writing is an attempt to crystallize and articulate the authenticity of its creator. Thus the fictional worlds portrayed, in which different types of heroes are immersed in the search for their genuine selves, actually represent the real, existential predicaments of these authors, who, in confronting these issues, are trying to become authentic themselves. This will be particularly clear in Kierkegaard's case. The link between the thematic and rhetorical qualities of these works and their authors' existential projects heightens the reader's sense of authenticity and enhances the perlocutionary import of these works. Authenticity is a subjective pathos, requiring subjective and privileged access; this access is best obtained from the perspective of the personal dramas, agonies and doubts reflected in these writings.

IV

Because of its intimate relationship with the notion of authenticity, the most powerful and widely used literary means of enticing the reader is irony. One might even claim that the writings of the philosophers of authenticity are essentially ironic, since much of their apparent content is incommensurable with the underlying motive for their creation – to lure the reader towards a different life.[11] But how exactly does irony function as a royal path to authenticity? What accounts for its effectiveness?

There is little agreement among critics as to what irony is; some even claim that 'its very spirit and value are violated by the effort to be clear about it'.[12] Having devoted much effort to avoiding a definition of authenticity, it will now be useful for me to do the same with irony.

I begin with the following description of irony: 'The art of irony is the art of saying something without really saying it. It is an art that gets its effects from below the surface ... saying much more than it seems to be saying.'[13] The 'effect' that concerns us here is enticement, which cannot be achieved by direct propositional language. Indirect enticement requires disguise, masking. As critics have noted, irony is often characterized by the following features: it involves a multi-layered figure of speech; it entails an incongruity between the overt and the implied levels; and the speaker pretends ignorance of the deeper level.[14] In other words, the ironic writer presents a text in such a way that the reader or listener is moved to reject the overt, literal meaning and seek an implied contradictory or inexplicable sense. As regards authenticity, the effect of a particular type of irony is especially important. I refer to the irony that indirectly casts doubt on the validity of prevailing values and thereby arrests or lessens the reader's motivation to continue upholding them. This effect is achieved by the simulated adoption of another's point of view for the purpose of ridicule, by reducing this point of view to absurdity (as exemplified by Kierkegaard's treatment of the aesthetic life), or by depicting the psychologically disastrous consequences of clinging to prevailing values (a technique used by Nietzsche). This type of irony, implying that no vindication of the values under attack is possible, is helpful in the search for authenticity, which necessarily involves transcending the prevailing ethos of objectivity in favour of a less-defined openness of mind, character and identity. Hence Wayne Booth's description of the writers of 'unstable irony' suits our philosophers of authenticity as well. They 'refuse to declare themselves, however subtly, for any stable proposition, even the opposite of whatever proposition their irony vigorously denies'.[15]

We should bear in mind, though, that authenticity is not to be confused with nihilism – ultimately, it is an ethic stressing an undogmatic attitude towards other values and beliefs and towards one's self. 'Unstable irony' is used to destabilize our fixed inauthentic selves and pave the way to spontaneity and indeterminacy, for steady progress towards becoming what one freely wills. Irony, likewise, does not express nihilistic attitudes, but, rather, stems from genuine beliefs and critical attitudes toward the prevailing values. It purports to undermine what is considered worthy of admiration by exposing the absurdity and hypocrisy involved in trying to translate 'ought' into a viable social 'is'. Hence Kierkegaard, who makes the most extensive use of the ironic posture in his attempt to attain authentic faith, claims that 'irony makes things manifest'.[16]

One of the main elements of irony, conspicuous in Plato's Socrates, is a pretence that the ironist is accepting the views of his or her adversary. The ironist seems to adopt the prevailing ethic, but this attitude gradually becomes, to use Hegel's phrase, 'scornful laughter' directed against the values and modes of life held in high esteem by the ironist's interlocutor before their encounter. Readers spontaneously join in this laughter, unaware that their own will to uphold prevailing dogmas is thereby arrested.

Another salient feature of irony (also noticeable in Socrates) is the opposition between literal meaning and intended meaning. A dialectical tension exists between the dynamic attraction to the intended meaning and the repulsion engendered by the literal or expressed meaning. Hence the effectiveness of the ironic posture in the struggle against the ethic of sincerity, honesty and honour, the classic example of which is Mark Antony:

> For Brutus is an honourable man,
> So are they all, all honourable men.
> (*Julius Caesar*, III.ii.84–5)

The ethos of honesty and sincerity is diametrically opposed to irony. One who upholds it believes in what he preaches, whereas the ironist says that which he does not believe, and believes that which he does not say. In practice, however, what takes place is somewhat different: the ethic of honesty demands that one comply with prevailing norms, but often one's feelings are not in accord with this ethic. This is especially true of times when the normative fabric is in decline – when authoritative institutions, such as Christianity in Kierkegaard's and Nietzsche's age, deteriorate, losing their vital motivating content, with only the external shell left intact. At these moments, the effectiveness of irony is manifest. The emptiness of the ethos that has lost its driving force is the perfect background for the ironist's projection of her emerging selfhood.

Irony is the art of unmasking by means of 'honest', 'objective' convention, namely, everyday language. In the ironic situation, however, language becomes a fifth column which eventually overwhelms the readers, upsetting their illusions of being authentically 'honest'. Irony succeeds because it uses the rhetoric according to which one lives one's life.

A frontal attack on the ethos of 'honesty', on the other hand, would surely fail, since 'honest' individuals would find it difficult to admit, even to themselves, that they are not truly honest and that their apparent conformity with the letter of their ethos is not motivated by a genuine commitment to its spirit. Irony uncovers the shallowness and superficiality of this ethic indirectly, avoiding direct confrontation with the external shell protecting the void. A direct assault would only provoke a defensive response, making real change even less likely.

Though the ironic idiom apparently uses the objective language of the prevailing ethos, the essence of irony is the indirect but intentional persuasion to transcend that framework. The ironic technique of enticement uses the language of the reader to take the reader beyond the ethos from which this language derives its meaning.

This explains why irony is so rarely used by the 'sincere' educator. Sincerity and honesty preclude any disparity between the external and the internal. Irony, by its very nature, especially when the ethos of honesty is in decline, implies that there is no correspondence between external and internal. Yet though it affirms the distinction between the two, it confounds the appearance/essence dichotomy and creates confusion as to which is which. Authenticity emerges from this challenge to long-accepted metaphysical distinctions. Irony teaches us to suspend belief in the usefulness of the distinction, but does not repudiate its existence. Rather, it prepares us to live beyond such artificial categories, unsettling our dogmatic beliefs, and humbles us by making us reconsider the notion that we have fixed and ultimate essences.

Irony also facilitates the emergence of authenticity by helping the individual to become detached from her self. All creation requires detachment. The writer, for example, scrutinizes her writings as if they were someone else's. The same is true of the authentic formation of the self. Irony brings out the self-detachment needed to transcend subjectivity, and enables the individual to refocus, as it were, on the emerging authentic self. The ironic posture, and especially self-orientated irony, enables us to take ourselves lightly, keeping us from regarding ourselves in terms of rigid a priori essences. It allows us to pass from the domain of Being to the pathos of Becoming, from inauthenticity to genuinely authentic modes of life.

On this account, an ironic person does not commit suicide. According to existentialist teaching, suicide is a philosophical mistake: in contemplating suicide one regards one's self as a defined entity whose essence cannot be changed. The spirit of irony, by contrast, aims at changing one's personality and its attendant circumstances; in spite of its negative tactics, irony is ultimately positive. The ironic stance assumes that a person is free not only to change her or his own self but also to create it at will. It thus differs from nihilistic cynicism, which denies all values, including those of authenticity and self-creation. Cynicism, and perhaps sarcasm as well, are expressions of despair and defeatism. Irony is the voice of commitment and caring, the optimistic call to innovation and formation, rebirth and transformation. Irony is negation of the negative – the ethic which has lost its validity; cynicism is its passive acceptance. Cynicism seeks to avoid unfavourable situations by escaping, by shying away from, any constructive confrontation. Irony resolves problems by aborting stale commitment to prevailing norms and opening up new directions. As Kierkegaard notes, 'irony and resignation are two opposite poles'.[17] Cynicism is premised on thoroughgoing passivity, on acceptance of 'familiar evils', whereas irony seeks to alienate us from them by inciting us to restore our selves and create a new ethic. At the very least, it calls for readiness for the pathos of constant change, exhorting us to be faithful to the scripts we write for ourselves.

This call must be internalized by those who seek authenticity, who feel the urge to forge genuine selves beyond conventional community values and modes of behaviour. Hence irony's potential influence is limited to those in whom it finds existential resonance. Not all of us are willing to become what we are; not all of us possess the courage to shake ourselves free of the conformist mob. Many of us lack the power to challenge public opinion, and fear the solitudes of authenticity. Literary enticement to authenticity is thus directed at the courageous few who are able to bear the uncertainty of the search for authenticity and the pain that will be incurred in the often frustrating search. But for those who do dare to enter this adventurous life of overcoming oneself and creating it anew, irony is like the garments of the ancient Greek statues: it not only veils but also reveals that which it veils – the path to authenticity.

Notes

1   'Twilight of the Idols', in *The Portable Nietzsche*, ed. and trans. W. Kaufmann (New York: Viking, 1954), p. 470.

2   Thus, e.g., Rennie, the 'inauthentic' heroine of Barth's *The End of the Road* (New York: Doubleday, 1958), tells Jake (the character striving to attain authenticity) that Joe (a parody of an 'honest' man) is genuine because '*Real* people aren't any different when they're alone. No masks. What you see of them is authentic' (p. 70). Then Jake, stating that 'nobody's authentic', persuades Rennie to spy on Joe, who is discovered parading naked in front of the mirror, talking nonsense, picking his nose and masturbating all at once. For another example of a parody of existentialism, see B. Vian, *L'écume des jours* (Paris: Pauvert, 1963).

3   Cf. D. Cohn, *Transparent Minds: Narratives Modes for Presenting Consciousness in Fiction* (Princeton, NJ: Princeton University Press, 1978).

4   *Les Mots* (Paris: Gallimard, 1964), p. 89; *The Words*, trans. B. Frechtman (New York: George Braziller, 1964), p. 69. At the end of this personal account Sartre concludes with a tone of resignation: 'I lost myself' (p. 153). His companion, Simone de Beauvoir, testifies in her autobiography that her quasi-autobiographical novel *The Mandarins*, which 'described certain ways of living after the war' (as Sartre's trilogy *Roads to Freedom* depicted certain ways of living during the war) was really 'an evocation'. Two pages later she claims that 'one defect of diaries and autobiographies is that usually what "goes without saying" goes without being said, and thus one misses the essential', namely, that these are disguised forms of enticement and evocation. See Simone de Beauvoir, *Force of Circumstance*, trans. R. Howard (Harmondsworth: Penguin, 1968), pp. 282, 284. Cf. Nietzsche's *Ecce Homo: How One Becomes What One Is*, which is a fictional 'autobiographical' account of Nietzsche's life and intellectual development. The same can be said of Kierkegaard's *The Point of View for my Work as an Author*.

5   S. Rimmon-Kenan, *Narrative Fiction: Contemporary Poetics* (London: Methuen, 1983), p. 2. Also see her discussion of the importance of events and actions in narrative texts (pp. 15–28, 61–3); and Wallace Martin, *Recent Theories of Narrative* (Ithaca, NY: Cornell University Press, 1986), pp. 81ff., 173.

6   A concise and systematic exposition of Jaspers's key notion of *Grenzsituationen* is found in his *Philosophy*, trans. E. B. Ashton (Chicago, Ill.: University of Chicago Press, 1969–71), vol. II, pp. 178ff.

7   *The Portable Conrad*, ed. M. D. Zabel (New York: Viking, 1947), p. 573.

8   'Schopenhauer as Educator', in Friedrich Nietzsche, *Untimely Meditations*, trans. R. J. Hollingdale (Cambridge: Cambridge University Press, 1983), p. 129.

9   J.-P. Sartre, 'Existentialism is a Humanism', in *Existentialism from Dostoevsky to Sartre*, ed. and trans. W. Kaufmann (Cleveland, Ohio: Meridian, 1956), pp. 291, 300.

10   Camus, *The Outsider*, pp. 113–16.

11   We shall see in Chapter 5 that this claim applies even to Heidegger.

12   Wayne C. Booth, *A Rhetoric of Irony* (Chicago, Ill.: University of Chicago Press, 1974), p. ix and the last sentences in the book.

13   D. C. Muecke, *The Compass of Irony* (London: Methuen, 1969), pp. 5–6.

14   See ibid., pp. 19–20, and D. C. Muecke, *Irony and the Ironic* (London: Methuen, 1970), p. 39. Cf. Samuel Johnson's admirably concise definition of irony: 'A mode of speech of which the meaning is contrary to

the words', quoted in D. J. Enright, *The Alluring Problem: An Essay on Irony* (London: Oxford University Press, 1986), p. 5.

15   Booth, *A Rhetoric of Irony*, p. 240.

16   *Journals of Søren Kierkegaard*, ed. and trans. A. Dru (London: Oxford University Press, 1938), p. 159.

17   *Søren Kierkegaard's Journals and Papers*, ed. and trans. H. V. Hong and E. H. Hong (Bloomington: Indiana University Press, 1967), vol. II, p. 250.

3

Kierkegaard's ironic ladder to authentic faith

The search for authenticity in modern Western thought begins with the desperate journal entry, dated 1 August, 1835, of a 22–year-old Dane: 'the thing is to find a truth which is true *for me*, to find the idea for which I can live and die'.[1]

Kierkegaard was not talking about objective cognitive truth; nor was he referring to the intellectual act of rationally explicating some kind of philosophy. He wanted to create a quality of life, a pattern of life which would be true for him and would enable him to be true to himself. The creation of authentic life is an existential vocation; it has nothing to do with theoretical speculation. Kierkegaard stresses this point in the next entry in his journal, claiming that he wants

> *to lead a complete human life* and not merely one of the understanding, so that I should not . . . base the development of my thought upon . . . something that is called objective . . . but upon something which grows together with the deepest roots of my life.[2]

He asks: 'What is truth but to live for an idea?' Here we encounter the insight that authentic life has less to do with a specific concrete content, a 'what', than with some particular path, with a 'how'.

Another existential leitmotif hinted at here is the bond which must link the act of philosophizing with the personal life of the philosopher. Doctrine and life must overlap. Kierkegaard was the first thinker in modern times to insist on making the process of philosophizing a relevant and formative force in his own life, as an explicit protest against the objective and non-personal style of traditional philosophy, epitomized by Hegel.

A note written by Kierkegaard four years before his death indicates the practical objective of his philosophizing: 'my task has continually been to provide the existential corrective by poetically presenting the ideals and inciting people'.[3] Indeed, the passage points to three main themes dominating the literature on authenticity: (1) the existential, as opposed to purely theoretical, aim of changing the reader's life; (2) the poetic-literary means employed by the philosopher to achieve this aim; (3) the indirect tactics used to incite and entice the reader to seek authenticity.

At the outset, Kierkegaard found himself deeply confused as to the proper 'anchor' for his quest to form his own identity. In one of the most important entries in his voluminous journal he tells us:

> I have looked in vain for an anchorage in the boundless sea of pleasure and in the depth of understanding. . . . But the pleasure did not outlast the moment of understanding and left no profound mark upon me. It seems as though I had not drunk from the cup of wisdom, but had fallen into it. What did I find? Not my Self, which was what I was looking for. . . . And so the first thing to be decided, was the seeking and finding of the Kingdom of Heaven. . . . Although I am still far from having reached so complete an understanding of myself, I have, with profound respect for its significance, tried to preserve my individuality – worshipped the unknown God.
>
> (Dru, pp. 17–19)

When people are confused as to their self-identity, a serious quest for genuine self can begin. When one is painfully conscious of the danger of abandoning one's self, a cry for authenticity is heard. Indeed, given the negative sense of the notion of authenticity, discussed above, and commonsense psychology, one might dare to put forward the following rule: only one who has deeply experienced the conflict between authentic and inauthentic patterns of life and has frequently struggled to decide between them can become conscious of the importance of being authentic. Only such a person will recognize the vital significance of authentic identity and strive to make it an operative value in his life. We set about looking for our selves when we feel we are actually experiencing the disintegration of our selves and our own identity. The role of these existential predicaments explains the tendency of the philosophers of authenticity to engage in self-questioning and self-analysis; to probe the innermost layers of their selves and their turbulent lives. Continuous self-examination helps one to see that, to use Sartre's words, one is not what one is, and one is what one is not.

From the first words he puts down, Kierkegaard reveals a fundamentally religious personality. In his actual life, however, he did not always feel or live religiously, and was diverted many times on to different paths. His personal solution to this conflict was to return to or recover an abandoned religious 'Self'. Hence his insistence on connecting authenticity with genuine faith and his appeal to his readers to return to the origins of Christianity, to original, authentic faith. In a posthumously published book, he asserted: 'I am and was a religious author ... the whole of my work as an author is related to Christianity, to the problem "of becoming a Christian", with a direct or indirect polemic against the monstrous illusion we call Christendom.'[4] Kierkegaard is thus determined to entice his readers to 'leap' into and embrace passionately the genuine 'religious sphere' of existence, to 'become Christian' and live intensely, fulfilling all the demands of a faith that can transform the whole of life.

I

Kierkegaard's demand that we reshape and reform our selves is also one he made of himself. Kierkegaard's efforts are directed to the problem of how 'to *become* a Christian', not how to *be* one. His personal life and writings are a persistent quest for authentic selfhood,[5] and he indirectly entreats his readers to undertake a similar journey.

Many psychobiographical interpretations of Kierkegaard attempt to reduce his writings to his life, and in particular to various vague or hypothetical psychological and physical maladies[6] – they are a 'symptom of his sickness',[7] deriving from sado-masochism, neurosis, schizophrenia, manic-depressive psychosis, and other disorders. I believe, however, that it is Kierkegaard's writing, rather, that defines his life, crystallizing and forming it by bringing forth the personal authenticity he so desired. The psychobiographical treatments consistently misinterpret the fundamental drive of Kierkegaard's philosophizing and blindly assume it revolves around events of the past rather than concern for the future.

While Kierkegaard's philosophical activity originates in the problematic predicaments of his life, it seeks a wider resolution of this existential confusion. Moreover, to regard Kierkegaard's writing as solely concerned with his own existence is mistaken: it also directs itself to the problems of the *reader* and the 'age'. Otherwise, Kierkegaard would have been quite content to leave his philosophical meditations in the form of personal journals and would not have bothered with tiresome and costly publication for the general public. To reduce Kierkegaard's thought to his life deprives readers of the 'corrective' he seeks to give them.

The problematic relation between Kierkegaard's life and his writings can be described as an existential dialectic of authenticity. As we saw, the problem of personal identity and Kierkegaard's perplexity about what he was and what he had to do to attain authentic selfhood brought him to write and to philosophize. However, the actual act of writing was in turn the means that allowed Kierkegaard to reach the threshold of authenticity. By dealing with the question of 'how to become what one is', Kierkegaard gradually became what he was - an individual with a strong religious pathos. As we have noted, this religious bent was initially problematic for him.[8] However, this ambivalence regarding religion settles as, in his writings, Kierkegaard discusses and resolves conflicts between different existential views of life. Kierkegaard utilizes quasi-Hegelian dialectic - the explication of an already given content by elevating (*aufheben*) it from the obscure and indefinite complex which contains a destructive antithesis to it. However, while Hegel deals rationally and systematically with the explication of the Absolute Spirit pervading history, Kierkegaard uses indirect and non-rational enticement to uncover, intensify and reactivate, in his own life and in the lives of his readers, the hidden and implicit sources of their authentic selves. The target of the dialectical process is shifted from the totality of the universe to the solitary 'inwardness' of the individual.

Kierkegaard's literary work functions as a sort of temporary scaffolding to be abandoned once it has served its purpose, namely, to evoke and inspire readers to live authentic lives and to do so intensely 'without regrets'. Like anyone else who tries to write, at the beginning Kierkegaard has only vague, implicit intuitions and insights about the matters he intends to examine. As the act of writing progresses the structure of one's ideas gradually comes into focus and defines the whole composition. The very act of writing becomes part of what is being communicated to the writer and then to the reader. This is particularly true in Kierkegaard's case, since what he intends to communicate is not a theoretical 'content' but a moral directive.

To attain authenticity, Kierkegaard must first generate meaning in his life. The sheer arbitrariness of life, and our lack of control over it, create the illusion that existence is a product of blind chance and we are without responsibility for its course. This leads to evasion of freedom and abandonment of the search for authenticity. Kierkegaard's writings attempt, among other things, to portray the 'stages on life's way' (to use the title of one of his books). They constitute a concrete and inspiring example of how the existential dialectic of authenticity has actually worked in the life of the author. Kierkegaard states in his journals: 'My writing is essentially my own development', and says that in writing he came to understand himself.[9] This development as a writer, and also as a person, eventually brought him to the point where, in 1848, the time had come to abandon his indirect tactics and 'come forward personally, definitely, and directly as one who wished to serve the cause of Christianity' (Dru, p. 259).

Hence it is of little importance to try and correlate the stages of existence portrayed by Kierkegaard in his works with different phases of his actual life. To find out, for example, whether Kierkegaard was actually an aesthetic type who lived an aesthetic life – according to his own definitions – while he was writing his aesthetic works is secondary to the main question: what he tried to do *in* his writings, and what he attempted to communicate *by* them. In any case, his journals do not reveal the secrets of his personal life, since they deal mainly with the future and not the past or present. They are concerned with the Self to come and not with the already-existing person. Even his 'formal' biography, laboriously pieced together from the manifold personae which Kierkegaard intentionally proffered, has little to offer. We ought not to forget, as Kierkegaard reminds us, that at the time he wrote his aesthetic works, published pseudonymously, he also wrote numerous Christian 'Edifying Discourses' published under his own name. On the other hand, even during the so-called 'religious' stage of his life he wrote an 'aesthetic' work. And witness his own statement:

> The religious is present from the beginning. Conversely, the aesthetic is present again at the last moment. After two years, during which religious works only were published, there follows a little aesthetic article.[10]

The desperate cry for authenticity cannot be mechanically deduced from the actual life-experiences of the man Søren Kierkegaard. What is of importance for us is the fact that this individual strove, by means of his writing, to intensify both his sense of authentic selfhood and the religious pathos he felt at the outset, a pathos which gradually gained the upper hand. The existential dialectic of authenticity Kierkegaard used, and perhaps also lived by, shaped his life and gave it a definite direction, but it is presented to us for our own use, as it was presented to his own generation. As such, it must be taken seriously by all who are moved by a similar existential aim: to become what we are.

II

The attempt to encourage authentic modes of living in his contemporaries, the second leitmotif of Kierkegaard's writings (the first being the inward intensification of his own self), gives rise to the obvious question: what was so wrong with Kierkegaard's age that he felt compelled to offer a 'corrective'? What was there to correct? The answer can be found in the first sentence of the essay 'The Present Age', published in 1846 under Kierkegaard's own name: 'Our age is essentially one of understanding and reflection, without passion.'[11] Kierkegaard's contemporaries indulge in 'the coils and seductive uncertainty of reflection', which kills action and brings them to '*inertiae*'. Much as Nietzsche asserts 'Knowledge kills action; action requires the veils of illusion',[12] Kierkegaard holds that action requires passion, which is lost when the individual sinks into the bottomless pit of reflection. Too much analysis leads to paralysis, and since 'man stands or falls by his actions', there is no way to attain authenticity without significant life-shaping action. To counter this tendency to 'over-reflectiveness' that hinders the emergence of authenticity, Kierkegaard attempts to wake us from our existential slumbers by infusing us with passion, the motivating force for action.

By passion Kierkegaard does not mean any emotion that affects us, but rather, emotion originating in the first days of Christianity, more precisely, in the sufferings of Jesus Christ on the Cross: an overpowering emotion that changes, or even ends, one's life.

To be sure, his age is also pervaded by the ethos of sincerity and Hegelian 'Reason', an ethos which has led his generation into apathy, lack of commitment, shallowness, and evasion of any decisive and determined course of action. Kierkegaard did not want to abolish this ethic completely, but only to 'correct' it. He wanted to infuse his age with passion, contending that passion together with sincerity of intention produces authenticity.[13]

To become existentially committed and to act decisively, Kierkegaard holds, one must feel passionately about the object of one's commitment. Sincere intent alone is not sufficient. This addition of pathos to the ethos of sincerity – an empty and meaningless ethic that had lost its driving force – is Kierkegaard's main contribution to the emergence of authenticity. Kierkegaard envisages genuine thinkers in constant opposition to their age. And even if he intended only to 'correct' a lukewarm and flabby age, his thought was revolutionary and was regarded as such by his contemporaries, as his conflicts with the established Church and the Hegelian outlook attest.

We must remember that in speaking of 'Reason', and of the reflection which kills action, and hence individual authenticity, Kierkegaard was not referring only to Hegel's immanently unfolding Reason in universal history. To be sure, he claims in many places that the sway of Hegelianism is responsible for the dissolution of the self: it favours the overwhelming objectivity of abstractness over subjective individuality. Here, however, Kierkegaard has in mind reason as 'the calculating intelligence' (*PA*, p. 35). He refers to the human intellect, whose overpowering primacy was transforming everything into ideas which no one was able to experience 'completely and personally'. 'And thus', Kierkegaard adds, 'as one longs for the clink of real money, after the crackle of bank-notes, one longs nowadays for a little originality' (ibid., p. 40). Here we find another meaning of authenticity, in addition to passionate commitment, namely, the return to the genuine origins of our selves, our feelings and our beliefs. This notion of originality is consistent with Kierkegaard's view of the Christian faith, which for him starts and ends at Calvary.

Moreover, Kierkegaard believes that intellect and reasoning are the main ways in which people escape their selfhood. Our intellect rationalizes away all avenues to authenticity. It provides people with rationalizations for not becoming what they are. And Kierkegaard, who spent much time and energy on rationalizing his life in order to escape from commitment and from his genuine self, was well aware of this. Since Kierkegaard felt that 'for the individual as for the generation no task is more difficult than to escape from temptations of reflection' (ibid., p. 42), he attempted to make passion for authentic action a counter-temptation.

Another aspect of the 'present age' that requires 'correcting' has to do with 'the levelling process' that is an outcome, on the sociological and theoretical levels, of the abstract and 'passionless' nature of reflection. This levelling process is a symptom of the victory of abstraction over the individual, and that of 'the committee' over personal commitment. The modern individual is 'lost' in the crowd and 'at a loss' without the crowd. The anonymity of man, and his impersonal education in industrial society, the 'abstract power' of the state, change him into a 'phantom' in 'the public . . . which is a monstrous nothing'. It destroys his individuality, externalizes his 'inwardness' and makes him forget what it means to be a genuine self. This shallow and confused age relies on statistics, making public opinion the criterion of truth. It demands that the levelling process also expresses itself sociologically in the form of 'mathematical equality'.

Kierkegaard was well aware that his antidote – passion – might bring with it 'atrocious sins' (ibid., p. 43). But this risk is worth taking because it is the only thing that can also bring us to 'the good' and to the performance of 'great things'. What must be pointed out, however, is that in this small but brilliant book the genuine either/or emerges: not the earlier either/or between the aesthetic and ethical spheres of existence, but the real existential choice – to become a selfless 'nothing at all', in the midst of the abstract collective 'public' and 'a deathly silence', or to become a genuine and concrete individual by committing the 'leap of enthusiasm', the 'leap into the arms of God' – either to embrace the authentic faith or to become a two-dimensional phantom. It is true that 'enthusiasm *may* end in disaster, but levelling is *eo ipso* the destruction of the individual' (ibid., pp. 68, 50, 82, 54). Thus Kierkegaard here posits a genuine choice: either religious authenticity or nothing.

Clearly, however, he prefers the dangers of an authentic pathos of faith to an ethos resulting in the levelling and annihilation of selfhood. One of his reasons is that in addition to himself 'there are still people who passionately want to be what they ought to be' (ibid., p. 44), who long for something higher and more meaningful in the midst of ongoing levelling processes in the social, political and intellectual spheres. Kierkegaard wants to make this inclination explicit, to speed it up and broaden it, by harnessing to it the motivating passion, that is, by using the very forces now directed toward the destruction of individuality.

Here we arrive at the dialectic of Kierkegaard's indirect enticement. By employing the very forces that prevail in his age and hinder the emergence of authenticity he wants to assist us in overcoming them. Thus, as he repeats several times, 'reflection is not the evil'; it is 'not in itself something harmful'. On the contrary, it is necessary to utilize its terminology, which was very much in vogue at the time; and Kierkegaard employs the prevailing views of aesthetics, ethics and Christian sentiments to impel his readers to eventually adopt their antitheses: authentic faith and genuine selfhood. Thus, for example, he hopes that from the ideal of the equality of men will emerge the passionate belief in 'the equality of all men before God' (ibid., p. 57).

Generally speaking, Kierkegaard believes that out of Hegel's 'system' of Reason and the levelling ethic a genuine individual will emerge. And since this antithetical process lacks the deterministic necessity of Hegel's rational dialectics, Kierkegaard wants to further it and overcome those trends that go against it. It is true that 'the time has come for work to begin, for every individual must work for himself, each for himself', but Kierkegaard, becoming 'unrecognizable' and hidden 'like a plain-clothes policeman' (ibid., p. 81), will indirectly assist these individuals 'to make the decision which he himself has reached' (ibid., p. 80). The 'plain-clothes policeman' appears once again as a 'secret agent' (p. 82). Kierkegaard pictures himself as a spy in 'the present age' (that is, in the enemy camp): one who steals information, ideals and vocabularies from the prevailing ethos and brings them to his isolated place 'before God' to use against 'the Public'.

Kierkegaard believes that his call to us to take the painful road to authenticity may yet succeed because of the decline of the 'present age' and its prevailing ethos. Two strong powers of his age had lost their authority. On the religious plane, there had been a watering-down of Christian faith to a comfortable code of shallow bourgeois ethics.[14] On the intellectual level, the Hegelian system, as an empty abstraction, had lost its motivating and inspiring power. Truth and morality had given way to oratory. Word and gesture had replaced life. The time had come for the subjective pathos of authenticity.

In the twilight of the prevailing ethic and ideals, we have to rely on ourselves alone. Kierkegaard wants to speed up this process with his enticing tactic of using the ideals of Hegel's philosophy, Kant's ethics, and the residue of Christian sentiment – but with the goal of overcoming their present decadent forms and correcting them. Kierkegaard subjectifies the Hegelian notion of objectivity; he employs the aesthetic and deepens it to its destruction; he adopts ethical generalizations and personifies them. These 'correctives' work by taking a notion and intensifying it until it becomes an antidote to that very notion.

III

Why did Kierkegaard employ indirect tactics rather than argue directly and rationally with his readers? What accounts for his tortuous device of publishing 'aesthetic' works under various pseudonyms, and what is the relation between this tactic, which Kierkegaard calls 'indirect communication', and his goal of enticement?

Kierkegaard wrote many of his books under different *noms de plume*. He followed this practice in all the works he later called his 'aesthetic' corpus, from *Either/Or* (1843) onwards. These pseudonyms were not intended to conceal his authorship, which was common knowledge in the then small town of Copenhagen and was on file with the government censor long before his explicit acknowledgement in 'A First and Last Declaration', appended as an afterthought to the *Concluding Unscientific Postscript*. In this note Kierkegaard states that 'in the pseudonymous works there is not a single word which is mine'. It is not he but fictitious authors who wrote those 'aesthetic' books. In this 'first', but not the 'last', 'declaration', Kierkegaard says: 'My pseudonymity or polynymity has not had a causal ground in my *person* . . . but it has an *essential* ground in the character of the *production*.'[15]

First, the use of pseudonyms has to do with Kierkegaard's own dialectic of authenticity. Being the author of the pseudonymous 'authors', each representing a certain view of life in as ideal a form as possible, Kierkegaard maintains poetic distance from his creations. In his pseudonymous writings he is neither an aesthetic person nor a moral one nor does he embrace religious faith genuinely and passionately like his Abraham; he is all of these and, because of this, none at all. But principally he is the Kierkegaard of the late 'Christian Discourses', written under his own name, who wants 'to become' an authentic 'Christian'. But still he cannot identify authentically with any of the imaginary writers' statements. In order to crystallize his existential chaos into an authentic wholeness he has to detach himself mentally from the aesthetic experiences he has had in his life and from the ethical aspirations that have driven him. To 'become a Christian' Kierkegaard needs to intensify his religious sentiments; to create a passionate pathos. The existential process of attaining authentic selfhood always implies overcoming those elements in our lives and characters that hinder this process. Thus Kierkegaard's detachment from the aesthetic pathos, from the ethical-reflective ethic, and from inauthentic Christianity, help him control these dimensions of his personality for the sake of his own religiosity. You can become what you are by *not* being what you are not. By not identifying himself with the aesthetic life-view and/or bourgeois ethic in his pseudonymous writings, Kierkegaard became a writer whose 'last group [of writings] is exclusively religious', as he testifies in his *Point of View* (*PV*, p. 13). He ultimately found his identity as a religious author; his existential confusions were overcome by his creations. In this Kierkegaard is like his God, who 'communicates in creating, so as, by creating, to *give* independence over against Himself' (*CUP*, p. 232). Kierkegaard, like God, wants to create his own authentic self by indirect communication.

Yet his indirect communication is not only an expression of his own existential search for authenticity. It is also directed at persons whose 'existence presents itself to them as a confusion' (*CUP*, p. 236). Their confusion, however, is blunted by the prevailing ethos of reflection, which puts them in a state of inertia. Kierkegaard does not disdain shocking them because what he most wants to do is to change them. However, to shock them he first needs to attract their attention. One way to do so is to provide his aesthetic books with 'the interest of novelty' by using pseudonymous masks. This succeeded, at least according to his testimony, in the case of *Either/Or*, which 'caused almost a riot, so that the book was bought, and is even supposed to be sold out' (*CUP*, p. 254). Masks attract audiences: we want to know who is behind them. Our curiosity is aroused and we read the disguised book, opening ourselves to indirect enticement.

In this respect the technique of indirect communication serves as an initial stage of the enticement procedure. But what accounts for the indirectness of the enticement itself? Kierkegaard provides several hints, one in *Point of View*:

Assuming then that a person is the victim of an illusion, and that in order to communicate the truth to him the first task . . . is to remove the illusion – if I do not begin by deceiving him, I must begin with direct communication . . . but an illusion stands in the way. . . . What then does it mean 'to deceive'? It means that one does not begin

43

directly with the matter one wants to communicate, but begins by accepting the other man's illusion as good money.

(p. 40)

And in the *Postscript* he says: 'the art of communication . . . becomes the art of *taking away*, of luring something away from someone' (ibid., p. 245). Kierkegaard wishes to dispel the illusion that we are authentic Christians and authentic human beings. He wants 'to take away' the Hegelian rational ethos of objectivity and reflective life and to lure us into the pathos of authenticity. But one cannot openly communicate one's intention of enticing the reader, just as one cannot deceive somebody by announcing this intention to him. To present the way to authenticity we must first 'take away' the illusion that one is already authentic. But we cannot achieve this directly because it will cause resistance. Kierkegaard's aesthetic works are acceptable to his contemporaries, who live and think in 'aesthetic categories' yet delude themselves that they live in a 'Christian' age. Thus Kierkegaard speaks the aesthetic language of his age to lure his audience to a different existential sphere. He confesses: 'The deception consists in the fact that one talks thus merely to get to the religious theme' (ibid., p. 41).

But there are still more fundamental reasons for Kierkegaard's method of indirect communication. Other features have an even deeper 'essential ground in the character of the production'. The use of varied literary forms and unsystematic writing suggests that there is no objective or rational way in which Kierkegaard's views about authenticity can be presented or argued for. Since authentic passionate commitment has no concrete, cognitive content, one has no recourse but to the indirect arousal of the desired pathos. Kierkegaard's unique style intrigues and fascinates us and creates a suitable psychological atmosphere for change. To affirm his existential claim about 'truth as subjectivity', about authenticity as a personal appropriation of the pathos of sincere commitment and free choice, Kierkegaard uses indirect communication, above all to change the reader, not just to enlighten him. Enlightenment is the aim of direct communication free of personal passion and paradox. It tries to provide us with 'objective' opinion and information, much of it completely irrelevant to our most urgent existential concerns. Its recipients are therefore the 'paragraph-eaters' who 'have forgotten what inwardness is'. 'Suppose,' Kierkegaard says, 'a man wished to communicate the conviction that it is not the truth but the way that is the truth, i.e. that the truth exists only in the process of becoming ... and hence that there is no result', then 'the difference between subjective and objective thinking must express itself also in the form of communication suitable to each'. But 'direct communication presupposes certainty' and 'certainty is impossible' for anyone in the process of becoming authentic.[16]

Kierkegaard aims to inculcate in us the pathos of authentic religious sentiments which cannot be communicated or aroused by traditional philosophical language that aspires to create an objectively transparent atmosphere. Moreover, this language, at least in Kierkegaard's time – the reference here is to Hegel – was used for the conceptual explication of reality and the constitution of a total system that transforms the individual into an abstract entity and estranges her from her search for authenticity. Any attempt to reach the subjective sphere with this argumentative, objective language is bound to fail. This is well understood by Kierkegaard, who says in his diary: 'the subjectivity ... existing [existerende] in isolation wants to communicate himself, something he cannot possibly do directly, since it is a contradiction. One may very well want to communicate himself, like the person in love, but always indirectly' (Hong, I, p. 259). You cannot convince someone to love you passionately, but you can entice him into it. Moreover, you cannot convince someone that you love him intensely by using rational and direct arguments. You will be much more convincing if you show him indirectly, namely, by sincerely committed and passionate actions. Kierkegaard's writings are just such acts of enticement. His writing, taken as a whole, with its inherent existential dialectic of authenticity, provides a personal example of this indirect mode of trying to establish one's authentic selfhood.

Kierkegaard was deeply convinced that certain things are vital but cannot be directly expressed by means of propositional language, be it as univocal as is possible in everyday language. Certain things – especially authentic pathos devoid of any definite and rational content – cannot be spoken of propositionally. Here we see a certain similarity between Kierkegaard and Wittgenstein, the well-known last proposition of whose *Tractatus Logico-Philosophicus* states that anything we cannot speak about directly 'we must pass over in silence'. Wittgenstein was in no doubt that everything of importance, especially the ethical, is inexpressible; the *Tractatus* was the impossible attempt to express it. Wittgenstein was a good Kierkegaardian, since Kierkegaard likewise thinks that the 'things' of paramount importance for one's life cannot be spoken of directly and must be made manifest indirectly if we are to be enticed to follow them. The affinity between the two thinkers is evident from Wittgenstein's admiration for Kierkegaard and his claim 'There are, indeed, things that cannot be put into words. *They make themselves manifest*. They are what is mystical.'[17]

The fictional author of *Fear and Trembling* is Johannes *de silentio*. Kierkegaard believes that it is possible to indicate the patterns of authenticity and subjectivity indirectly, to feel and portray them poetically, to reveal them in outstanding and fictional individuals. It may even be possible to describe them as existential possibilities, to be chosen freely by readers. In other words, it is feasible to talk about them indirectly without taking them as, or making them into, direct propositional objects. Thus Kierkegaard does not talk to us directly, but creates imaginary characters and writers who speak to each other without ever reaching any definite conclusion, as in Plato's aporetic dialogues. If no definite conclusions are drawn in a work which dramatically engages the attention, readers are enticed into considering the issue for themselves and concluding subjectively from their individual points of view. The imaginary characters forcefully express their respective life-views, and the reader is incited to take sides by making an existential decision to adopt for himself one of these possibilities, notably the religious one, in which the required passionate commitment will help him attain genuine selfhood. Kierkegaard's challenge needs no reply. We need only consider it and become what we are.

Thus the purpose of philosophical discourse in Kierkegaard is completely different from that in Hegel, which is rooted in the tradition of the *vita contemplativa*. Kierkegaard seeks to move us to a *vita activa* of free and decisive choices and authentic actions that can create genuine selfhood. He asks us to overcome our tendency to find refuge from our selves in the world and flee from the subjective reality of choice into the domain of speculation. In the world of *theoria*, in the Greek sense of speculation and observation, rationalization may gain the upper hand over rationality, and the impersonal and cold objectivity of reflection or 'overreflectiveness' may swallow up the passions of living persons. Hence the dominance of Hegelian philosophy was regarded by Kierkegaard as proof that his age had 'forgotten what inwardness is'. Thus he 'maintained an indirect polemic against speculative philosophy', declaring against Hegel that 'truth is subjectivity'.[18]

It is important to realize in this context that Kierkegaard was not denying the traditional definition of truth as correspondence between thought and reality. It would be self-defeating to argue for a theory that subjectivity is truth. His conception of subjectivity and truth gives philosophy a totally different context from that provided by the various epistemological answers to perennial philosophical problems. By declaring truth to be subjectivity, Kierkegaard tried to shift the attention of philosophers and their readers from objective knowledge to subjective and existential concerns – identity, genuine selfhood and authenticity. He sought a truth which was 'true for him', with which he could identify, and which he could appropriate into his innermost self to become what he authentically was. And since passion and sincerity of active commitment are authenticity, Kierkegaard sought the object that would be able to incite in him the highest passion possible. For him, this object was the Christian God. Since *'the objective accent falls on WHAT is said, the subjective accent on HOW it is said'* (*CUP,* p. 181), and since to be true to one's self lies in the 'how' of the subject's relationship, the fullest authenticity attainable by human beings is in the relationship in which the subjective element – the passion with which one holds to an object – reaches its highest intensity. 'But the passion of the infinite is precisely subjectivity, and thus subjectivity becomes the truth' (*CUP,* p. 181). This 'truth' is not cognitive but conative. It has to do with actions, passions and sentiments – in short, with the pathos of 'inwardness' and authenticity. In this context 'truth is subjectivity' means truth as authenticity rather than truth as the objective value of the propositional content of sentences about reality or about other sentences: it is the internal harmony and correspondence between our hearts and our actions, not that between our sentences and external objects.

Kierkegaard is aware that he cannot convince us rationally to choose this search for harmony. Such a directive would be self-defeating, since one cannot force authenticity. One can lead rational people to the waters of choice, but one cannot make them drink. He thinks, however, that one can make them thirst for their selves. The function of Kierkegaard's enticing philosophy is to make our mouths dry, to heighten rather than to slake our thirst for subjectivity. Pseudonyms, humour and, above all, irony – all help him indirectly to discredit common refuges from authenticity: the shelters devoid of significant existential import where we become inauthentic, one-dimensional objects. Irony is especially helpful in indicating the way, pointing to that which cannot be said. Ironic statements are ambivalent, carrying a surface affirmation subtended by an unspoken negation. Irony helps to portray a given pattern of life and, as it were, assert it while simultaneously denying it; the reader is left wondering what is actually true, and has no choice but to choose for himself. Thus irony is both a kind of a-rational literary affirmation and a refutation.

IV

Irony is the main device Kierkegaard used to entice his readers to espouse the inexpressible patterns of authenticity. It is not surprising, therefore, that in his Master's dissertation, *The Concept of Irony* (1841), he examined the philosophical significance and existential potential of the ironic stance.[19] This book was written under his own name and not under one of the many pseudonyms he used for his 'aesthetic' writings, which are ironic *par excellence* since their external content is incompatible with the underlying motive for their production. *The Concept of Irony* has special relevance because of its conclusion: 'As philosophers claim that no true philosophy is possible without doubt, so by the same token one may claim that no authentic life is possible without irony.'[20]

The main part of the dissertation portrays Socrates as an ironic subject confronting the prevailing ethos. In Socrates, Kierkegaard depicted himself. He saw himself as a Christianized analogue of Socrates, as a 'gadfly' of the 'present age' who used irony to sting people into perceiving the inauthenticity of their Christianity. In Kierkegaard's eyes, Socrates was a turning-point in the course of history since he was the first to proclaim the rights of subjectivity over objectivity. He sought to move the centre of gravity from the traditional objective morality of custom to subjective morality based upon individual free conscience: 'The standpoint of Socrates is subjectivity, inwardness reflecting upon itself, [which] in relation to itself loosens and dissolves the existent.'[21] Socrates thus won 'negative freedom' (freedom from the conventional-social conditioning of the prevailing ethic). Using irony, Socrates actually confronted the ethic of honesty and sincerity. He was, according to Kierkegaard, the first thinker heroically and self-consciously to lead the individual revolt against objectivity. He thus opened the way to an authentic subjective self, relatively independent of social and political institutions. The Socratic model showed Kierkegaard that irony can be the highroad to speaking of authenticity, since it uses conventional language to undermine traditional values.

On this Socratic basis Kierkegaard defines irony as 'infinite absolute negativity' (*CI*, p. 276). With his aporetic irony, Socrates became 'estranged from existence', hovering 'in ironic satisfaction' above the determinants of self, such as state, society and religion. Like Kierkegaard, Socrates stood in opposition to a world in decline, to an ethic which had lost its validity. He had arrived on the scene in an age when the divine was becoming extinct, before its incarnation in the body of Christ. He therefore had no choice but absolute negativity, offering no positive content but the negative freedom of reflection. Having none of Kierkegaard's notions of the pathos of passionate commitment to faith, he could not become the thinker of authenticity. His irony was infinite negativity, since sheer reflectiveness, without positive existential content, opens itself to doubt. With no reason for discontinuing the process, it finally 'dissolves' everything, paralysing any definite action short of its own destruction (witness Socrates' self-inflicted death-sentence).

Yet Kierkegaard was attracted to this picture of Socrates as ironic subject in an age of religious decline, where the pathos of subjective inwardness was swallowed up by the superficial objective ethic, itself on the verge of decline:

> With every turning point in history there are two movements to be observed. On the one hand, the new shall come forth; on the other, the old must be displaced . . . and seen in all its imperfection, and here we meet the ironic subject. . . . The ironist has advanced beyond the reach of his age and opened a front against it. That which shall come is hidden from him, concealed behind his back, but the actuality he hostilely opposes is the one he shall destroy.
>
> (*CI*, pp. 277–8)

The ironic subject, therefore, has no choice but to speak the language of the declining ethos of his age while aiming at a new, as yet unborn ethic. By doing this he entices us to forgo our inauthentic illusions and selves and marks the way to the pathos of authenticity.

Kierkegaard here emphasizes that irony is 'a negative concept': it 'established nothing, for that which is to be established lies behind it': hence its intimate relation with authenticity, which is also a negative notion in a negative age, that is, in an age which has lost its objective ethos. Irony alone cannot establish a new ethic, but by negating the discredited ethic it can augur the birth of a new one. Hence Kierkegaard concludes: 'Irony is like the negative way, not the truth but the way' (*CI*, pp. 50, 278, 340). It is the way to subjectivity as the 'truth' of one's 'inwardness', being, perhaps, only a transitional step before a new or renewed objective ethos.

Irony is negative in another sense too, since its basic feature, as Kierkegaard puts it, is to affirm the opposite of what is meant or felt: the essence (meaning) is not the appearance (the ironic figure of speech or phrase). In this respect it is the language of the genuine poet, portrayed poetically as 'an unhappy man who in his heart harbours a deep anguish, but whose lips are so fashioned that the moans and cries which pass over them are transformed into ravishing music' (*Either/ Or*, I, p. 49).

Another facet of irony has direct relevance to the enticement to authenticity: 'The ironic figure of speech cancels itself, however, for the speaker presupposes his listeners understand him, hence through a negation of the immediate phenomenon the essence remains identical with the phenomenon' (*CI*, p. 265). Ironic communication is contingent upon the reader's understanding that he faces irony. But only one who seeks authenticity, who stands beyond the 'present age' of dishonest honesty and feels the urge for a genuine self, is able to see that he confronts an ironic situation. Just as only one with a sense of humour can appreciate jokes, so only a person who can feel that his self is not his own can respond to the ironic tactic of enticement. This is what Kierkegaard means by 'Irony is a determination of subjectivity' (*CI*, p. 275). The individual determined to form his own self and become an authentic person is the proper target for the ironic posture.

This brings us to Kierkegaard's notion of irony from the perspective of the individual who adopts irony as a total existential attitude to life:

> No authentic human life is possible without irony. When irony has first been mastered it . . . limits, renders finite, defines, and thereby imparts stability, character, and consistency. . . . He who does not understand irony and has no ear for its whisperings lacks *eo ipso* . . . the absolute beginning of the personal life.
>
> (*CI*, pp. 338–9)

By irony 'mastered' Kierkegaard means irony that is consciously used as a method and instrument and not as an end in itself. As an end in itself it can mislead and destroy. If we are not able to direct it to attaining our own purposes, then 'irony is an abnormal development which, like the abnormality of the livers of Strasburger geese, ends by killing the individual' (Hong, II, p. 262). It drives us to a reflective regression *ad infinitum*, without repose or stable commitment, until it paralyses our will to live. This is exactly what happened in the case of Socrates, who, according to Kierkegaard, lacked the stabilizing content of passionate faith. 'Therefore Socrates' influence was simply to awaken – midwife that he was – not redeeming except in an inauthentic sense' (Hong, II, p. 256). But if one uses irony in a constructive and controllable way, then it becomes a 'guide' and a means for moulding one's genuine self. This is the 'truth of irony' about which Kierkegaard speaks at the end of his dissertation. To form freely one's own self one must first detach oneself from it and work on it from the outside, as it were. Here, the ironic posture helps significantly. Mastered irony allows one to judge one's values as if they were someone else's. It helps one to detach oneself from the prevailing values and modes of behaviour and yet to act within that ethos, to transform it from within. Moreover, if one succeeds in detaching one's own self from the 'levelling' processes of the 'present age' this shows that one still has a subjective self to be detached from, which may encourage attempts to make it into a genuine self by free and fearless commitment to authentic acts of faith. This is the reason for Kierkegaard's 'definition of irony' as 'the fusion of a passionately ethical view, which inwardly lays infinite stress upon the self – and of education which outwardly (among others) abstracts infinitely from the personal I' (Dru, p. 139).

Here Kierkegaard calls the search for authenticity 'a passionately ethical view'. This fits well with my interpretation of his notion of authenticity as 'a passionate and sincere commitment or act'. Though the 'maximum' passion is to be found in religious faith, sincerity is an ethical category. The concept of authenticity thus does not belong exclusively to the religious realm. The concern of any individual with the character of his own self is obviously an ethical issue. Although according to Kierkegaard the genuineness of the self is grounded in passionate faith, this should not prevent us from seeing that his concern with authenticity makes him an existentialist moralist *par excellence*. For authenticity is not a quality one either possesses or lacks; it is an attribute of the will to be able to create one's genuine self. It characterizes the subject not just as part of nature, but as part of the moral realm. Against the impersonal and impassive objective ethic of tradition, Kierkegaard emerges as a moralist of the subjective pathos of authenticity. In moving from ethics to morality he uses ironic communication aimed at enticing us to follow the same path. The irony which seeks to help us attain this intense authenticity 'is really the deepest irony. . . . But to excavate in the middle of "Christendom" the types of being a Christian – this is the most intensive irony' (Hong, II, p. 277).

V

Kierkegaard's ironic ladder to authenticity has three rungs – the aesthetic, the ethical and the religious – the first two of which will produce despair. The reader's motivation to go on living inauthentic modes of life is arrested by these ironic descriptions. These accounts of possible life-styles show disastrous consequences from the psychological point of view and pave the way to the existential change of the reader's way of life and his self. Kierkegaard describes these steps as 'views of life', 'existential categories', 'spheres of existence', 'modes of existing' or 'stages on life's way'. As fundamental existential commitments which by definition cannot coexist, they are incompatible with one another.

The incompatibility of these life-styles, however, stems not only from the existential and psychological point of view but also from theoretical considerations given by Kierkegaard. Each 'sphere of existence' contains its own system of values. The choice must be made without any guiding meta-principle but by an a-rational 'leap' of free choice which cannot be further defended. Kierkegaard strives to adopt religious faith, but for him this concrete appropriation is not the 'absolute truth' but only his *own* passionate commitment. Here lies the main difference between Kierkegaard's existential dialectic of authenticity and the Hegelian dialectic of Absolute Spirit. In the former there is a conspicuous lack of a rationally necessary transition from one form of life to another, reason having been dethroned from its ultimate role as the driving force of dialectics. Lacking ultimate authority, reason itself becomes open to challenge by the individual, who can always ask: 'Why be rational at all?' Thus choice and spontaneous freedom are reintroduced by Kierkegaard, and the Kantian and Hegelian rational or ethical way of life is just one possibility among many. Man can no longer live under the illusion that the choice and, therefore, the responsibility for a system of values is out of his hands. For Hegel, freedom consists simply in following Reason, but for Kierkegaard following anything means giving up one's freedom and hence one's authenticity.

Free choice is the mark of the 'truly existent individual' – setting him off from the 'crowd'. Kierkegaard's point here has little to do with the metaphysical problem of freedom and determinism. His concern is with our subjective inward life and intentions. He does not question our belief and feeling that we have freedom of choice and does not consider the traditional philosophical problem of whether one actually is free. Kierkegaard 'brackets' the external world.

His existential version of dialectic is individual, passionate and discontinuous, proceeding by sudden leaps and crises. Man is a living passion, not abstract reason. Hence the individual's conflicting courses of action exist side by side without being synthesized. Conflict is present in any sphere of existence to which one commits oneself. Unlike Hegel's dialectic, there is no necessary transition from one sphere to another, no compromise or 'mediation' (to use a Hegelian concept) between them, and no rational resolution of their 'opposition'. The individual faces 'paradoxes', that is, opposed ways of life or alternative courses of action, and a choice must be made. This is exemplified in the title of the work, where the two spheres of existence, the aesthetic and the ethical, are described: *Either/Or*, as opposed to Hegel's 'both . . . and . . .'.

Here we face a serious problem in interpreting Kierkegaard's doctrine of possible life-views. At first the existential spheres are presented as equally valid possibilities, and as such Kierkegaard cannot directly show which is preferable. Later, however, he presents them as stages, as an actual progression from aesthetic to ethical and finally to fundamental religious commitment.[22] This ambiguity persists throughout Kierkegaard's writings and is neatly expressed by contrasting the notions of 'spheres' (*Spoere*), which can be simultaneously present and overlapping, and 'stages' (*Stadier*), which must be successive temporary steps. But in what sense are the earlier stages inferior to the final one?

Some commentators have provided vague or partial answers to these questions. They speak, for instance, about 'a mounting hierarchy of existential fullness' and about 'the development of the individual self'.[23]

It should be pointed out that the existential movement towards authenticity has nothing to do with a concept of 'development' or with the widespread notion of 'self-realization'. Kierkegaard's notion of authenticity is not about the realization or fulfilment of one's self but about its spontaneous creation. The self is something that should be created and formed, not something possessing an intrinsic essence to be further developed.

Moreover, authentic selves do not exist; there are only certain individuals who carry out authentic acts and live authentic modes of life, in contradistinction to persons (in the Latin sense of *persona* as a player's mask) who escape the responsibility and 'dizziness' of freedom into inauthentic ways of living. Thus authenticity has nothing to do with quantities and sequences in time but has to do with the quality and origin of action. In various psychoanalytic analogies and psychological interpretations of Kierkegaard's 'stages' as 'self-development' the time factor becomes crucial, but in a philosophical sense succession in time is irrelevant. An act either is or is not authentic. One cannot stipulate degrees of authenticity and progressive levels of its so-called realization. Hence there are no 'stages' of authenticity, and the notion is applicable only to the rhetoric of enticement.

Still, there is one important sense, beyond the rhetoric, in which the idea of stages is relevant to Kierkegaard's notion of authenticity: 'Johannes Climacus being purely subjective . . . shows that there is a "how" which has this quality, that if *it* is truly given, then the "what" is also given; and that it is the "how" of "faith". Here quite certainly, we have inwardness at its maximum' (Dru, p. 355; cf. *CUP*, p. 248).

Kierkegaard, referring to 'Johannes the Climber' (the pseudonymous writer of the *Postscript*, where the stages are arranged in a sevenfold scheme), postulates that if passion is 'truly given' it will result in authentic action. Maximum authenticity will be found in the realm of faith, where the 'how' and the 'what' overlap. But if Kierkegaard speaks of 'inwardness at its maximum', does this mean that there are lesser degrees of authenticity?

Not necessarily, as is already evident from the eloquent maxim presented under Kierkegaard's own name in his *Edifying Discourses in Various Spirits* from 1847: 'PURITY OF HEART IS TO WILL ONE THING'.[24] On my reading, this means that authenticity is sincerity of intention ('purity of heart') along with passion ('to will') directed at 'one' object. This 'thing', according to Kierkegaard, is 'Good' or 'God', but especially one's own self. That is, authenticity consists in acts of willing passionately and sincerely to become a genuinely authentic individual. Hence becoming authentic requires perpetual movement without definite results. It is 'the way which is the truth'.

The scheme of existential spheres can also be said to contain 'stages' in terms of the intensity of the passion involved. Aesthetic objects annul passion, thereby destroying authenticity. Because of its reflective and abstract nature, the ethical object, though preserving the sincerity of intent (sincerity being in itself an ethical category), cannot enlist the optimal intensity of passion required for authentic acts. Hence, Kierkegaard asserts, it is only in the religious sphere that the 'what' does not destroy the 'how'. Appearing as an infinite being, it incites the most intense passion, and vice versa: a certain manner of willing and intending – infinite, that is, absolute and unconditional passion – gives the 'what' of faith. But it should be stressed that these internal stages of intensity of passion do not result in overall stages of 'developing' authenticity, since in Kierkegaard authenticity is possible in the sphere of faith alone. Thus here we have internal stages but an external dichotomy between the spheres.

The stages, however, are significant for the indirect tactic of enticement. Kierkegaard needed to arrest the most widespread modes of living, which, he held, were aestheticism and Romanticism. His age, which lacked passion, had 'no values' and was on the verge of completely losing the individual self. Kierkegaard, therefore, used aesthetic-Romantic categories to inject a passion of commitment into the prevailing 'apathy'. Moreover, Kierkegaard could not help having aesthetic tendencies himself. He had to start from the aesthetic modes of living in order to overcome them in his own person as well as in his 'age'. In his era of 'Christendom' without genuine 'Christians' there were many more 'honest persons' than authentically faithful individuals. Because of these historical, tactical and existential considerations, Kierkegaard begins with the 'aesthetic sphere', then moves to the 'ethical sphere'.

The place accorded to the ethical sphere may also be connected with Kantian ethics and the Hegelian notion of *Sittlichkeit*. To understand Kierkegaard's claim in the *Postscript*, 'The ethical and the religious stages have in fact an essential relationship to one another' (p. 261), we have to realize that the Kantian and Hegelian ethic of sincerity and honesty, which constitutes a social and bourgeois way of life, paves the way for Kierkegaard's morality of authenticity.

We should also keep in mind that Kierkegaard's tactical 'stages' of enticement were related to his own life-experiences. Here his problematic use of the notions of 'spheres' and 'stages' becomes part of a personal dialectic. At the beginning the young Kierkegaard faced simultaneous overlapping spheres of existence. Later he formed his own self by actualizing existential spheres of possibility. Then he realized that there was a 'method in his madness', namely, that there was a unifying dialectical movement prompting him to 'leap' from one sphere to another. Thus at the beginning there were only 'spheres' (a term frequently used in his earlier books), but retrospectively they became 'stages' – in his life as well as in his writings.

Using the rhetoric of irony, Kierkegaard strives to entice us to choose freely, passionately and sincerely, that is to say, authentically. But to do so we must first 'relate' earnestly to our own selves. To clarify this crucial point and the driving motive behind Kierkegaard's ironic and evocative presentations of the first two modes of existence, I now turn briefly to his image of man:

> Man is spirit. But what is spirit? Spirit is the self. But what is the self? The self is a relation which relates itself to its own self. . . . Man is a synthesis of the infinite and the finite, of the temporal and the eternal, of freedom and necessity. . . . A man who has no will at all is no self.[25]

I interpret this enigmatic (almost Hegelian, one might say) text as follows: man is a spiritual self trying to unite contrary tendencies of soul and body, of possibility and necessity. To exist is to be in the process of becoming one's self. It means using one's freedom for self-creation and self-transcendence, refusing to let the 'finite' or the passive elements of our facticity determine who we are. By a conscious and committed 'relation' to ourselves and by concentration on creating ourselves we are continually ('eternally') becoming authentic individuals. Authenticity, or the quest for it, is, then, the 'way' which determines what we really are – indeterminacy. A man who does not 'will' or does not accept this perpetual movement towards self-creation dissolves his own self either by not really choosing (the aesthetic predicament) or by choosing a dispassionate part or role in an abstract wholeness (the ethical). Always to have to choose freely and create one's own self is to be in a constant state of 'dread'[26] or anxiety, but to give up this quest means to be rid of one's self and to be in despair. And, indeed, every project begins in dread while the first two modes of life end in despair. This follows from Kierkegaard's expositions of the aesthetic and the ethical life-styles from which he wants to liberate us by his ironic indirect communication.

In the first volume of *Either/Or* Kierkegaard uses the term 'aesthetic' in its most comprehensive sense, derived from the Greek *aisthesis*, which literally means sense-perception and observation. This sphere is that of sensual immediacy and passive absorption in external circumstances, where immediate pleasure is sought by employing one's natural endowments and given conditions. The aesthete avoids decision either through immersion in sensuous inclination or through endless and fruitless reflection. He is striving not to form his own self, but only to create the right circumstances for intensifying his pleasure from external objects. In this sense he is actually not choosing his self, but rather using with sophistication the aesthetic element by which 'he is immediately what he is': pure natural facticity. In this sphere, therefore, there is no trace of self-creation, and the already-given raw material of one's senses and inclinations plays the major, or the only, role. From this point of view, the 'Judge' who is supposedly the author of the second volume of *Either/Or*, presenting the 'ethical sphere', is right in accusing the aesthete of living negatively by refusing to choose at all, of remaining essentially passive in his aesthetic pursuits.[27] Since the aesthetic sphere is characterized by the absence of genuine choice – choice that fundamentally changes and forms one's self – freedom is not exercised at all and there is no place for authenticity.

The latter is also suppressed by the continued escape from sincere commitment to any potential object that might satisfy the aesthetic urge. This happens because beyond the constant threat of pain and frustration there is the even greater danger of boredom due to the unceasing repetition of the same or similar stimuli. Kierkegaard ironically 'translates' the first chapters of Genesis in describing this 'root of all evil' for the aesthete:

> The gods were bored, and so they created man. Adam was bored because he was alone, and so Eve was created. Thus boredom entered the world, and increased in proportion to the increase of population. . . . To divert themselves they conceived the idea of constructing a tower high enough to reach the heavens. This idea is itself as boring as the tower was high. . . . The nations were scattered over the earth, just as people now travel abroad, but they continued to be bored. . . . The English are in general the paradigmatic nation.
>
> (*Either/Or*, I, pp. 282, 286)

As a remedy against boredom Kierkegaard suggests the 'Rotation Method' (from which the above passage is taken). This essay is one of the best examples of his irony. The aesthetic mode is reduced to absurdity by his advice to escape the imminent boredom by constant and 'prudent' changes and artificial intensification of aesthetic stimuli. Kierkegaard suggests several principles for the aesthete 'to find diversion' and as a way of avoiding commitment: develop the art of forgetting, *Nil admirari*, 'keep the enjoyment under control', 'never enter into the relation of marriage', hold 'fast' to life of sheer 'arbitrariness', and so forth. All these maxims can be summed up as the project of perpetuating one's indeterminacy by absolute non-commitment to anything, not even to one's own self, which is completely dissolved during this process. No genuine choice is made because nothing significant must happen. One's inherent needs for eternity, transcendence and meaning are repressed but nevertheless demand fulfilment. The outcome is a pervasive feeling of estrangement, 'melancholy' and 'despair'. One loses one's own self in the aesthetic mode of life but cannot get rid of the psychological effects accompanying this loss of self. All this is beautifully though indirectly portrayed in Kierkegaard's ironic descriptions. If being ironic in general means 'intending to be interpreted as having a meaning different from one's words',[28] then here we have irony at its best, since Kierkegaard presents the aesthetic sphere from within, as it were, right up to its most extreme manifestations. Behind his romantic portrayal Kierkegaard points to the hell which looms for any resident of this aesthetic 'paradise'. This hell, if felt by the reader, freezes any desire to live that kind of life.

The possibility of authenticity in the aesthetic domain is also thwarted by lack of genuine passion. Kierkegaard conceived of strong passion for, or intensive emotional attachment to, particular objects, as the optimal expression of freedom and authenticity. In the aesthetic sphere, however, this is not the kind of passion that drives one's actions; there is only 'the emptiness of a blind and noisy enthusiasm' (*Either/Or*, I, p. 286). In this reflective and diluted age it is not passion that holds the reins but 'apathetic' and 'calculating' feelings.

If, dissatisfied with the aesthetic mode of existence, one 'leaps' desperately to the ethical sphere, one is no better off as far as authenticity is concerned. In his understanding of the ethical sphere, Kierkegaard was dependent on Kant's popular version of moral philosophy. He believed the ethical domain lacked the passion required for authenticity, that duty swallowed up love.

However, the superiority of the ethical to the aesthetic with respect to authenticity - given the sincerity of intention, free resolution of one's will, and commitment to one object – is apparent rather than real. Because of its abstractness, universalism and formalism, the ethical depersonalizes the self, suppressing its spontaneous and passionate expression. The equilibrium or integrity between the conflicting elements of self is shaken. Moreover, the demand for absolute conformity prevents the emergence of the unique individual. Another important reason for the breakdown of the ethical sphere is the fact that 'ethics points to ideality as a task and assumes that man is in possession of the conditions requisite for performing it. Thereby ethics develops a contradiction, precisely for the fact that it makes the difficulty and impossibility clear' (*Concept of Dread*, p. 15). Since one is unable to enlist the help of passionate commitment to fulfil high ethical standards, and because of their very ideality, the ethically oriented individual recognizes his failure to achieve this goal, 'goes bankrupt' and feels guilty. He begins to blame himself and try harder, but to no avail. Despair makes him feel a sinner and he assumes the notion of 'original sin'. With the notion of sin 'there has come to the fore a category that lies entirely outside its provinces' (*Stages*, p. 430). The individual is now ready to adopt the religious way and try to regain equilibrium between what he ought to be and what he is, and so to establish inner harmony between his conflicting aspirations. He becomes motivated to assume the quest for authenticity. This is the sense of Kierkegaard's claim that 'the ethical sphere is a transitional sphere', that 'the religious' sphere becomes 'that of fulfilment' (*Dread*, p. 17; *Stages*, p. 430). Kierkegaard's attitude to ethics is thus essentially a critique of Kant, who argued for the autonomy of ethics.

Without the passion of faith, ethics cannot stand alone. Even the ethical claim for universality cannot be validly maintained, for extreme existential situations far exceed the scope of ethics and do not fall under the ethic of honesty and sincerity. One such extreme situation is the case of Abraham, who scandalously (at least to the ethical mind) attempts, on God's orders, to sacrifice his son Isaac. Kierkegaard's poetic description of this exception undermines the claim of ethics to universality and 'freezes' the willingness of those trying to attain authenticity to follow the ethical code blindly. Kierkegaard concludes his enticement by presenting us with a case of authentic faith, where the utmost passion enables us to commit ourselves intensely to the formation of our own selves.

VI

That it is impossible to point to concrete living or dead individuals as authentic figures does not stem solely from the fact that authenticity 'begins precisely there where' the ethos of objectivity and rationality 'leaves off' (*FT*, p. 64), taking with it all public criteria of judgement. Kierkegaard holds that it also has to do with the intrinsic nature of authenticity, which revolves around the innermost self and the subjective 'inwardness' of passion. Outwardly the authentic hero may even look like a 'tax-collector', like any philistine exercising his conventional and ethical modes of living. But inwardly it is a different story altogether. Abraham's self, tested and forged by the dreadful encounter with the Absolute, acquires a qualitatively new nature. Kierkegaard uses this point to reject 'the familiar philosophic maxim' of Hegelian philosophy 'that the external is the internal, and the internal the external' (*Either/Or*, I, p. 3). At one point, Johannes *de silentio*, the pseudonymous author of *Fear and Trembling*, characterizes faith as 'the paradox that inwardness is higher than outwardness',[29] whereas in the ethical sphere, the moral agent's rational (Kantian) duty is to 'become revealed' and to express his subjectivity 'in an outward way'. While the ethic of honesty is objective, public and transparently manifested, the pathos of authenticity is concealed, radically subjective, and externalized only rarely, in momentous acts of 'truthfulness'.

The individual always finds it difficult to be sure of his authenticity. In diametrical opposition to Hegel's image of man, the knight of faith, renouncing the universal language of reflective thought, cannot become intelligible even to himself. 'Abraham', the paradigmatic knight of faith, 'keeps silent – but he cannot speak'.[30] His immediate, faithful and private relation to God makes it impossible for him to speak to Isaac or to anyone else. Kierkegaard interprets the Biblical story as Abraham's attempt to test his religious commitment by an extraordinary act of faith. Only such an act, analogous to those in certain extreme situations described by other writers, can attest the authenticity of the believer. In other words, by his determined act to sacrifice his dearest for the sake of God, Abraham proves to be an authentic believer. This explains why, in an essay on authenticity in the sense of *auctoritas* (possessing original or inherent authority), Kierkegaard answers the question of how an Apostle can prove he has authority as follows: 'An Apostle has no other proof than his own statement, and at the most, his willingness to suffer anything for the sake of that statement.' The Apostle, like St Paul, is no 'genius', but 'a simple man'. He cannot prove that he has 'divine authority', but it remains his responsibility to see that 'he produces that impression'. In other words, one cannot prove that one is authentic but one can feel in one's innermost self the need for authenticity, and thus seek it constantly. This mode of living may shape such a personality so that by sheer force it conveys its authentic 'authority'. The latter, unlike genius, is not 'marked out by natural gifts', but is formed continuously by one's own efforts, sufferings and self-overcomings.[31]

Abraham cannot analyse himself or immerse himself in endless reflection. Because of his great passion, he is not paralysed at the moment of truth – or rather of truthfulness. For Kierkegaard the ideas of passion and uncertainty are interrelated; it is the most uncertain thing that excites our most burning passion. Thus Abraham has to risk the possibility that it is not God who summons him to sacrifice Isaac, but Satan, or an unconscious urge, or a delusion. After all, Abraham's decision to sacrifice Isaac might be a horrible temptation, what Kierkegaard terms an *Anfechtung* in several places.[32] This is the 'dread' that makes Abraham choose the quest of authentic faith. Here, not reflection, but only action, can attest to the self's authenticity. The act in which 'the knife glittered' was the act of infinite and absurd faith that caused Abraham to believe deeply 'that God who requires it of him should the next instant recall the requirement'.

According to ethical standards sanctioned by society, the universal always takes precedence over the particular.[33] Yet the paradox of faith is that the particular becomes higher than the universal by virtue of its passionate relation to the Absolute. Even the murder of one's son can be a holy act, if done at the behest of God. Faith is a passion which begins at the point where reason ceases to operate; it means believing the absurd, contrary to all rational, earthly calculations. Because it is a relationship between the finite and the infinite, between the ephemeral and the absolute, it supersedes all else. The 'absolute duty' to God (who, by virtue of being Absolute, is not bound by morality) renders all other ethical obligations relative. Thus, after despairing of the 'ethical sphere', when we realize our inability to live up to the abstract and categorical demands of morality – this realization being sparked by Kierkegaard's description of the ethical sphere – and after Kierkegaard has managed to uncover our repressed passion, we are psychologically ready for the final stage of his enticement to 'leap into' the authenticity of faith. But are we ready, for the sake of our authenticity, to perform the 'teleological suspension of the ethical' and behave like Abraham, who 'by his act . . . overstepped the ethical entirely' (*FT*, p. 69)?

Thus it seems that the first modern philosopher of authenticity was willing to involve us in a serious clash between this authenticity and ethics. His version of the story of Abraham suggests that the road to authenticity may even pass beyond rational communication and the ethos of honesty. But to attain authentic life we should not hesitate to enter this zone even at the terrible price of crucifying our understanding. It is possible to argue against Kierkegaard that if the crucial factor in authenticity is the 'how' of passion, does it not follow that on his view it is better to be a zealous Nazi than a lukewarm Christian? Is Abraham the highly esteemed knight of faith or just a zealous murderer? If an authentic mode of living requires an individual's total and passionate commitment and uncompromising rejection of anything that is alien or contradictory to it, could it be that a passionate Nazi or religious fanatic is to be regarded as an authentic subject and deserving our highest esteem? Such questions were directed to Kierkegaard by various unsympathetic critics. Using my presentation of his position, I think a partial defence against such attacks can be mounted.

As we saw, Kierkegaard holds that authenticity is formed by a kind of correlation between the 'what' of commitment and the 'how' of committing oneself. Kierkegaard seems to think that any *idée fixe* or ideology directed towards a finite and limited object, such as the thousand-year *Reich*, cannot in principle incite the 'endless passion' required for acting authentically. Only an infinite and absolute object or paradox can evoke the required absolute passion. Our authenticity may emerge only through the 'suspension' of reason and logic. But for this we need an object, like that of Christian faith, which will demand that we do exactly that, namely, bracket out our morality codes.

However, one may object and argue that, psychologically at least, it is still plausible that even a finite object, such as my love for a woman, can incite me to such a degree of passion that I may sacrifice everything to preserve my absolute commitment to her. And indeed Kierkegaard describes love in terms similar to those he uses for faith, saying: 'Love is a passion whose pathos is immediate' (*CUP*, p. 345). It seems that there is no obstacle to becoming passionately committed to a contingent and finite object, whom I may love just as authentically as I may believe in the Absolute. Why, then, is it only the Absolute God who has the capacity to overwhelm me so passionately that my faith in him is the only genuine expression of an authentic commitment?

One possible answer to this question, which will perhaps be regarded as scandalous by believers in any version of a transcendent God, is that this kind of faith is an expression of the ultimate paradox and requires man's most sustained creativity. To create God requires the utmost passion possible of man. I do not refer here to an actual creation but to the intentional constitution of the relation to an object which by this very relation becomes the Absolute. In his story of Abraham, Kierkegaard implies that the existential experience, which makes the 'knight of faith' affirm the command subjectively and regard it as coming from God, grants this God the status of being an absolute entity for Abraham. In order for the Absolute to become an Absolute for me and to demand of me 'an absolute duty', this Absolute is completely dependent upon my subjective interpretation of him as the Absolute. Here we reach the climax of the paradox: despite Abraham's awareness that the Absolute is dependent upon his decision to make him so, a fact that may destroy the immediate relation towards him, Abraham acts as if this Absolute has an objective authority to be the Absolute! Though the Absolute depends upon one's subjective decision, one has to accept him, as does Abraham, as if he is the objective Absolute *per se*. Thus God is intentionally created in our hearts, though we obey him as ontologically aloof, in heaven.

Kierkegaard maximizes and sharpens the distinction between man and God in order to make religious faith the most authentic and authoritative thing imaginable. The gap between God and man is infinite because it is man who made it, creating religions of transcendence. We should remember that both Abraham and Jesus were founders and originators of specific faiths, and since originality is part of the meaning of authenticity, both may legitimately be regarded, as indeed they are, as authentic 'knights of faith'. Whereas the most passionate lover is only forming passion in his inwardness and directing it to an already existing individual, the 'knight of faith' creates first the object of his faith and then the passion involved in the faithful commitment to this object. Thus the intimate correlation between the 'how' of faith and its 'what' is entirely of his making. Therefore it is only this formative relation that can create the self's authenticity. To create one's own self, one must first overcome one's sensual nature (aesthetics), then universal reason; only then can one become what one intrinsically is: the sole creator of one's self and God. For this the utmost passion, commitment and self-overcoming are needed. One must be deeply immersed in the search for authenticity. In ethics we have a similar 'what/how' correlation but, because of the abstractness of its objects and the amount of rational reflection involved, passion evaporates and the subject cannot become truly committed to the object of his creation.

But is not the correlation between object and subject a relic of traditional rationalism? It seems that in the most radical subjectivism we still find some residue of rational objectivity. But does this diminish the thrust or the revolt of authenticity against the ethic of objectivity?

And, in the final analysis, why is it valuable to be 'a truly existent individual'? Why is it better to suffer the agony and dread of authenticity than to be secure in the comfort of conventional public values such as, for example, honesty? Kierkegaard does not pose this question and does not feel discomfort about both denying any ultimate criterion for evaluation and positing authenticity as a value according to which actions are to be measured.

Notes

1 *The Journals of Søren Kierkegaard*, ed. and trans. A. Dru (London: Oxford University Press, 1938), (henceforth Dru), p. 15. Following Kierkegaard, I use 'individual', 'subjectivity', 'spirit', 'inwardness' and 'authenticity' interchangeably in this chapter.

2 Ibid., p. 16.

3 *Søren Kierkegaard's Journals and Papers*, ed. and trans. H. V. Hong and E. H. Hong (Bloomington: Indiana University Press, 1967) (henceforth Hong), vol. I, p. 331.

4 *The Point of View for My Work as an Author: A Report to History*, trans. W. Lowrie, ed. B. Nelson (New York: Harper & Row, 1962) (henceforth *PV*), pp. 5–6.

5 This was also perceptively observed by M. C. Taylor, *Kierkegaard's Pseudonymous Authorship* (Princeton, NJ: Princeton University Press, 1975), p. 5, and implied in Jean Wahl, *Études Kierkegaardiennes* (Paris: Aubier, 1938), esp. pp. 257–62.

6 For helpful summaries of various psychological and physiological analyses of Kierkegaard, see A. Henriksen, *Methods and Results of Kierkegaard Studies in Scandinavia: A Historical and Critical Study* (Copenhagen, 1951), pp. 66–128; M. Grimault, *La Melancholie de Kierkegaard* (Paris, 1965); H. Fenger, *Kierkegaard: The Myths and their Origins*, trans. G. C. Schoolfield (New Haven and London: Yale University Press, 1980), pp. 62–80. Against the reductive tendency, see

the classic essay of T. Haecker, *Kierkegaard the Cripple*, trans. C. Van O. Bruyn (London: Harvill, 1948).

7 J. Thompson, *The Lonely Labyrinth: Kierkegaard's Pseudonymous Works* (Carbondale, Ill.: Southern Illinois Press, 1967), p. xiii.

8 In the journals we can sense a gradually growing identification of the maturing young man with Christianity. At the beginning (1838) he asserts: 'I mean to labour to achieve a far more inward relation to Christianity; hitherto I have fought for its truth while in a sense standing outside it' (Dru, p. 59). A short time later, in 1839, Kierkegaard admits to 'having wasted the strength and courage of his youth in rebellion against Him' (ibid., p. 73). In 1848 and 1849, when he had reached religious maturity and stopped using pseudonyms, he stated unqualifiedly: 'The relation to God is the only thing that lends significance' (ibid., p. 241); 'I delineate Christianity . . . and consider that to be, quiet literally, my calling, to which I have been led in the most curious way from my earliest years' (ibid., p. 333).

9 Dru, p. 258; cf. another passage: 'The wrong path lies all too near, the wish to reform and awaken the whole world . . . instead of one's self' (ibid., p. 319).

10 *PV*, p. 12. The article mentioned is 'The Crisis and a Crisis in an Actress's Life' published in the July 1848 issue of the Danish journal *The Fatherland*.

11 *'The Present Age'* and *'Of the Difference between a Genius and an Apostle'*, trans. A. Dru (New York: Harper & Row, 1962) (henceforth *PA*), p. 33. The same point is already made by Kierkegaard in the 'Diapsalmata' of the early (1843) *Either/Or*: 'Let others complain that the age is wicked; my complaint is that it is paltry; for it lacks passion. Men's thoughts are thin and flimsy like lace, they are themselves pitiable like the lacemakers' (vol. I, trans. D. F. and L. M. Swenson (Garden City, NY: Doubleday, 1959), p. 27). Cf. his *Concluding Unscientific Postscript*, trans. D. F. Swenson and W. Lowrie (Princeton, NJ: Princeton University Press, 1941) (henceforth *CUP*), p. 345.

12 Friedrich Nietzsche, *The Birth of Tragedy*, trans. W. Kaufmann (New York: Random House, 1967), p. 60. This is especially true, Nietzsche says, of Hamlet.

13 This formula came to my mind after reading Kierkegaard's admonition that his age 'being without passion has lost all feeling for enthusiasm and sincerity' (*PA*, p. 39).

14 See, e.g., his *Attack upon 'Christendom'*, trans. W. Lowrie (Princeton, NJ: Princeton University Press, 1944).

15 *CUP*, first page following the end of the text. Kierkegaard's instruction

to his printer to print this appendix without numeration was kept to the letter (and the number) in the English translation.

16 *CUP,* pp. 72, 68, 68n., 236, 245n. Cf. J. Rée, *Philosophical Tales* (London: Methuen, 1987), pp. 114-20.

17 Ludwig Wittgenstein, *Tractatus Logico-Philosophicus,* ed. and trans. D. F. Pears and B. F. McGuinness (London: Routledge & Kegan Paul, 1961), p. 151, proposition 6.522. See also M. P. Gallagher, 'Wittgenstein's Admiration for Kierkegaard', *Month,* 29 (January, 1968), 43-9. It seems very likely (see P. Gardiner, *Kierkegaard* (London: Oxford University Press, 1988), p. 115) that the following remark made by Wittgenstein refers to Kierkegaard: 'An honest religious thinker is like a tightrope walker. He almost looks as though he were walking on nothing but air. His support is the slenderest imaginable. And yet it really is possible to walk on it' (*Culture and Value,* trans. P. Winch (London: Oxford University Press, 1980), p. 73).

18 *CUP,* p. 236, and chapter II of Part Two, pp. 169-224. Since almost every work on Kierkegaard deals with his polemic against Hegel, I will not dwell on it here, especially as it is only one part of his critique of the 'present age'.

19 *The Concept of Irony with Constant Reference to Socrates,* trans. L. M. Capel (New York: Harper & Row, 1965) (henceforth *CI*).

20 *CI,* p. 338. And see the last thesis (*xv*), where he formulates this idea as follows: 'As philosophy begins with doubt, so also that life which may be called worthy of man begins with irony' (p. 349).

21 *CI,* p. 190. In this dissertation, Kierkegaard uses Hegel's famous distinction between objective morality or *Sittlichkeit* and subjective morality or *Moralität* (individual conscience).

22 A concise outline is provided in *CUP,* pp. 261-5, and a more elaborate and poetic presentation in *Stages on Life's Way,* trans. W. Lowrie (Princeton, NJ: Princeton University Press, 1940).

23 See J. Collins, *The Mind of Kierkegaard* (London: Secker & Warburg, 1954), p. 46; and Taylor, *Kierkegaard's Pseudonymous Authorship,* p. 74. Taylor also provides an informative exposition of the basic ways in which the stages have been understood by commentators (pp. 62-77).

24 *A Kierkegaard Anthology,* ed. Robert Bretall (Princeton, NJ: Princeton University Press, 1946), p. 271. Cf. Kierkegaard's 'poetic' description of himself as an individual whose 'purity of heart was to will only one thing' (*PV,* p. 103).

25 *'The Sickness unto Death' and 'Fear and Trembling',* trans. W. Lowrie (Princeton, NJ: Princeton University Press, 1954), pp. 146, 162. (*Fear and Trembling* is henceforth referred to as *FT.*) Cf. the following pas-

sage from his journals: 'It is not true of the human race, as it is with animals, that each individual is only a particular instance or copy. The person who really becomes spirit, for which he is intended, at some point takes over his entire being (by "choosing himself", as it is called in *Either/Or*)' (Hong, p. 31). Interestingly enough, the motto for the first volume of *Either/Or* is taken from Edward Young, the eighteenth-century poet who asked the essential question regarding authenticity: 'Born Originals, how comes it to pass that we die Copies?'

26 *The Concept of Dread*, trans. W. Lowrie (Princeton, NJ: Princeton University Press, 1944), pp. 139–45.

27 For the quotations above, see *Either/Or*, vol. II, trans. W. Lowrie, p. 182. For the Judge's arguments, see ibid., pp. 170–82, 215–20.

28 Cf. Rée, *Philosophical Tales*, p. 27.

29 *FT*, p. 79. Kierkegaard is not very consistent in his distinction between 'paradox' and 'absurd', but he hints at the following difference: whereas 'absurd' describes actions or behaviours performed in a context devoid of any rational reason or justification, 'paradox' portrays a situation of conflict between two or more accepted modes of life, theoretical doctrines and sets of values, each containing its own principles. Cf. Kierkegaard's own statement: 'That there is a difference between the absurd in *Fear and Trembling* and the paradox in *Concluding Unscientific Postscript* is quite correct. The first is purely personal definition of existential faith – the other is faith in relationship to a doctrine' (Hong, vol. I, p. 8).

30 *FT*, p. 122. This fundamental loneliness of Abraham is also present in another fictional hero of authenticity – Nietzsche's Zarathustra.

31 'Of the Difference between a Genius and an Apostle', (see n. 11 above), pp. 105, 93–4.

32 E.g. *FT*, pp. 79, 124. This notion of negative enticement is analogous, as we shall see in the next chapter, to Nietzsche's concept of *Verführung*.

33 Interestingly, Kant, who worked out in detail a conception of religious life 'within the limits of Reason' and ethics 'alone', considers this same issue, namely, whether or not a father could be 'ordered' by God 'to kill his son who is, so far as he knows, perfectly innocent'. He concludes that since the moral law, being universal, cannot grant any exception to its maxims, and since such a command contradicts morality, it 'cannot, despite all appearances, be of God' (*Religion within the Limits of Reason Alone*, trans. T. M. Green and H. H. Hudson (New York: Harper & Row, 1960), p. 82). See the reference to the Abraham-Isaac story on p. 175. This view is rejected by Kierkegaard as too easy a way out of the paradox of faith.

4

Nietzsche's pathos of authenticity

Nietzsche did not use the term 'authenticity' explicitly, but it is possible to locate its origin in his recurrent distinctions between *Wahrheit* (truth) and *Wahrhaftigkeit* (truthfulness): 'a proof of truth is not the same thing as a proof of truthfulness ... the latter is in no way an argument for the former'.[1] This notion of *Wahrhaftigkeit* is virtually a synonym of the Heideggerian term *eigentlich* and of what in the later existentialist literature is called *authentic*. Since there is no necessary logical connection between truth and truthfulness, Nietzsche could admire Schopenhauer and Socrates while rejecting their doctrines. The shift from philosophy to philosophers, and that from the traditional meaning of truth to personal authenticity, show up repeatedly in Nietzsche's treatment of the history of philosophy. In his lectures on the Presocratics he declares: 'The only thing of interest in a refuted system is the personal element. It alone is what is forever irrefutable.'[2]

One of the basic intuitions of Nietzsche's thought is the concept of complete immanence, formulated in sections 108-25 of *The Gay Science*. Transcendental entities or supra-natural powers do not exist; there is no 'pure reason', no other world, no domain different from or superior to our own. After the 'Death of God' one has to adopt for oneself the God-like role of being the originator of truth and of one's own self. The absence of a 'pre-established harmony' between our cognitions and reality permits us to shift our emphasis to the creation of our own genuine selves.

We can attain 'truthfulness' only if we accept life in all its harshness and its complete immanency. If an individual is prevented from genuinely creating and expressing his self, a deepening alienation develops between him, his 'civilized' acts and his civilization. This is, then, the positive task of Nietzsche's philosophy: to assist us in overcoming culture's repression and entice us into uncovering and reactivating our own creative powers.[3]

Nietzsche rejects the entire philosophical tradition of rationalism and the ethos of honesty and sincerity from Descartes onwards. But it would be a mistake to suggest that he is pre-eminently an anti-rationalist who wishes to suppress all knowledge and reflection in favour of a 'return to nature'. The rational-Apollonian principle of self-knowledge, first described by Nietzsche in *The Birth of Tragedy*, is also an integral part of his thought on authenticity. An individual's life comprises a boundless number of experiences and notions, including a tremendous burden of superfluous information. Through awareness of one's authentic needs one may organize and refine this chaos into a harmonious, sublimated whole. Initially, the self is a bundle of conflicting desires and an array of contradictory possibilities. The self's unity is a function of its own decisions and creations.

It appears that two seemingly contradictory models of authenticity are in Nietzsche's thought. The first model (whose historical roots are, perhaps, to be found in Rousseau) derives its inspiration from the biological metaphor of a plant actualizing the potential of the seed. It assumes the individualistic thesis, namely, that 'every man is a unique miracle',[4] a unique aggregate of drives and wishes. One becomes authentic, according to this model, if one manages to manifest this complex fully in one's lifetime. The second model employs the metaphor of art and artistic creation. The search for authenticity is seen as the wish to reflect one's own indeterminacy by spontaneous choice of one out of the many possible ways of life. The individual is a kind of artist who freely shapes his self as a work of art.

It would be a mistake, however, to think that Nietzsche embraced these two models equally. The second conception, that of artistic creation, is surely primary. Nietzsche rejects crude naturalism and determinism and does not believe that the innateness of one's individualistic nature completely determines one's self. Nietzsche is less concerned with biological nature and more with cultural conditioning and formative influences which blindly shape one's character. To become 'what we are' is not to live according to our so-called 'innate nature', but to create ourselves freely. To that end we have to know ourselves to distinguish what we can change in ourselves and in the external circumstances that have shaped us; we must realize what we have to accept as inevitable, and must do so in the heroic manner of *amor fati* (love of fate).[5] The concept of self-overcoming (*Selbstüberwindung*), which is central to Nietzsche's thought, would become meaningless were the biological model really dominant.

The notion of self-overcoming is the key to the meaning of the will to power, a pivotal notion in Nietzsche. This is illustrated in *Thus Spoke Zarathustra*, where Nietzsche discusses the will to power in terms of the unceasing will to overcome one's self. The will to be rid of the superfluous elements of one's character and culture indicates spiritual maturity. If one were to ask Nietzsche the purpose of this self-over-coming, his answer would be, to attain maturity, authenticity and power. In this respect the will to power is of a piece with the quest for authenticity – the will to become the free author of one's own self. The optimal will to power is expressed by the ideally authentic *Übermensch*. If this will is diminished in quality, the tendency to escape from the task of creating one's self and to identify with the 'herd' will intensify. One endowed with a will to power of higher quality and greater vitality will manifest the 'master morality' and authentic life patterns, in contrast to the 'slave morality' typical of those possessing lesser power (*Macht*). The latter, however, may be endowed with greater physical force (*Kraft*). Nietzsche's distinction between *Kraft* and *Macht*, which cannot be elaborated here,[6] represents his philosophical emphasis on the transition from sheer physical force and brutal violence (*Gewalt*) to spiritual-creative power which is necessary if one is to attain authenticity.

I

Nietzsche's use of an artistic model of authenticity begins in *The Birth of Tragedy* (1872), where he delineates an 'Apollonian principle' which exercises its drives in direct opposition to the 'Dionysian barbarian' instincts. It does this through the creation of sophisticated images, and the imposition of order and a causal network on to the world.

The subjugation by Apollo of the unrestrained drives of the Dionysian barbarian is the source of art in general. This synthesis provides 'the metaphysical comfort' which allows man to affirm existence despite its horrors. By this process, through which man is purified of his cruder components, he himself is transformed into an object of art, into an artistic sublimation: 'He is no longer an artist', Nietzsche tells us, 'he has become a work of art.'[7] This, in fact, is the image of the authentic individual who individualizes and creates himself. In this act of creation, creator and creation merge; and any possible alienation between man and his created objects is overcome, since these objects become an integral part of his own self. For Nietzsche, the work of art is a product of the transforming of man's drives. It is this sublimation by art, this artistic mode of being in the world, that enables one to remain oneself and continue to live. Art protects man from the fear of existence and the struggle with absurd reality, without repressing his instinctual Dionysian elements. On the contrary, art allows them to be manifested by transforming the world into an 'aesthetic phenomenon', rendering it enjoyable in spite of its inherent pain.

One Apollonian principle, expressed in the command 'know thyself', is self-consciousness. This means knowing one's own instinctual desires, being aware of one's hidden wishes and of one's genuine, Dionysian character. At the same time it recommends coming to terms and living with them in a well-functioning and authentic manner. The really powerful person, though cognizant of sickness, affirms life and health. Apollonian culture recognizes only the rational principle in nature and in its own creations. It therefore perpetuates an illusion regarding its true origins. This illusion prevented the Greeks from attaining authentic existence. For this reason, Nietzsche ultimately rejects the purely aesthetic solution and corrects it by proposing a concept of existence stripped of veils and self-deceptions. This attitude is characteristic of the *Übermensch*; it leads to the acquisition of profound self-knowledge by destroying our various rationalizations through a process of 'unmasking'.

The process of attaining authenticity by unmasking begins to emerge in Nietzsche's 'Schopenhauer as Educator', where he claims that human nature is 'a thing dark and veiled' (SE, p. 129). Although potentially creative and powerful, man is afraid of expressing himself freely, fully and uniquely, and hides behind various dogmas. He typically prefers empty generalizations to his own remarkable particularity. This motivates Nietzsche's unmasking method, which attempts to free human individuality from such masks. Unmasking functions as a vehicle of authentic existence by exposing the individual's dependence on external conditioning and internal deception.

A critical challenge to Nietzsche's pursuit of the authentic personality is that of gaining access to the innermost self – the 'veiled' self carefully guarded by a complex of psychological defences. Suspecting the reliability of introspection, Nietzsche prefers a more indirect course, the investigation of exemplary figures and models which allow the development of self-identity through assimilation:

> Let the youthful soul look back on life with the question: what have you truly loved up to now, what has drawn your soul aloft, what has mastered it and at the same time blessed it? Set up these revered objects before you and perhaps their nature . . . will give you a law, the fundamental law of your own true self.
>
> (SE, p. 129)

We are at liberty to shape our identity and ideals by freely choosing our educators; indeed our 'educators can be only our liberators' (SE, p. 129). This freedom makes us responsible for our characters just as artists are responsible for their creations. The path to this creation of an authentic self follows the leads of one's educators. By subjecting our intuitive admiration for exemplary figures to self-analysis, we come to realize what we genuinely value and who we really are. Nietzsche is not propounding an 'ethics of self-realization'.[8] This ill-chosen term distorts Nietzsche's view, since it presupposes a given personal self and clearly rests on the biological model of authenticity. Nietzsche, however, makes it clear that becoming one's true self is a perpetual movement of self-overcoming, a free creation of one's own perspectives.

Nietzsche is well aware of the strong pressure exerted by social convention and educational systems. Hence the road to authenticity and spontaneous creativity requires the two stages described by Nietzsche's Zarathustra: 'the spirit becomes a camel; and the camel, a lion; and the lion, finally, a child'.[9] The individual ('the lion') must liberate himself from 'the camel', i.e. from all the external layers imposed on him by institutional conditioning. Only then, after attaining a childlike state of 'innocence' (Z, p. 139), can he proceed to the second stage, in which he consciously adopts and assimilates moral norms. These norms may well reflect the traditional values discarded in the first stage; it is not their content that matters, but the unconstrained *manner* in which they are adopted.

II

Nietzsche's philosophy and the literary means he employs to present it are meant to lure his readers into joining the search for authenticity.

This is the only alternative left after the 'death of God'; the ability to embrace this alternative is indicative of the *free spirit* par excellence'. Like Kierkegaard, Nietzsche presents the 'coming generations' with the 'terrifying Either/Or: "Either abolish your reverences or – *yourselves!*" '[10]

Nietzsche's ultimate objective, then, is to make possible a creative and authentic life in a world without dogmatic beliefs. The death of dogma will not lead to the disintegration of one's self, but rather will liberate one's creative resources, repressed until now by morality. It will open new horizons to new beliefs, but these will function solely as life-enhancing and self-crystallizing 'perspectives'. Once they have lost their usefulness, such beliefs will be discarded and replaced by other perspectives.

Hence, Nietzsche's philosophy is to be regarded as a means: 'a mere instrument' to entice us to form our authenticity. In view of this, Nietzsche is one of these 'philosophers of the future' who may have a right to be called 'tempters' (*Versucher*). The appropriate aphorism concludes with the words: 'This name itself is in the end a mere experiment, and if you will, an enticement.'[11] Nietzsche's play on the words *Versuch* (hypothesis or experiment) and *Versuchung* (temptation or enticement) points to one of the most significant features of his philosophy, namely, that it is a sophisticated mode of enticement. Nietzsche speaks of the nature of this 'enticement' in terms of an 'experiment' that directs one's efforts toward one's own power and tests one's ability to reach and activate it in one's life (*BGE*, sec. 41).

Nietzsche distinguishes between the positive enticement to authentic pathos – the *Versuchung* – and the negative seduction (used, e.g. by Christianity), which he calls *Verführung*.[12] This distinction is one reason why Nietzsche calls himself the 'Anti-Christ'. He is like the early Christians insofar as he uses the same tactics of enticement as they used to attract mankind to 'negative' ideals. But Nietzsche is also their opponent since against the Christian gospel of salvation from the hardship of life he posits its antithesis: salvation from this negative salvation by incitement to create an authentic self.

Nietzsche is aware that his enticement is not for everyone and sees different reactions to it as indicating different types of power:

What serves the higher type of men as nourishment . . . must almost be poison for a very different and inferior type. . . . There are books that have opposite values for soul and health, depending on whether the lower soul, the lower vitality, or the higher and more vigorous ones turn to them: in the former case, these books are dangerous and lead to crumbling and disintegration; in the latter, herald's cries that call the bravest to their courage.

(BGE, pp. 42–3)

Three kinds of responses to Nietzsche's challenge are implied in this passage: the 'inferior type' of disintegrated and inauthentic self is confused and escapes from the burdensome 'self-overcoming' it entails; the 'higher type' of adequate, genuine self accepts it and becomes more powerful and independent; the authentic *Übermensch* does not respond to this enticement since he does not require it. Such avoidance of Nietzsche's challenge does not stem here from weakness of the will but from a surplus of power.

This view of Nietzsche's writing as a means for the enticement of the reader may explain its peculiar nature. Nietzsche intended his books for the few who would really understand and benefit from them. They aim to shock and attract us, softening and reducing our resistance. It is not by accident that in several places Nietzsche insists on the close connection between his goal as a philosophical *Versucher* and his peculiar literary style.[13] 'Whatever is profound loves masks', declares Nietzsche, and whatever forms one's self loves the enticing and ironic mask behind which lies 'so much graciousness in cunning' (*BGE*, pp. 50, 51). Nietzsche's enticing literature then becomes 'the path to the fundamental problems' (ibid., p. 32). However, being only a path, it is naturally abandoned once it comes to an end. Nietzschean philosophy becomes, then, a sort of temporary scaffolding, or provisional 'hypothesis'. It is a metaphoric structure in the original meaning of the term *meta-phora* (change of form), to be abandoned once it has served its purpose. Wittgenstein's well-known analogy from the penultimate sentence of the *Tractatus Logico-Philosophicus* is similar to Nietzsche's conception of philosophy here: 'one may well want to look out over the topmost rung of the ladder, but one ought not want to stand on it'.[14]

III

Nietzsche's ladder does not create the self and postulate its powerful patterns *ex nihilo*; it merely explicates them and calls for their crystallization and re-activation. This is the main meaning of Nietzsche's focal statement that the philosopher's 'thinking is, in fact, far less a discovery than a recognition, a remembering, a return and a homecoming to a remote, primordial, and inclusive household of the soul' (*BGE*, sec. 20). This motif of a return or homecoming to some previous genuine state of the self is characteristic of many thinkers on authenticity. Kierkegaard, for example, expressed it by an attempt to incite readers to return to the original sources of the early Christians.

In any case, Nietzsche's teaching on power is not an induction or an experimental hypothesis. Apart from the method of unmasking, it clearly contains an explicative and typological dimension, in contrast to the constructive and explanatory aspect of the empirical sciences. This dimension is expressed in Nietzsche's descriptions of the different patterns of power and in his distinction between its two central manifestations: the positive, which I take to be the authentic, and the negative, or inauthentic.

Negative power, or inauthenticity, is symptomatic of a weak self, lacking in power but incessantly attempting to obtain it:

> There are recipes for the feeling of power, firstly for those who can control themselves and who are thereby accustomed to a feeling of power; then for those in whom precisely this is lacking.
>
> (*D*, sec. 65)

Clearly, no positive power is exhibited in the satisfaction derived from abusing and dominating one's fellow-beings. The negative power of one with a feeble sense of selfhood expresses itself not spontaneously but derivatively. It is fundamentally deficient, and hopelessly strives to encourage and fortify itself by means of abuse, cruelty and the 'drive to distinction' (ibid., sec. 30). By contrast, one who possesses genuinely positive power, the really authentic self, needs neither the approbation of his surroundings nor the medals and titles that allegedly attest this power; nor does such a self require the various pleasures stemming from abusive domination in order to intensify the 'feeling of power' – for it is already intrinsically a part of him. This is the man who 'becomes what he is' without deviously manipulating his surroundings or deriving his sense of potency and selfhood from transcendental ideologies or political banners.

Nietzsche portrays in detail the cunning, devious mechanisms by which people of negative power reinforce and affirm their selves. One such strategy is to establish the morality of duty, thus assuming a sovereignty over other individuals. Certain 'rights' are granted, but in return for these rights people are required to accept certain duties and to concede others' rights in return. Thus all are trapped in a network of duties and rights which eventually strengthens the defective powers of persons subscribing to the moralities of duty.

Nietzsche's elaborate criticism of the current ethic can be constructive only if guided by a regulative idea of an alternative moral pattern. He does not posit power against morality, but proposes an active morality of positive power that expresses courageous creativity. He contrasts the characteristic features of these two moralities: 'All actions may be traced back to evaluations, all evaluations are either *original* or *adopted* – the latter being by far the most common' (*D*, sec. 104, p. 60). Nietzsche maintains that the main reason for the latter is moral cowardice (*D*, sec. 101), which shuns the authentic expression of intrinsic power. The mechanisms for adopting traditional morality include blind internalization of external maxims, making them into habit, the 'second nature' of a 'camel'. This given, habitual ethic, conditioned in childhood (*D*, sec. 104), stands in contrast to the creative and authentic evaluations made by a mature selfhood.

Nietzsche, however, in explicating various moral phenomena, was not searching for new, esoteric values; he sought to re-activate authentic modes of living. This can easily be seen by looking at some of the descriptions of positive power in his writings. We do not find any original or new values there, but rather values that have already appeared in traditional philosophical ethics: self-sufficiency, heroism, creative sublimation of instinct, intellectual tolerance, generosity, nobility, courage, vitality, self-control, faith in oneself, the ability to accept contradiction, the lack of bad conscience, and the like. Most of these values can be found in the ethics of Plato, Spinoza and Kant, to all of which Nietzsche frequently refers. (By the term 'ethics' I mean a doctrine aiming at a rational justification of moral norms.) However, like Kierkegaard, Nietzsche did not believe that we are capable of providing any such rational foundation. This is especially the case with his ideal of authenticity which reigns supreme 'beyond the good and the evil' – beyond the ethos of sincerity and objectivity. This, of course, raises the question: why should we prefer authenticity to negative power, if neither can be transcendently justified? Why should we prefer the authentic *Übermensch* to the ordinary man? Or, to put it directly: why be a moral agent at all?

Nietzsche was aware of this meta-ethical question, which he called 'the problem of morality itself' (*BGE*, sec. 186). Like Kierkegaard's Abraham, Nietzsche's Zarathustra could not provide a rational answer to this question. He could only repeat the 'terrifying Either/Or: "Either abolish your reverences or - *yourselves*!" '; these 'reverences' are our convenient clinging to the prevailing ethic, which has lost any existential appeal. The dissolution of our selves, however, 'would be nihilism' (*GS*, sec. 346, p. 287), and Nietzsche encourages us to will, to create or actualize our authentic selfhoods simply because it would be spiritual suicide to do otherwise.

The wish to meet the challenge of authenticity must already be implicit, and it is the task of Nietzschean enticement to intensify it. There is thus no contradiction between the fact that Nietzsche gives no esoteric prescriptions, and his calling on us to live creatively and originally. Originality, Nietzsche believes, springs from the inherent sources of the self and lies in the manner in which it operates, not in its external manifestations. On Nietzsche's view, his own originality is not exercised by founding a new and unique set of moral values, but, rather, by elucidating already existing values and by giving them new names. 'What is originality?' Nietzsche asks, and answers: 'To see something that has no name as yet and hence cannot be mentioned although it stares us all in the face' (*GS*, sec. 261). Such is the notion of authenticity or *Wahrhaftigkeit* that he attempts to confront us with so that we adopt its patterns.

By enticing us to create our own selves, Nietzsche strives to assist us to overcome the impediments that have hitherto inhibited us. Nietzsche assumes that the mental powers to create our selves are deeply rooted in us, but because of various psychological handicaps, such as cowardice, we have repressed them. These handicaps have been projected as an ideological network, and Nietzsche uses his unmasking 'hammer' to shatter such repressive 'idols', to overcome them while freezing our faith in them.[15]

There is a striking similarity between Nietzsche's tactic of 'coolly placing on ice' (*EH*, p. 284) and Socrates' *aporia*. Socrates seeks to freeze the listener's belief in *x*, for example. by showing him that this logically entails a belief in *y*. The listener is not ready to endorse belief in y because of his belief in the set of values, p, s, t ... which are incompatible with belief in y. Nietzsche employs almost the same procedure. He shows his readers, by means of psychological and genealogical unmasking, that the effects of their inauthenticity include stagnation, inhibition of creativity, depression and, above all, dissolution of their selves – effects most of us consider undesirable. The enticing thrust of authenticity, therefore, is not, and cannot be, presented directly and prescriptively. Rather, the indirect process of 'freezing' is employed, showing that the prevalent norms originate inauthentically and that the effects of our blindly accepting them are harmful to our selves.

IV

In Nietzsche the genealogical method is also designed to explain why the *Übermensch* is 'Utopia' (nowhere). What accounts for the historical supremacy of the 'slave morality' over the 'masters' who exhibit genuine power and superior authentic moral capacity? Nietzsche himself declared that he wrote *On the Genealogy of Morals* to deal with this very issue. The third essay in this work answers 'the question whence the ascetic ideal, the priests' ideal, derives its tremendous *power* although it is the *harmful* ideal *par excellence*, a will to the end, an ideal of decadence' (*EH*, p. 312; cf. *GM*, Preface, sec. 6).

Nietzsche's descriptive analyses have shown that '*Morality in Europe today is herd animal morality* ... beside which, and after which many other types, above all *higher* moralities, are, or ought to be, possible' (*BGE*, p. 115). Nietzsche's moral philosophy is meant to incite revolution in the realm of human conduct by arousing our thirst for authentic selfhood. Hence he abandons the explicative approach and adopts the genealogical method. He does not merely wish to 'freeze' completely the declining prevailing ethic, but also to find suitable conditions for the formation of authenticity. Nietzsche is convinced that understanding the historical-psychological circumstances that nurture 'herd' morality will help us grasp the conditions required for establishing authentic patterns. His lengthy answer to the question raised above can be summed up as follows: it is not some inherent flaw in the ideal of authenticity that prevents its predominance, but rather the relative strength of the opposing patterns, arising from negative power, and ensuring their victory.

Nietzsche's genealogy also attempts to examine the most important question concerning authenticity, namely, whether the *Übermensch* can in principle develop and live in society as such. Granted his emphasis upon the immanence, autarchy and extreme individuality of authentic power, is it compatible with morality? Since Nietzsche affirms 'a community' (see, e.g., *GM*, second essay, sec. 9) and does not seek to destroy it, he must explain how the morality of authenticity is at all possible within the social context and analyse the nature of the interaction among its members. This is what he does in his genealogical inquiry, where he maintains that genuine justice is possible only within a social fabric composed of equally powerful members (ibid., sec. 8). He declares that recognition of the value and freedom of others originates in egoism (*BGE*, sec. 264). Only an individual who possesses an abundance of positive power and firm authentic selfhood is able to grant similar rights and freedoms to all those whom he recognizes as his equals. He is not afraid that this might diminish or destroy his own authentic power. It is the self-affirmation of one's power and virtues that psychologically enables (but, of course, does not necessitate) the affirmation of the other and *his* authenticity. Human egoism and emphasis on authenticity do not contradict the moral order; indeed, Nietzsche thinks, they create the conditions for its proper functioning.

Moreover, if we are not convinced by this argument, the genealogical account also attempts to show that the moral patterns of positive *Macht* were occasionally manifested within some social and historical context. Witness his remarks about 'an ancient Greek *polis*, or Venice' and his references to Rome and the Renaissance.[16] He also shows that external factors were responsible for their disappearance. Historical testimony thus seems to show that there is no essential contradiction between Nietzsche's morality of authenticity and social reality; in principle the path to their mutual reconciliation remains open.

V

Alas, the story is far more complicated. Authenticity denotes, among other things, a state of integrity between the innermost self and its external manifestations, whatever their form and content. As we know from Kierkegaard, it is a subjective pathos of inwardness which in principle cannot be judged by any external and objective criterion.

Only the individual who strives to attain authentic life is able to feel whether he or she has been successful. Nietzsche is aware of this:

> One should not dodge one's tests, though they may be the most dangerous game one could play and are tests that are taken in the end before no witness or judge but ourselves.

(BGE, sec. 41)

At this point a crucial question arises: do the powerful need a society at all? Is it not the case that the need for others indicates a feebleness and insufficiency of positive power or authenticity? In answer, Nietzsche may point out that the powerful and authentic man is not identical with an omnipotent and absolutely perfect God. There is no upper limit to power, and there is no optimum for authenticity. Moreover, cultural enterprises necessarily require the association and collaboration of various creative powers, each contributing its distinct capacities to the common enterprise. To make the personal and social manifestation possible, any creation, even the most individual and idiosyncratic, requires the linguistic and social fabric as a necessary condition. There is no power without creation and form-giving, as there is no authenticity without some sort of determined action. Hence there is no power and no authenticity without society, and their essential manifestations are impossible apart from any social context.

Further, since absolute authentic power never actually exists, and since there is no creation *ex nihilo*, powerful and authentic individuals need each other, and need society and culture as the vital working framework within which they create themselves and their objects. Society itself obviously also requires morality to organize and consolidate it. Nietzsche, then, is not a negating 'nihilist'; he does not wish to overthrow society and go beyond its limits. The 'Antichrist' within him does not make him into an anarchist.

However, here we have arrived at the crux of the matter: the cry for authenticity appears at the twilight of the rational ethic – at the 'twilight of the idols'. It is an explicit expression of revolt against the spirit of objectivity. Thus it is inconceivable to have a fully authentic individual living in society, which by nature is founded upon a set of objective norms and a common ethos. To clarify this point let me draw an analogy from the domain of psychoanalysis.[17] If neurosis is, as Freud claims, a natural outcome of the repressive society, which is founded upon such repression, can we imagine a society where there are no neurotic people? This question remains valid even for a society all of whose neurotic individuals have successfully undergone psychoanalytic treatment. But once they try to live in that society under, more or less, the same conditions as caused their neurosis in the first place, will they not to some degree regress? The same consideration is relevant to the individual whose quest for authenticity is supposedly finally fulfilled. Since such a person continues to be a member of society, the processes of social conditioning and levelling will continue to exert their inauthenticating effects. Moreover, imagine a society where authenticity became a general norm: such a society would either be destroyed or would destroy that authenticity, which would be manifested precisely in those individuals who attempted to overcome its ethic and exhibited the spirit of revolt. Hence the search for authenticity faces what seems to be a paradoxical situation: it cannot be materialized without society, nor can it be lived within its framework.

Nietzsche's genealogy cannot provide us with the sought-after empirical evidence that authenticity has been common among human beings in any given society historically. He had no objective criteria for 'judging'. Yet, I think, he was well aware of the difficulty of trying to allow for the 'ought' of authenticity within the social 'is'. The fact is that he leaves this issue intentionally vague in the closing sentence of his book, where Zarathustra, who personifies the ideal of authenticity, leaves his 'cave' in order to do – what? To return to society? It is far from completely clear: 'Thus spoke Zarathustra, and he left his cave, glowing and strong as a morning sun that comes out of dark mountains' (Z, p. 439). The metaphor of a 'sun' implies that Zarathustra, not being able to become part of the human-social nexus, is like the sun, which, not being part of the earth, only warms it from above. Zarathustra can only inspire us to try and become authentic, to be what we really are. Authenticity is a kind of regulative and corrective ideal rather than a manifestly viable norm.

VI

Hence we must understand Nietzsche's basic idea of the 'transfiguration of all values' not as radical abolition of the inauthentic ethic, but as a gradual approximation to authenticity. This process is constantly taking place 'within a *single* soul' (*BGE*, sec. 260, p. 204) vacillating between opposed modes of living. Thus Nietzsche is not proposing a new ethics, but, rather, is describing the transitory sentiments and mental states of the individual, 'the true pathos of every period of our life', containing, among others, 'the pathos of nobility and distance' and 'the Yes-saying pathos'.[18] It should be noted that Nietzsche occasionally identifies the 'will to power' with pathos: 'The will to power is not a being, not a becoming, but a *pathos.*'[19] As an inward experience, the various sentiments, temperaments, emotional states and types of pathos of the personality require no definite ontological status or metaphysical commitment; hence they are the most relevant factors in the discussion of authenticity, which likewise shuns such constraining categorizations.

It is important to stress that the central notion of Nietzsche's philosophy is not the will, but the *feeling* of power. Indeed, Nietzsche denies the existence of the will as such, opposing what he considers an invalid transition from 'the feeling of *will*' to the concept of 'the will itself' (*GS*, sec. 127). The intensification of the 'feeling of power' is reflected in a tendency to see it in ontological terms, but the will is a fictitious entity. Nietzsche rejects any reification of the will and conceives of volition only in terms of functions and activities: there is no will but only 'willing' (*GM*, first essay, sec. 13). The phrase 'will to power' does not express an ontological principle referring to some entity underlying the phenomenon of pathos. Nietzsche might have seemed more consistent, then, if he had used the expression 'the pathos of power' or 'authenticity' instead of 'the will to power'. Here, as elsewhere, his language is not altogether compatible with the central direction of his thought. (We should also recall that the term 'the will to power' occurs most frequently in the text so titled, a text which Nietzsche did not officially authorize for publication.)

It follows that within the framework of Nietzschean philosophy we cannot speak about authentic character or self. Authenticity is a predicate not of character or the self, but merely of acts and pathos. It describes acts but not constant essences. In extreme situations, where the general and objective norms are no longer applicable, authentic acts can emerge and become conspicuous. However, these acts in themselves cannot become new or renewed norms and moral prescriptions:

> Suppose nothing else were 'given' as real except our world of desires and passions, and we could not get down, or up, to any other 'reality' besides the reality of our drives.
>
> (*BGE*, sec. 36)

This immanent human reality excites the various types of pathos in any transitory period of our life. Nietzsche identifies 'the reality of our drives' with 'the development and ramification of one basic form of the will - namely, of the will to power' (ibid., p. 48). The concept of 'the will' is superfluous here, or at least empty of rational and purposive meaning, and the identity between pathos and power is again emphasized. On this point we should heed Heidegger's warning not to be led astray by Nietzsche's language - 'will' is 'only a word',[20] to which we succumb 'owing to the seduction (*Verführung*) of language' (*GM*, p. 45), as Nietzsche himself cautions us. Wittgenstein's remark in *Philosophical Investigations* that 'philosophy is a battle against the bewitchment of our intelligence by means of language' would draw a sympathetic response from Nietzsche.

The will in Nietzsche is no more than a fluid collection of affects and a bundle of different types of pathos. His concept of power refers to the pathological function that externalizes the various transitory types of pathos. Power transforms moments of pathos into interpretations and perspectives through which they become enduring creations. No one perspective is more correct than another, just as there is no one pathos which is truer than others. All types of pathos are of equal epistemological legitimacy. The whole complex of possible moments of pathos and their correlative perspectives is collectively subsumed under the rubric 'power'. Nietzsche does not reject the 'negative' (inauthentic) types of power/pathos because they are less true. They are rejected as detrimental and destructive to his ideal of the pathos of authenticity, which is concretized in the notion of the *Übermensch*, in whom the will to power becomes identical with the will to authenticity. Nietzsche is aware that such a personality cannot be realized completely; the *Übermensch* provides only a regulative idea, a model to approximate and emulate. It is a corrective to the overemphasis on the equality, the objectivity, the levelling processes of modernity that result in dissolution of the self. And indeed Nietzsche does not offer concrete examples of the *Übermensch*, always being careful not to attach to it any historical name:

> To be a human being with one elevated feeling - to be a single great mood incarnate - that has hitherto been a mere dream and a delightful possibility; as yet history does not offer us any certain examples.
>
> (*GS*, sec. 288)

In the absence of a historical example that could provide an appropriate model, Nietzsche relied on his literary imagination. Zarathustra became a literary paradigm of how art could lead to authenticity. Sublime, enticing descriptions rather than authoritative prescriptions are offered to awaken us from our inauthentic slumbers. Nietzsche's tactics of enticement were intended to induce in us the desire for the pathos of authenticity. As for those already searching, Nietzsche tries to entice them to intensify their quest.

The attempt 'to become who you are' must be carried out alone, through one's own mental resources. Nonetheless, it is possible to arouse, to educate and to entice others to do this without constraining their free self-achievement. And Nietzsche even attempts to fortify this autonomy by deliberately introducing a sceptical element into his enticing 'ladder'.

VII

Nietzsche's theory of perspectives and its sceptical ramifications are yet another pedagogical means to entice the reader to seek authenticity beyond the ethos of sincerity and objectivity. Nietzsche tries to lead us to that authentic state of 'higher human beings who desire and provoke contradiction', since in his eyes 'the ability to contradict . . . is still more excellent and constitutes what is really great'. This is 'the step of steps of the liberated spirit' (GS, sec. 297). Nietzsche tries to entice us into making this 'step' with his perspectivism. He is well aware that his teachings regarding authenticity are not valid in the classical logical sense. He provokes us to challenge his view: 'Supposing that this also is only interpretation – and you will be eager enough to make this objection? – well, so much the better' (BGE, sec. 22). His scepticism highlights the peculiar status of his philosophy: it stands or falls neither on its rational validity or invalidity, nor on its truth or falsehood, but only on the degree of its allure. It is supposed to help us to live authentically in a purposeless world which '*may include infinite interpretations*' (GS, sec. 374). The truth value of his philosophy is an irrelevant issue in the context of this project. His enticing discussions and literary presentations deliberately abjuring any cognitive foundation are exclusively directed towards evoking the emotional pathos that expresses and stimulates one's power to become 'what one is'.

This becoming is a dynamic and a-rational process; hence no eternal value is capable of expressing it. Indeed, authenticity does not attach itself to fixed values. Rather, as Nietzsche stresses (*BGE*, sec. 41), drawing a model of authentic life-patterns, it is determined by impermanence, its positive pathos. At every stage of his philosophizing, Nietzsche is conscious that this stage is actually only a 'step' to overcome and proceed further: 'Those were steps for me, and I have climbed up over them; to that end I had to pass over them. Yet they thought that I wanted to retire on them.'[21] Here, however, we reach the limits of our capacity to speak rationally in a world of chaos and pathos without a *logos*. And perhaps Nietzsche intended to bring us to this ultimate boundary in order to help us transcend his own thought as well, thereby assisting us to reach real maturity of positive power: standing on our own feet and throwing away all crutches, including Nietzsche's.

Nietzsche's Zarathustra incites us as follows: 'This is my way; where is yours? – thus I answered those who asked me "the way". For *the* way – that does not exist' (*Z*, p. 307). At every stage Nietzsche tries to entice us to overcome even his own thought and influence. This is the real meaning of his saying: 'It is part of the humanity of a master to warn his pupil about himself' (*D*, sec. 447).

Now we are in a better position to grasp why Nietzsche's enticement includes a sceptical component ultimately intended to help us overcome even his own allure. But what sense can one make of an enticement which also includes deterrents? It seems that Nietzsche believes that when we have reached the advanced stages, and have overcome the emotional barriers and the ethic of objectivity and honesty, we will have discovered and built up enough power and immunity to be able to withstand this scepticism and even 'joyfully' embrace it, showing that we have really attained authentic power.

Moreover, any process of enticement also tests our ability to be enticed. Thus Nietzsche, by means of his perspectivism, introduces the self-checking mechanism designed to test the genuine power of the enticed person. He introduced perspectivism explicitly in the fifth book of *The Gay Science*, which was added only in the second edition in 1887,[22] the year in which he started to write his *Genealogie*, the final rung of his ladder to authenticity. The whole process is actually a dialectical one: the more efficiently power is uncovered and reactivated, the greater the likelihood that the individual will persevere through the more advanced stages, being able to withstand both the test of scepticism and the reality looming at every step on the road to authenticity. If we have already reached this point, our power will have been most favourably revealed. Only then will Nietzsche be able to throw away the philosophical crutches he has given us and send us to our own walks of life and their authentic manifestations: 'And if you now lack all ladders, then you must know how to climb on your own head' (Z, p. 265).

Notes

1 *Daybreak*, trans. R. J. Hollingdale (Cambridge: Cambridge University Press, 1982) (henceforth *D*), sec. 73; p. 73. Also see *The Gay Science*, trans. W. Kaufmann (New York: Vintage, 1974) (henceforth *GS*), sec. 357; *Beyond Good and Evil*, trans. W. Kaufmann (New York: Vintage, 1966) (henceforth *BGE*), sec. 1.

2 *Philosophy in the Tragic Age of the Greeks*, trans. M. Cowan (Chicago, Ill.: Henry Regnery, 1962), p. 25.

3 Thus Nietzsche's morality of power ultimately turns out to be the means by which all his earlier and later views 'become . . . more and more firmly attached to one another, entwined and interlaced with one another': *On the Genealogy of Morals*, trans. W. Kaufmann (New York: Vintage, 1969) (henceforth *GM*), Preface 2, p. 16. This interrelation of central Nietzschean concepts and motives transforms what would at first seem a loosely connected and aphoristic body of work into a positive and comprehensive philosophy of authenticity – and, moreover, one which can be discussed coherently.

4 Friedrich Nietzsche, 'Schopenhauer as Educator', in *Untimely Meditations*, trans. R. J. Hollingdale (Cambridge: Cambridge University Press, 1983) (henceforth *SE*), p. 127.

5 See Friedrich Nietzsche, *Ecce Homo*, trans. Walter Kaufmann (New York: Vintage, 1967) (henceforth *EH*), p. 258, where he says: 'My formula for greatness in a human being is *amor fati*: that one wants nothing to be different. . . . Not merely bear what is necessary, still less conceal it . . . but *love* it.'

6 This distinction between *Kraft* and *Macht* is crucial to any understanding of Nietzsche's mature doctrine of power: see Jacob Golomb, *Nietzsche's Enticing Psychology of Power* (Ames: Iowa State University Press, 1989), pp. 179–221.

7 *The Birth of Tragedy*, trans. W. Kaufmann (New York: Vintage, 1967) (henceforth *BT*), p. 37.

8 W. Kaufmann, *Nietzsche* (Princeton, NJ: Princeton University Press, 1968), p. 158.

9   'Thus Spoke Zarathustra', in *The Portable Nietzsche*, trans. W. Kaufmann (New York: Viking, 1954) (henceforth *Z*), p. 137.

10 *GS*, sec. 346, p. 287.

11 My translation from *BGE*, sec. 42; cf. *BGE*, sec. 205. Nietzsche's play on the words *Versuch* (hypothesis or experiment) and *Versuchung* (temptation or enticement) is not, as Kaufmann claims in his translation (*BGE*, pp. 52-3 n. 26), unintentional. It points to one of the most significant features of Nietzsche's philosophy, namely, that it is a sophisticated mode of enticement.

12 See, e.g., *GM*, first essay, sections 8, 9.

13 See, e.g., *BGE*, sec. 295. Cf. Alexander Nehamas's discussion of the philosophical significance of Nietzsche's literary styles in his *Nietzsche: Life as Literature* (Cambridge, Mass.: Harvard University Press, 1985).

14 *Human, All Too Human*, trans. R. J. Hollingdale (Cambridge: Cambridge University Press, 1986) (henceforth *HH*), p. 23.

15 An illuminating example of such a 'freezing' process, based upon an implicit set of values latent within ourselves, can be found in his analysis of the ascetic ideal, to him the ultimate expression of inauthenticity: see esp. *GM*, third essay, sec. 23.

16 *BGE*, sec. 262; *GM*, first essay, sec. 16.

17 Though not so alien to Nietzsche, who has clearly anticipated Freudian thought and such notions as sublimation, repression, the unconscious, and interpretation of dreams: cf. Golomb, *Nietzsche's Enticing Psychology of Power* (cited n. 5 above).

18 *GS*, sec. 317, p. 252; *BGE*, sec. 257; *EH*, p. 296.

19 *The Will to Power*, trans. W. Kaufmann and R. J. Hollingdale (New York: Vintage, 1967), sec. 635, p. 339; cf. T. B. Strong, *Friedrich Nietzsche and the Politics of Transfiguration* (Berkeley: University of California Press, 1975), p. 257.

20 M. Heidegger, *Nietzsche* (Pfullingen: Neske, 1961), Bd I, p. 650.

21 'Twilight of the Idols', in *The Portable Nietzsche*, trans. Kaufmann, p. 472.

22 Mainly in the fifth book of *The Gay Science*, which was added only in the second edition of 1887 (*GS*, sec. 373, 374, etc.) and in the posthumous fragments from this period.

5

Heidegger's ontology of authenticity

The philosophical birth of the concept of authenticity was impeded by two acute problems: how could authenticity be recognized, and how was it to be implemented? The former arose from the fact that neither Kierkegaard's authentic faith nor Nietzsche's pathos of authenticity could be identified by objective criteria. How could one rationally evaluate one's progress towards achieving authenticity? The second problem was whether the authentic individual could, in principle, emerge and live in society as we know it. Those for whom authenticity is at the very heart of the existential challenge must explain how its ethic is possible. As we saw in the preceding chapters, no satisfactory solutions to these problems were devised by the early existentialists.

The second generation of thinkers on authenticity, notably Heidegger and Sartre, tackled these problems by systematically ontologizing the idea of authenticity. By turning from the informal nineteenth-century notion of authenticity as pathos to its systematic twentieth-century version as phenomenological ontology they betrayed the true spirit of this ideal. Camus's revolt against this development, and his attempt to return to Nietzschean intuitions, came too late. Indeed, as a result of Heidegger's impact on current Continental philosophy, authenticity has been denuded of its vitality. The Heidegger–Sartre betrayal, does, however, expose the fundamental either/or: one opts either for authentic personal pathos or for a Kantian and/or Hegelian ethics. There can be no Kantian or Hegelian authenticity.

On the surface Heidegger might seem like an old-fashioned system-builder striving to attain objective truth. Seeking 'to interpret the meaning of Being',[1] he employs the heavy academic jargon usually associated with Kantians and Hegelians. The attempt to lay a foundation for 'fundamental ontology' leads him to the apparently speculative question of 'what we really mean by the word "being" (*BT*, p. 19). Thus his philosophical concerns appear to be detached from existential issues and he seems indifferent to Kierkegaard's and Nietzsche's goal of promoting authenticity and enticing their readers into adopting it.

In fact the question 'What does it mean to be?' has nothing to do with 'soaring speculation', since it is 'of all questions, *both the most basic and the most concrete*' (ibid., p. 29). Answering this question can have a concrete impact on one's life. Despite his claim that he can only analyse but not affect us, Heidegger recognizes the necessity that 'out of reflection we receive instruction'.[2] Like Kierkegaard and Nietzsche, he tries to motivate us to change our lives, or at least our perceptions of them. Even in his later writings, the attentive reader cannot fail to discern, behind the tone of passive resignation, his determination not to let human selves remain as they are: 'what is at stake is a transformation in man's Being itself'.[3]

Heidegger contends that before answering the classic metaphysical question ('What is?') we must first ask the meaning of 'is' in general. Such an inquiry must start from the notion of authentic *Dasein*,[4] an entity which genuinely exemplifies its Being. Hence even a purely ontological orientation requires the notion of authenticity, which becomes central to Heidegger's early philosophy. It is often incorrectly believed, however, that Heidegger's sole concern is with the classic ontological question of being – 'What exists?' He holds, rather, that to answer it adequately one must first ask: 'What is the meaning of "is", of Being?' Until we have answered this question, answers to the former, so abundant in metaphysics, are meaningless. But to ask it is not to assert that the issue of authenticity is of secondary importance, that it is solely a means to disclose what really matters to Heidegger: the meaning of Being. This is so obvious that I would not have stated it were it not for the fact that many people seem to deny this.[5] In any event, authenticity is a genuine 'is-ness' (*Existenz*); hence to ask about the meaning of Being is to look for the meaning of authenticity.

To be *Dasein* is to ask these questions. They become an issue only for an authentic Being, whose authenticity is 'hidden' but nonetheless given 'beforehand' (*BT*, p. 25). The very search for authenticity 'constitutes its meaning' (ibid., p. 59) and discloses the seeker's authenticity. To be authentic *Dasein*, therefore, is to grasp that one cannot become authentic as an ontic entity among entities, as a static being, but only as the asking, searching Becoming, that is, as a transcendent consciousness, whose projected intentionalities become authentic 'only by anticipation' (ibid., p. 310). This point will become clearer when I discuss Heidegger's notion of 'Being-towards-death'.

Meanwhile we should bear in mind that Heidegger asks two cardinal questions: first, the a priori ontological structure of Being that allows one to become aware of one's authenticity or inauthenticity (the problem of recognition) and, second, the a priori conditions required for authentic Being to be viable at the ontic level as well (the problem of implementation). The quest for (the meaning of) Being and the quest for authenticity are inextricably linked and even, in a sense, coterminous, since 'Every doctrine of Being is *in itself alone* a doctrine of man's essential nature',[6] which is the capacity for inquiring into its own Being while being open to the call of authenticity.

But if Heidegger denies any connection with existentialism, if he is uninterested in philosophical anthropology, why does he occupy such a central role among thinkers about authenticity? If his sole concern is what it means to Be, how can he contribute to the ethical dilemma of the possibility of authenticity?

Heidegger touched on these questions: 'To accomplish means to unfold something into the fullness of its essence . . . to lead it forth into this fullness – *producere*.'[7] Heidegger tries to promote authenticity by unfolding its meaning into 'the fullness'. Since 'thinking acts insofar as it thinks' (*LH*, p. 193), insofar as Heidegger is preoccupied with the ontological investigation of authentic Being, his thinking acts on his readers by providing them with the necessary a priori framework for their morality. Ethics cannot exist apart from fundamental thinking, Heidegger states, for thinking that is truly fundamental 'is in itself the original ethics' (*LH*, p. 235). One of the conclusions of Heidegger's inquiry into authenticity is its priority over morality. Authenticity is the fundamental a priori condition for a viable ethics. To paraphrase Kant, ontic inquiry without an ontological framework is blind; ontological investigation without the ethical import (of enticement) is empty.

In 1927, Heidegger declared the practical import of his philosophy: 'Philosophy is the *ontological corrective formally* pointing out the ontic.'[8] Elsewhere Heidegger reiterates the relevance of philosophy to life: 'it is the authentic function of philosophy to challenge historical Dasein and hence . . . granted that *we* cannot do anything with philosophy, might not philosophy, if we concern ourselves with it, do something *with us*?'[9]

The meaning of authenticity, as Heidegger may have learned from

Kierkegaard and Nietzsche, cannot be found by studying concrete persons within a specific society. Only a transcendental point of view provides answers to the two problems posed above: authenticity can indeed be defined a priori and is socially viable, because it is an ontological existential. However, here lie the roots of Heidegger's betrayal of the Kierkegaardian and Nietzschean conceptions of authentic life. Harnessing the open-ended notion of authenticity to a systematic yoke leads to its being swallowed up by ontology on a grand scale, and becoming an *essential* relation between the self and the world. And thus Heidegger, in his later writings, shifted his focus from the ontology of *Dasein*'s authenticity to Being itself. This minimized the voluntaristic and human elements of authenticity still found in *Being and Time* and contributed further to its betrayal.

Heidegger's question about Being can be rephrased in terms of authenticity: What is an authentic *Dasein*? How is its authenticity lost? How is it regained and acted on in the social sphere? While addressing these questions, this chapter presents and questions Heidegger's ontology of authenticity as a possible solution to the problems associated with this notion in previous writers.

I

A significant area of affinity between Heidegger and earlier proponents of authenticity lies in his attempt to entice his readers. This exhortatory endeavour is ironically concealed under the technical jargon of his seemingly neutral writings. His insistence on the objective validity of his ontological explications and his use of the phenomenological method to attain apodictic results keep him from using an emotional tone. With Heidegger we appear to return to the objective language of traditional philosophy, which shuns any such pathos as seems to obscure the natural light of our reason and the clarity of 'the things themselves' (*BT*, p. 49).

To what extent does Heidegger belong with those philosophers who sought to change their readers' lives and selves? On the surface, Heidegger was more interested in changing the course of the history of philosophy, which had forgotten 'the question of Being' (ibid., p. 2), than in changing his readers' modes of existence. His interests appear professional rather than existential, and his teaching aspires to enlighten rather than to convince. He even provides a philosophical argument for this absence of any explicit attempt to influence readers directly. Referring to *Dasein*'s authentic 'ontological possibility', he says:

> Let Dasein itself project itself upon this possibility, without holding up to Dasein an ideal of existence with any special 'content', or forcing any such ideal upon it 'from outside'.
>
> (*BT*, p. 311; cf. ibid., pp. 315–16)

Authenticity must emerge from *Dasein*'s own self, not from pressure, manipulation and incitement. In *Being and Time* Heidegger seems to side with Hegel's opposition to any kind of philosophical evocation by insisting on the non-evaluative, ontologically neutral character of his analyses (ibid., p. 211). Yet this is incompatible with the appreciation of the evocative import of Kierkegaard's philosophy expressed in his remark that there is much 'to be learned philosophically from [Kierkegaard's] "edifying" writings' (ibid., p. 494). Heidegger also quotes Count Yorck's description of his own philosophy approvingly: 'The practical aim of our standpoint is one that is pedagogical in the broadest and deepest sense of the word . . . to make possible the moulding of individuality' (ibid., p. 454), and admits that his 'preparatory existential-temporal analytic of Dasein is resolved to foster the spirit of Count Yorck' (ibid., p. 455).

The contradiction can be reconciled when we take his insistence on neutral interpretation as part of a sophisticated enticement tactic. Here I agree with Harries that '*Being and Time* can be read as an edifying discourse disguised as fundamental ontology', and with Rorty's comment that Heidegger's ' "most elementary words" are words designed to express the predicament of the ironic theorist'.[10] If one of the components of irony is a simulated innocence and the pretence of avoiding any judgement, then here we have an ironic posture at its best. Looking closely at Heidegger's basic distinctions, we cannot but feel that the terms he uses for authentic modes of life as opposed to inauthentic ones are charged with evaluative connotations and associations of which he is well aware. He employs these provocative terms to make us more self-conscious, and thereby to awaken our readiness for change in our lives.

Heidegger calls the inauthentic manifestations of human being 'the "falling" of Dasein' (ibid., p. 219; *Verfallen* connotes deterioration and collapse). He then tries to convince us, ironically, that his term does not express any negative evaluation, but is used to signify that Dasein is proximally and for the most part *alongside* the 'world' of its concern . . . Being-lost in the publicness of the 'they' . . . fallen away from itself as an authentic potentiality for Being its Self.

(ibid, p. 220)

But surely 'Being-lost' is bad: nobody wants to be lost or to fall. The very term 'fall', when addressed to a mainly Christian public, arouses negative associations of which Heidegger, as a former student of theology, was quite aware.

He speaks of the inauthentic 'evasive concealment in the face of death' (ibid., p. 300), of the 'illusion' and the 'failure' to recognize one's authenticity (ibid., p. 301). These terms are hardly neutral. Can we accept unreservedly Heidegger's reassurance that an expression such as 'idle talk' (the inauthentic counterpart of authentic 'discourse') 'is not to be used here in a "disparaging" signification' (ibid., p. 211)? When Heidegger describes *Dasein's* movement towards the inauthentic mode of Being as a 'downward plunge' into 'the groundlessness and nullity of inauthentic everydayness' (ibid., p. 223), does this come across as a purely neutral description?

Heidegger might argue that such terms are negative only in everyday language, but from the perspective that seeks to explicate the a priori essence of Being such terms are neutral, with none of the a posteriori connotations ascribed to them by the 'anyone'. Even so, the reader encounters these terms in an ontic way, namely, with naive pre-onto-logical associations. Such a predictable reception of Heideggerian ter-minology is crucial here: it may provoke the reader into the very mood Heidegger wishes to excite. In the middle of his laborious ontological investigations, we find the beautiful Latin fable of *Cura*, who 'shaped' *homo* 'out of *humus* [earth]' (ibid., sec. 42). Why does Heidegger bring this 'pre-ontological' story here 'though its demonstrative force is "merely historical" ' (ibid., p. 241)? It is clear that the fable is used as a 'force' to effect the reader's 'transformation into that which he can be in Being-free for his ownmost possibilities' (ibid., p. 243). Thus, we cannot fail to sense a prescriptive undertone which also reaffirms his thesis that, for man, to be is to care about one's sense of authentic Being and self (ibid., pp. 175, 240).

Heidegger's use of seemingly neutral terms is intended to counter the 'seductive' forces prevalent in the inauthentic public realm. Like Nietzsche, who used the term *Verführung* for negative seduction, Heidegger regards the public as trying to seduce *Dasein* to think and behave as it does: 'The dominance of the public way' is such that 'in no case is a Dasein untouched and unseduced' (*unverführt*; ibid., p. 213). *Dasein* is seduced into believing that adopting 'their' way of thinking and living will ensure a full, genuine and tranquil life. 'However, this tranquillity in inauthentic Being does not seduce (*verführt*) one into stagnation and inactivity, but drives one into uninhibited hustle' (ibid., p. 222). Heidegger's language is plainly evaluative, at least from the point of view of the layperson. Since his books are available to the public, they constitute enticing counter-seductions for the fallen *Dasein*, who may be moved by the evocative etymologies, the contrasting pictures of authentic and inauthentic *Dasein*s, and the literary digressions.

However, if authenticity is an a priori ontological phenomenon, what is the point in enticing us to *be* what we already necessarily are? The answer is that we are authentic solely as possibilities still to be ontically actualized. To be ontologically authentic is not yet to become authentic, and it is to entice us into becoming what we are that Heidegger resorts to phenomenological explications and ironic presentations.[11] Following Kant, he urges us: 'You must, because you can!'

II

Dasein is not an entity like material things, which are merely 'present-at-hand', but a process of becoming aware of its ownness and concerned with the meaning of Being. It can exist either authentically or inauthentically. By realizing my possibilities, by creating and 'winning' myself, reflecting on the meaning of Being and being concerned about its development, I am authentic *Dasein*. My existing is fully determined by my own choices. The intimate relation between Heidegger's *eigentlich* (authentic, genuine or real) and *eigen* (own) is lost in English. The possibility of inauthentic existence is also mine. But in this case I grasp it not as an indefinite existence but as an entity among other entities, as sheer facticity. I let my existence be determined and defined by others, thereby changing its meaning from existence to essence. My ownness becomes otherness and I lose myself by my own actions.

Unlike previous thinkers who arrived at the notion by examining inauthentic patterns of life, Heidegger starts with a positive definition. Both authenticity and inauthenticity are defined positively, for the latter, as a modification of authenticity, also has a positive ontological status. Heidegger's ontologizing leads to his making these modes into positive features of *Dasein*'s Being. Inauthenticity is not a mere negation of authenticity, but rather a distinct characteristic. Heidegger cannot define the meaning of Being by telling us first what it means not to Be. The positive approach to authenticity is reinforced by the method of going back to 'the things themselves' (*BT*, pp. 49, 50), namely, to *Dasein*s, analysing their structures and explicating their a priori meanings. Further, to attain an adequate description of the 'essence' (ibid., p. 67) of Being in its 'totality' a genuine specimen is needed, just as, in deriving the essential features of a circle, one must first contemplate a true representation of a circle, not a distorted copy. The same applies to inauthenticity. Heidegger's method requires that inauthentic Being be positive: one cannot 'uncover' what is not; therefore inauthenticity 'must be made accessible by a positive characterization' (ibid., p. 69) *'because* this phenomenon itself always gets "seen" ' (ibid., p. 85). Inauthenticity is doubly positive: it is a positive expression of *Dasein*'s mode, and it is indicative of another, more fundamental mode of *Dasein*'s Being – that of authenticity. Even if the mode of inauthenticity 'is only the mode of fleeing *in the face of it* and forgetfulness *thereof* [i.e. of the question of the meaning of Being]' (ibid., p. 69), this 'forgetfulness' points to the thing forgotten. Inauthenticity reveals what it betrays: the possibility of authenticity. Heidegger's advance over previous thinkers is found in this insistence upon grasping the phenomenon of inauthenticity positively. Here we find neither blunt condemnation nor rejection but a more balanced and empathetic understanding of this phenomenon. The twentieth-century processes of levelling, especially those rooted in technology and the global economy, may well have contributed to this more realistic attitude.

A problem, however, arises from regarding inauthenticity as an a priori 'structure of existentiality' (ibid., p. 69): how will it be possible to overcome it and regain an authentic sense of ownness? If *Dasein* is essentially bound to the inessential, if its nature is to flee from its primordial authentic Being and transform itself into an externally determined entity, what can induce it to forgo this betrayal and return to ownness? I shall look at these questions later. At this stage it suffices to note that inauthenticity is only ontologically but not ontically essential. Empirically, each *Dasein* preserves its free choice to decide whether it wants its authenticity or not.

The problem of recognizing authenticity and distinguishing it from inauthenticity finds its solution at the ontological level of inquiry. Though 'structurally' they are 'indistinguishable' (ibid., p. 70), since both belong essentially to the a priori constitutive structures of *Dasein*, they 'can be very well grasped ontologically' as two distinct modes of existence. The problem of recognition remains only at the ontic level. Still, this result is quite positive. The a priori possibility of authenticity, which may or may not find its actualization in the everyday lives of individuals, is assured.

Yet another problem which cannot be resolved at this stage is the question of priority. In one passage (*BT*, p. 68) Heidegger seems to imply that authenticity is ontologically prior to inauthenticity. A recurrent theme in Heidegger's writings is 'homecoming', regaining what was 'lost', indicating that he sees authenticity as primordial and, at least in time, prior to inauthentic modes of *Dasein*. But if inauthenticity also has 'mineness' as an essential character, in what way is authentic 'ownness' or 'mineness' prior to the inauthentic mode? How can one mode be prior if both are a priori essentials of the same *Dasein*? From the phenomenological standpoint, it appears that the two modes are structurally and essentially equally grounded in *Dasein*. Heidegger's later tendency to regard authenticity as fundamental (inauthenticity being its modification) is still latent at this point. Thus, when Heidegger speaks of authenticity, he refers primarily to the a priori ontological structure in every *Dasein*. Every human being must have this structure, but it is not the case that every ontological 'possibility' for becoming an authentic *Dasein* is ontically realized. For each *Dasein* also has the a priori potential to become inauthentic, to lose itself and never win itself, and is free to choose.

To be *Dasein* is to question the meaning of Being. It becomes an issue solely for an authentic Being, whose authenticity is 'hidden' but nonetheless given 'beforehand' (ibid., p. 25). The very search for authenticity 'constitutes its meaning' (ibid., p. 59) and discloses the seeker's authenticity. To be an authentic *Dasein*, therefore, is to grasp that one cannot become authentic as an ontic entity among entities, as a static being, but only as asking, searching Becoming, that is, as a transcendent consciousness, whose projected intentionalities become authentic 'only by anticipation' (ibid., p. 310).

III

The meaning of *Dasein*'s Being cannot be found in an isolated Cartesian subject, for *Dasein* is necessarily rooted in the world. Without the world there is no *Dasein*, hence no authentic *Dasein*. Heidegger's explication of 'Being-in-the-world' is an account of *Dasein*'s search for authenticity. The attitude of *Dasein* to its world is that of emotional and practical involvement in 'being-with', as opposed to the purely spatial and causal relationship of 'being-beside'. For *Dasein*, to be is always to be with something or to 'reside alongside' someone else as 'Being-with-one-another' (*BT*, pp. 80, 163). As *Dasein*, capable of inquiring into its own Being, human Being loses its role as a substantial subject opposed to other objects in the world. The traditional subject/ object distinction is inappropriate, for it presupposes understanding of what it means to be a subject or object.

As the hyphens indicate, Being-in-the-world is a '*unitary* phenomenon' (ibid., p. 78), the elements of which are inseparable. The relation between *Dasein* and its world is that of an intentional coexistence within a common system of meaningful symbols and social institutions. Grasping the 'mineness' of my Being cannot be achieved in a vacuum. My sense of my Being is possible precisely because it cannot be abstracted from the sense of 'mineness' that refers to my world. I am; I can reflect upon this because my Being is fulfilled and enfolded in the world. I am, *ergo* I am in-the-world. It is possible, however, to be in-the-world inauthentically.

'World' does not refer to the natural world, since 'Nature can also be when no Dasein exists.'[12] Nor does it confront us as a picture confronts observers who are not part of it. The world's relation to *Dasein* attests *Dasein*'s ecstatic and transcendental character. As aspiring, intending and projecting, 'Dasein has always already *stepped out beyond itself*, ex-sistere, it *is in* a world' (*BPP*, p. 170). *Dasein*'s mode of Being-in-the-world is not simply that of a fly in a bottle or a subject confronting an objective world, but that of an entity intimately immersed in it. *Dasein*'s world is of its making. In turn, it constitutes *Dasein*'s experiences, endowing them with meaning. I dwell 'within the world as projected by me'. To find my self through the world, I have to stand away (*ex-stare*) from it, but (and this is a crucial 'but') I must return to it and accept it as my 'homeland'. This is the returning of the *Sein* to *Da* (its world) after it has lost or abandoned it. To find one's self, one must lose it in the world. Estrangement from my world puts me in a state of ironic detachment from my self, enabling me to shape my self. Since, however, my sense of meaning (of what it means for *me* to be) is inseparable from the wider context of my Being-in-the-world, I cannot regain it without regaining the meaning of my Being-in-the-world and Being-with-one-another. I cannot be estranged from my world and at home with my self. Hence I cannot achieve my own sense of Being (my authenticity) apart from the community of other *Dasein*s and the meanings, institutions and relations which are 'tied up with Dasein's ownmost Being' (*BT*, p. 160). 'Being-in is *Being-with* Others' (ibid., p. 155), for 'Dasein, insofar as it *is*, has always submitted itself already to a "world" which it encounters, and this *submission* belongs essentially to its Being' (ibid., pp. 120–1). Heidegger stresses this idea of the inevitable sociability of existence. Thus, for example, he asserts that the 'so-called "private existence" is not really essential, that is to say free, human being. It simply insists on negating the public realm' (*LH*, p. 197). Only those who insist on presenting Heidegger's insight independently of its ontological frame can arrive at the bizarre conclusion that his philosophy leads to 'the ultimate loneliness of individual existence'.[13] In fact, Heidegger's elaborate ontological apparatus is introduced precisely to set the so-called 'solitary individual' firmly within the inevitable social context. The modes of Being-in-the-world and Being-with-one-another are necessary even in uniquely personal moments such as death.

To regain authenticity, inauthenticity must be overcome. To become my own authentic Being, however, I need others, and our common world as a horizon which defines my ownness *vis-à-vis* what is not genuinely mine. Heidegger concurs with Kierkegaard and Nietzsche that one becomes what one truly is by rejecting what one is not. For this one needs the world, which is partially one's own. Yet this partial possession gives rise to feelings of alienation: one becomes estranged from that which was not strange to one beforehand. Estrangement presupposes familiarity, as inauthenticity requires authenticity.

We begin to grasp the dynamics of the search for authenticity: (a) the starting-point is Being-in-the-World as 'necessary *a priori*, but . . . far from sufficient for completely determining Dasein's Being' (*BT* p. 79). My Being can be authentically mine or I can lose this mineness, becoming (b) inauthentic in this world. This is my free choice exercised at the ontic level to realize my possibilities. An ontological condition of my authenticity is (c) my feeling estranged within the world, losing it and becoming detached, and then (d) regaining authentic Being-in-the-world by 'homecoming', by overcoming the innate tendencies to inauthenticity which my Being-in-the-world and Being-with-one-another set in motion. This pattern presupposes that *Dasein* is a temporal Being; hence an ontological analysis of time and of *Dasein*'s temporality is introduced later on.

While the issue of the ethical viability of authenticity has to do with a '*what*' (*BT*, p. 71) and with a 'how', that of the identification and recognition of authentic Being is essentially one of 'a "*who*" (existence)'. Some progress has been made here, since Heidegger is in a better position to solve the problem of the 'how' by ontologically paving the way to ontic characterization. Kierkegaard and Nietzsche started from the solitary individual who strove to attain genuine self-hood in isolation from the common world and, after attaining authenticity, had to protect it from the inroads of society. Heidegger's picture is less Romantic and more modern. Throughout, *Dasein* is inseparably connected to its world, to the community of others and to history. The struggle for authenticity must necessarily be achieved within this framework. The question is not how one can maintain one's authentic self while living within society, but how to explain its loss in the first place. Heidegger answers by embarking on the analysis of everydayness, into which authentic Being falls.

IV

The 'anyone', which is nothing definite, and which all are, though not as the sum, prescribes the kind of Being of everydayness. . . . In these modes one's way of Being is that of inauthenticity and failure to stand by one's Self. . . . Dasein has . . . fallen away from itself as authentic potentiality for Being its Self, and has fallen into the 'world'. Fallenness into the 'world' means an absorption in Being-with-one-another, in so far as the latter is guided by idle talk, curiosity, and ambiguity.[14]

The delicate balance between my sense of Being and my sense of my world, which together constitute authenticity, collapses when 'proximally and for the most part' *Dasein* 'surrenders' itself to the world, becoming 'absorbed' by it. The world ceases to belong to me, and, by succumbing to its many distractions, I belong to it instead. When I lose my world, which becomes a strange and alienating objective world out there, I lose my sense of my own Being. I cease to be owner and master of my self and am owned by the public, the anyone. I become an entity 'within-the-world' (*BT*, p. 230), one object among many. Such an inauthentic *Dasein* becomes 'present-at-hand' for others, to be observed and defined, and 'ready-to-hand' – available for their manipulation. The victory of the anonymous world over *my* world perpetuates and even intensifies the process of becoming inauthentic. Echoing Kierkegaard's *The Present Age*, Heidegger claims that by losing my unique sense of Being, I let 'the real dictatorship of the anyone' (*BT*, p. 164) unfold and swallow my authentic Self, 'levelling' it 'down' to the 'averageness' of 'publicness' (ibid., 165). In the realm of inauthenticity 'everyone is the other, and no one is himself' (ibid., p. 165).

Living, as we must, in society, are we doomed to this anonymous hell, or can we resist these powerful forces that lead us towards inauthenticity? The expression 'proximally and for the most part', used by Heidegger frequently in reference to inauthenticity, is ambiguous, evading the question of whether inauthenticity is an essential and necessary mode of Being-in-the-world. However, the following crucial passage hints at the possibility of there being a community of authentic Beings-in-the-World:

> The Being-with-one-another of those who are hired for the same affair often thrives only on mistrust. On the other hand, when they devote themselves to the same affair in common, their doing so is determined by the manner in which their Dasein, each in its own way, has been taken hold of. They thus become *authentically* bound together, and this makes possible the right kind of objectivity, which frees the Other in his freedom for himself. Everyday Being-with-one-another maintains itself between the two extremes of positive solicitude – that which leaps in and dominates, and that which leaps forth and liberates. It brings numerous mixed forms to maturity; to describe these and classify them would take us beyond the limits of this investigation.
>
> (*BT*, p. 159)

When others regard me, and each other, as ready-to-hand objects to be used and manipulated, caring exclusively about their own concerns, interests and profits, inauthentic relations are established. 'Inconsiderateness' and 'indifference' as to my freedom and ownness are manifested, as they try to 'dominate' me. Yet there is also 'mature' interaction and 'authentic care'; unfortunately, Heidegger, limiting himself to description of the inauthentic fall, does not elaborate on it here. There is, however, the ontological possibility that human beings function in such a way that 'others are not proximally present-at-hand as free floating subjects along with other Things, but show themselves in the world in their special environmental Being' (ibid., p. 160). These are cases of 'solicitude' and 'authentically bound' relations in which people, including oneself, project themselves on to the 'same affair in common', 'caring for' (*Fürsorge*) each other's 'existence'. Such instances of mutual caring and respect for each other's well-being, for individual freedom and feelings of 'ownness', can be found, perhaps, in mature relations of love or marriage, which transcend satisfaction of symbiotic or egocentric needs. In them, the partner's project of being authentic becomes a 'common affair'. In such relations, which can also exist between friends, we can attain the 'right kind of objectivity', that which does not turn us into objects but provides a social framework in which to live significantly, according to one's own rights, working towards personal or shared goals.

But do not the prevailing social norms constitute insurmountable empirical obstacles to authenticity? *Being and Time* does contain descriptions of dramatic clashes between the anyone and the singular individual who attempts to attain authenticity (e.g. *BT*, p. 298); however, we do not find in Heidegger head-on confrontation between authenticity and the prevailing ethos. If one can maintain one's authenticity, ultimately society will not be able to take it out of one's hands. The fall to the inauthentic mode of Being is not directly caused by sociability, though social intercourse serves as a seductive medium for *Dasein*'s fall, and even '*aggravates* the falling' (ibid., p. 222). The reason for the fall is found in one's ontologically existential and immanent state of mind: anxiety.

Owing to 'the dominance of the public way . . . in no case is a Dasein untouched and unseduced' (ibid., p. 213) by the ontic pervasiveness and forcefulness of inauthenticity. Use of the neutral term 'temptation' (*Versuchung*, which also means test or experiment; *SZ*, p. 177), however, implies that *Dasein* need not necessarily succumb but can remain authentic. Inauthenticity does not have to be one's ultimate fate at the ontic level of public everydayness, despite the temptations and distractions of everydayness, and the pressure to lose one's self in the anyone's 'uninhibited hustle' (*BT*, p. 222). For if one is aware that these are merely temptations, one can yield, knowing that only temporary relief from one's struggle for authenticity is possible. By recognizing distractions for what they are, namely, enticements to self-abandon-ment, one increases the chance of climbing back from fallenness. If, however, one succumbs without this awareness, one is doomed to remain fallen. Like Nietzsche's tests (*Versuchungen*), designed to dis-tinguish the inferior from the superior, so Heidegger's idea of temp-tation differentiates *Dasein*s whose potential for authentic Being can be realized from inauthentic *Dasein*s. For the latter, temptation becomes seduction driving the *Dasein* to inauthenticity, in which it remains entrenched.

'Being-in-the-world is in itself *tempting* (*versucherisch*)' (ibid., p. 221), because it constitutes the most accessible route for falling into inauthenticity. But this does not mean that falling is an essential part of *Dasein*'s Being-in-the-world. Being-in-the-world and inauthenticity or fall are distinct; otherwise it would make no sense to speak of being tempted to fall. Nowhere does Heidegger identify Being-in-the-world with everydayness. However, such an identification is presupposed by those commentators who tend to regard Heidegger's ideal of authen-ticity as unattainable, impractical or a-social. If we recall Heidegger's remark about 'authentic' Being-with-one-another, it follows that falling is not an ineluctable aspect of *Dasein*'s social existence. Inauthenticity is 'for the most part' a pervasive feature of the world of the anyone, but not a necessary one. *Dasein need not* interpret itself along the lines of the public ethos. It can resist public self-interpretation and the temp-tation to merge with the anonymous anyone. It can cling to its own sense of authentic Being by regarding its basic condition of Being-in-the-world as a necessary 'test' of its authenticity. 'The laying-bare of Dasein's primordial Being must rather be *wrested* from Dasein by fol-lowing the *opposite course* from that taken by the falling ontico-onto-logical tendency of interpretation' (*BT*, p. 359). In Heidegger, as in Nietzsche and Kierkegaard, we can discern a kind of counter-temp-tation to the seductive everyday interpretation. Indeed, Heidegger's analysis of *Dasein*'s Being-in-the-world, in disclosing to the reader a viable ontological possibility for authentic Being, is just such a counter-temptation.

In addition to the seductive elements of everydayness that make *Dasein* forget its concern with its Being, another public mechanism can lead to self-abandonment. Being-in-the-world-with-one-another makes possible the comparison of one's self to other selves. *Dasein* 'compares itself with everything' and 'drifts along towards an alien-ation in which its ownmost potentiality-for-Being is hidden from it' (ibid., p. 222). By evaluating one's own achievements in terms of those of others, one lets the world intrude and destroy one's sense of self. The determination of one's self ceases to be one's own. It defines itself statistically until the average anyone swallows it. The way out is 'Beware! Don't compare!'

This is easier said than done. In Being-alongside-each-other and competing with one another, we naturally become entangled in the statistical framework of comparisons and alienation. In certain cases, though, we can free ourselves from these inauthenticating relations. Having 'the same affair in common', and being 'authentically bound together' (ibid., p. 158) let one overcome the tendency to compare oneself to others. Through preoccupation with the well-being of another or with one's contributions to 'the same affair', one measures one's efforts not in terms of others but in terms of what is left to be done. Within this type of interaction one feels and thinks authentically and directly without the mediation of publicness. The public, however, is not simply a source of seduction, but also deceives, covering up its fallenness with 'a sham of authenticity' (ibid., p. 223), and presenting it as self-fulfilment. Feeling the shame, one feels 'not at home' (*unheimlich*) and self-conscious. By contrast, the authentic *Dasein* feels *heimlich*, at home with its self.

But what exactly is *Dasein* promised? *Dasein* is seduced by the promise of '*tranquillity*, for which everything is "in the best of order" ' (ibid., p. 222). The bait which ensnares *Dasein* is the possibility of shaking off the anxiety *Dasein* necessarily feels in Being-in-the-world. *Dasein* loses its primordial sense of authentic Being not because it is Being-with-one-another but because it is essentially anxious. It can attain authenticity solely as Being-in-the-world, namely, when it faces and chooses possible ways or modifications of its own Being. We are fundamentally anxious, given our responsibility for our own Being. We are condemned to be free 'shepherds' of our authenticity; hence, we are condemned to anxiety. Feeling the authenticity of my Being invokes the *Angst* which makes me 'flee' and lose my sense of self; my immediate response to responsibility is anxiety.

This explains why authenticity is so hard to achieve and so transitory. The source of inauthenticity lies precisely in the gut feelings of selfhood. 'Anxiety throws Dasein back upon' its authenticity, but indirectly: by inciting one to flee one's authenticity, anxiety thereby discloses it. Since authenticity is always possible, one is always anxious. Indeed, to be anxious simply means to feel the inner call of authenticity. To evade this call is thus a way to overcome anxiety. But with its loss, we also lose our feelings of self. The 'everyday publicness of the "anyone" ', which 'absorbs' the anxious *Dasein*, serves as its 'tranquillizer' (ibid., p. 233). With an inauthentic self, one no longer feels the anxiety of freedom. One gives up one's authenticity to gain peace of mind, but one's mind becomes public property, estranged from its vital origins. Because escape inevitably discloses the thing one is escaping – namely, anxiety – there is no complete escape. Hence, the process of fleeing into publicness is saturated with 'latent anxiety' (ibid., p. 237), which makes one's Being aware of itself as anxious, thereby 'individualizing' it.

In *Angst* there is no definite intentional object; hence the very process of being anxious itself becomes the *noema*. That is, having no object, anxiety in its anxiousness feels its lack of an object; it feels *Nichts* (nothingness, non-Being). It responds by again experiencing anxiety. To eradicate this alienation, the self must be repossessed. Hence, anxiety discloses to *Dasein* that 'authenticity and inauthenticity are possibilities of its Being' (ibid., p. 235). Yet confronting these options and realizing that it is up to oneself to decide between them gives rise to 'real anxiety' in 'the very depths of [one's] Being' (ibid., p. 234).

But why does preoccupation with authenticity bring about such anxiety? The answer lies in the fact that to face one's self is to face one's facticity or finitude: the possibility of not being. It is to comprehend the ontological fact that our world is formed by us and that it is essentially immanent. In self-confrontation one understands that one is 'thrown' into a finite world and seized by a haunting anxiety in the face of certain death that cannot be rationalized away, for example, by projecting one's responsibility or salvation onto transcendental forces.

The motif of finitude and death recurs in Heidegger's Sisyphean circle of authenticity: (1) authenticity, or ownness of my Being-in-the-world > (2) anxiety in the face of (1) > (3) ownness lost by flight and fall into the anyone > (4) latent anxiety and the feeling of *unheimlichkeit* > (5) individualization > (6) authentic ownness of my Being > (7) anxiety in the face of (6), and so on unto death. Thus for Heidegger, unlike Nietzsche and Kierkegaard, the problem of the viability of authenticity has less to do with society and ethics than with the ontology of freedom. It is not society that is responsible for the dearth of authentic Being, but rather, the a priori anxiety built into Dasein. The most decisive factor in breaking through this circularity to a viable mode of authentic existence is Being-towards-death.

V

Together with others, one is, proximally and for the most part, inauthentic; then one dies alone, becoming authentic. Is this an accurate summary of Heidegger's account of authenticity? Several interpreters believe so, claiming that since authenticity can be attained only in isolation from the anyone, and since only death can bring about such isolation, only in relating to one's '*distinctively* impending death' (*BT*, p. 294) can one become authentic. This amounts to denying that authenticity can be a social mode of Being. Such a view was rejected by Heidegger, who repeatedly insisted that 'death belongs to Being-in-the-world' (ibid., p. 295; cf. p. 309). Authentically facing imminent death is an essential part of one's social relations. How is this claim to be understood?

At the intuitive level, it means that in a complete vacuum, in a social void, one cannot relate to death. In the absence of all sensory stimuli one cannot fathom what it means not to be. When there is nothing to lose, one cannot imagine what it means to lose one's World for ever. There is nothing within the immanent processes of Being that attests its Being-towards-the-end. Only as social, ontic Being-in-the-world can one gain awareness of the possibility of authentically comporting one's self towards one's death. This awareness, however, is not clearly demonstrable. Apodictic certainty of my own death is not rooted in hearing about or even observing others die but is found in anxiety. In anxiety 'Dasein finds itself *face to face* with the "nothing" of the possible impossibility of its existence' (*BT*, p. 310). Anxiety discloses that *Dasein*'s existence is temporary. To be is to be anxious because to be is to die. And if one can authentically or inauthentically be-in-the-world one can also authentically or inauthentically die.

Moreover, my mortality can have meaning for me only in the framework of limits. These limits are there because of others. For example, I can contemplate the world without me: others without myself. An authentic relation to one's death does not require individual isolation. It is a mode of Being-in-the-world and hence also of Being-with-others (see *BT*, p. 308).

One's authentic relation towards one's death does not exist in a vacuum; it assumes Being-with. One chooses one's ownness 'among the factical possibilities' (ibid.) within one's world. To choose authentic ownness meaningfully and freely one must prefer it to the inauthentic modes of relating to one's self. One must consider others' selves and other (inauthentic) ways of Being. Authentic acceptance of one's death liberates one from losing one's self in the inauthentic illusions of the anyone. Heidegger claims that 'freedom towards death' (ibid., p. 311) is freedom to be authentic. The possibility of one's ownmost sense of selfhood requires the possibility of losing one's own self in the everyday public. But death calls us back from this loss.

It is important to stress that freedom from the inauthentic modes does not mean freedom from concerned solicitude and authentic Being-with-one-another. Authentic Being-towards-death and detachment from the anyone does not isolate *Dasein* or make it unsocial. On the contrary:

> authentic Being-one's-self does not detach Dasein from its world, nor does it isolate it so that it becomes a free-floating 'I'. . . . [it] brings the Self right into its current concernful Being-alongside . . . and pushes it into solicitous Being with Others.
>
> (*BT*, p. 344)

Only a *Dasein* that is truly itself can be a truly concerned lover, spouse, colleague or friend. Freedom from inauthentic modes of Being towards death, by individualizing *Dasein*, makes self-possession possible. Far from leading to isolation, it creates the conditions for genuine sociability. Authentic dying enables me to open myself to the option of being authentically bound to others, of caring about them, say, as those who will survive.

Furthermore, Heidegger nowhere says that one can become authentic *only* in the mode of Being-towards-death. Granted, he holds that one reaches the most 'authentic certainty' in facing one's death, but this does not in itself preclude the possibility of authentic choices that have nothing to do with dying. When Heidegger envisages authentic life-patterns in reference to Being-with-one-another he does not necessarily presuppose dying. Still, death is decisive for authenticity, for several reasons.

First, death plays a significant role within Heidegger's inquiry into the meaning of Being. For one way to explore what it means to be is to investigate what it means *not* to be. Analysis of the meaning of one's death shows it to be that possibility in which one's selfhood is most forcefully revealed. If authenticity is the sense of one's Being, in death one reaches the culmination of one's potential for authentic Being. Moreover, truly to comprehend certain phenomena, one must consider them as wholes (*BT*, p. 348). This is especially true of authentic Being: what is authentic must be finite since one cannot *own* and grasp an infinite process or entity. Death enters life to conclude it, making possible its adequate explication. Hence, only Being-towards-death can be *fully* meaningful and authentic. Each time we entertain the possibility of dying we undertake an assessment of our Being. In our anticipation we define our existence.

Further, death highlights our reasons for adopting an inauthentic mode of Being-in-the-world. It is, indeed, the crucial boundary situation, for it is universally imminent, unlike other extraordinary circumstances that might befall us. Only death is inescapable. It is neither esoteric nor exotic. Everyone is equally concerned about and personally involved in Being-towards-death; hence we must all choose between inauthenticity and authenticity – there is no way out. To be is to be anxious, but to be also means to die. One dies one's life but does not live one's death. The most acutely felt anxiety is that which arises in the face of imminent death. To evade this unbearable 'state of mind' various ploys are resorted to. Inauthenticity is a formidable defence mechanism. By distracting myself from my ownness, by becoming an object among other objects, I try to be oblivious of *my* coming death. To escape my Being-towards-death, I try, by being inauthentic, not to live my own life. Suppressing awareness of my imminent death, I also hide from the significance of my life, and refrain from taking chances, from realizing my possibilities. To be afraid of death and not to accept this anxiety courageously is to fear life and jettison authenticity. One is not one's self because to be one's own self is to acknowledge the possibility of not being at all. One cannot die one's life when one's life is not one's own. One tends to inauthenticity not only because authenticity makes one anxious about one's responsibility for one's self in-the-world, but also because it appears an easy escape from anxiety in the face of death. But such defence mechanisms collapse with the awareness of impending death, forcing one to ask oneself: 'What does it mean for me not to be?' Since one cannot grasp nothing, one turns to the question of authenticity: 'What does it mean for me to be?' This puts the questioner in touch with her sense of ownness, with her authentic Being.

Yet another role played by death is in highlighting the unavoidable clash between the individual's sense of Being and the inauthentic ethos of the anyone. The statistical anyone 'never dies because it *cannot* die' (*BT*, p. 477). As an active participant in the ethos of everydayness, one cannot fully be in command of one's Being. Only an event which severs the bond with the anyone can set authenticity in motion. Being-towards-death is exactly such an event. It releases *Dasein* from the anyone but not, of course, from Being-in-the-world. As a result, the everyday public works hard to conceal authentic Being-towards-death, as it threatens to shatter the widely accepted illusions of the prevailing ethos and its elaborate schemes for fleeing death, such as 'tranquillization' (ibid., p. 298) and regarding death as solely for others, that is, as an objective entity present-at-hand for observation. The most vigorous clash between the will to authenticity and the inauthentic anyone is conducted under the shadow of death. By not permitting '*the courage for anxiety in the face of death*', the anyone does not permit the courage to be authentic.

Finally, by revealing the clash between my death and the ethos of the anyone, death also discloses *Dasein*'s will, an essential aspect of authentic Being:

> Our everyday falling evasion *in the face of* death is an *inauthentic* Being-*towards*-death. But inauthenticity is based on the possibility of authenticity. Inauthenticity characterizes a kind of Being into which Dasein can divert itself and has for the most part always diverted itself; but *Dasein does not necessarily and constantly have to divert itself into this kind of Being*. Because Dasein exists, it determines its own character as the kind of entity it is.[15]

Like Nietzsche's *Übermensch*, Heidegger's authentic *Dasein* is the author of its 'own character'. The voluntarism of authenticity is suppressed by publicness. *Dasein* is almost reduced to impotence in the face of the anyone, which forces itself on *Dasein*, seducing it into giving up its authentic ownness. The ethos of the anyone is so persuasive and pervasive that only death can 'wrench' one from its domination (*BT*, p. 307). Loss of authenticity can, however, be 'reversed' (ibid., p. 312) by a firm decision to stand up to it and not yield to its seductions. Being-towards-death enables one to do this most effectively. Because death is 'distinctively impending', we are forced to decide if we are to attain our authentic selves or lose them before the factual event of our dying. Again, it is not the case that one can only become authentic as Being-towards-death; rather, one can most *easily* attain authenticity in one's attitude to one's 'ownmost' death. One can be authentic in one's relations to significant others, for example, but here one cannot depend solely on one's will, but must take into account the other as well. One is, however, freer to shape one's attitude to one's death, since one's dying is 'irrevocably non-relational' and cannot be 'outstripped'. This is less true of other relations to one's self, such as self-love or self-image, for in these attitudes the element of anxiety is missing. The anxiety one feels in facing death must be accepted authentically. The voluntaristic aspect of the struggle is most pronounced in facing death and less so in the context of self-image, self-love, etc. The dimension of will makes authenticity possible, allowing 'impassioned **freedom towards death** – a freedom which has been released from the Illusions of the "anyone", and which is factical, certain of itself, and anxious' (*BT*, p. 311). This explains Heidegger's contention that, unlike the negative phenomenon portrayed in the psychiatric literature, anxiety 'liberates' one for authenticity (ibid., p. 395).

Being is an indefinite process of actualizing possibilities. To comport one's self authentically through this process is to accept it as sheer possibility. From the point of view of authenticity, possibility is more important than actuality, which is ontically tainted by inauthentic modes. The more firmly one grasps one's death 'as the possibility of the impossibility' (ibid., p. 307), the more death becomes 'Dasein's *ownmost* possibility' (ibid.). Authentic Being is attained by keeping one's death at bay: as non-actualized possibility. The more real this possibility becomes, the better one understands one's self as that possibility towards-death, and the less one is affected by inauthentic interpretations of one's dying.

The question might be asked: 'How do I know that I am anxious about death if anxiety by its very nature lacks a definite object?' What essentially lacks an object, in fact, is my authentic Being and my Being-towards-not-Being. Death is not an entity 'which is ready-to-hand or present-at-hand, but a possibility of Dasein's Being' (ibid., p. 305). It is not a phenomenon accessible to the inquiring mind; only the anticipation of death can be scrutinized. Authenticity lacks any definite object or content (ibid., p. 311) because it is the very process of owning one's self, of relating oneself to that pure possibility of Being. Death is the ideal means for assessing what cannot be directly perceived. As in searching for authenticity, so in anticipating death, the 'how' becomes the 'what'. How one accepts one's death becomes the 'what' of one's life. One cannot *fully* own one's sense of life, without owning (viz. anticipating) one's death, because authentic Being, as final, necessarily includes dying. Hence to be authentic is to be anxious about one's death without fleeing in the face of one's anxiety, to expect it courageously without denial. One can be anxious in the face of one's authenticity but not fearful of it, because fear always has a definite object. Authenticity, as sheer possibility, is indefinite and functions as a regulative ideal. This ideal can affect us profoundly, transforming our attitude towards our own Being.

Heidegger stresses death as an exclusive expression of ownness and hence as able to express and shape authenticity. But does he not over-emphasize the seemingly trivial fact that everyone dies their own death and that 'no one can take the Other's dying away from him' because 'death is in every case mine' (ibid., p. 284)? Is this unique to death? What about self-love, self-perception, and so on, or even loving, feeling and understanding? As intentional processes, all seem mine no less than my dying. Is it that by falling into the public realm of the anyone, my feeling of self, and all these intentional processes that constitute this self, are no longer mine, since I do not shape them freely? But this is also true of inauthentic Being-towards-death, the very notion of which presupposes that my Being-towards-death is not mine. So in what sense is my death uniquely mine?

One answer seems to be that death uniquely challenges the constitution of my world by reference to the future. More concretely, however, the exclusiveness of death has to do with the extreme anxiety that facing death evokes in us. We are almost irresistibly tempted to flee from it, but if we manage to overcome this urge, we emerge in firm possession of our selves. Dying is the ultimate test: if one can authentically hold on to one's self and freely face its demise, one can act authentically in other, less taxing, circumstances. Death is not the only authentic mode, but it can be the most revealing. In facing death one's authenticity is maximally disclosed, because the forces which work to suppress it are so very formidable.

Heidegger's analysis of guilt and the 'voice of conscience' is relevant here, since it discloses two far-reaching ramifications of his treatment of authenticity: (1) guilt and conscience are unmistakable indicators of the potential for authentic Being within the realm of inauthentic every-dayness. They attest the fact that authenticity is never completely suppressed by living within society, and hence, that it is indeed attainable; (2) guilt shows that authenticity, far from undermining society, is constitutive of morality.

The experience of guilt reveals the self in the full poignancy of its mineness, for the wish to own one's self indicates conscience. The radical responsibility of owning my self is fraught with conscience and hence with guilt: 'Dasein is essentially guilty' (*BT*, p. 353) because it is 'essentially something which can be *authentic*' (ibid., p. 68). Moreover, grounds for Being-guilty are amply provided by everydayness, which seduces us into betraying our authentic sense of responsibility for our selves. Since most of the time, even one who is determined to secure authenticity is lost in the anyone, self-betrayal is a common phenomenon of public everydayness. Hence guilt, by afflicting us, indicates that we can be authentic.

Dasein is always guilty because *Dasein*'s Being is not God's Being, that is, it is never completely actualized. Each choice (say possibility x over possibility y or z) dooms it to 'notness' (*Nichtigkeit*). The ability to be authentic is also *Dasein*'s ability to be inauthentic. But when *Dasein* attains authenticity, when it owns its self and disowns the not-selves, has its guilt been overcome? No. Because of its finitude, *Dasein* is always guilty. Authenticity is to be preferred, though, because by commitment to one's finite ownness, one accepts the eventuality of guilt. To accept guilt is to accept oneself as always responsible for one's own self. The attempt to escape this fundamental responsibility by falling is of no avail.

One never feels guilty about, say, developing diabetes. It is not of one's making, so one is not responsible and no guilt accrues. But when one does feel guilty, it is because of the real possibility of becoming authentic. Only transgression of a genuine possibility leads one to feel guilt and to attempt to relieve this guilt by establishing an ethic which suppresses the will to authenticity. Yet such an ethic need not prevail. By acknowledging one's finite ownness, one accepts responsibility and the eventuality of guilt. Attempting to escape by falling, one is no better off, for falling is not a viable solution to guilt and anxiety. Even within the depths of fallenness the call to authenticity is never completely suppressed. Falling makes the sense of guilt more acute, by attesting the attempt to flee responsibility for one's self. Thus Heidegger's drama of authenticity develops as follows: I first hear 'a *call*' (ibid., p. 314) to be authentic. I owe it to myself to own my self. I feel responsible and, in response, attempt to satisfy this call but, failing to do so, feel guilty. Guilt thus attests my primordial search for authenticity (ibid., p. 354).

This 'call' 'appeals solely to that Self which . . . is in no other way than Being-in-the-world' (ibid., p. 318). It is also heard by those who have already fallen into the world of the anyone. Thus authenticity is not a permanent mode of *Dasein*: it is a fluctuating state of mind, arrived at through an ongoing struggle against the pull of the public world. Given the powerful inauthentic elements which we necessarily encounter in the world and within ourselves, 'authentic resoluteness' is not just a momentary pathos or event or even an ultimate choice, but a resolve, which keeps 'repeating itself' (ibid., p. 355). By such perseverance the fallen *Dasein* is able to reach a state in which 'one's very lostness in irresoluteness gets undermined' (ibid., p. 356).

The call to authenticity is 'an abrupt arousal . . . it reaches him who wants to be brought back' (ibid., p. 316). Only one who, despite fallenness, is already in search of authenticity can 'hear' and respond to the call of conscience which emerges from the anyone. *Dasein* can hear because even in its most fallen state not the whole *Dasein* is immersed in the they-self: 'the caller is unfamiliar to the everyday they-self; it is something like an *alien* voice' (ibid., p. 321). It follows that *Dasein* is '*at the same time* both the caller and the one to whom the appeal is made' (ibid., p. 320). *Dasein* is *both* authentic and inauthentic: its authentic dimension calls, its inauthentic dimension is called upon. The unsuppressed potentiality for authentic Being within the inauthentic realm hears and responds. Even as fallen-in-the-world, *Dasein* is able to, and hence must, be authentic. The very phenomena of conscience, guilt and call attest the fact that the domination of the public is never so total as to prevent the call from being heard by that dimension of the self which is not totally obliterated: 'The irresoluteness of the "anyone" remains dominant notwithstanding, but it cannot impugn resolute existence' (ibid., p. 345).

Authenticity, as *Dasein*'s 'resoluteness' to heed the call to ownness, is possible even within the adverse circumstances of inauthenticity, because ontologically authenticity is the most fundamental and primordial existential. Heidegger's ontology solves the question of the social viability of authenticity. 'Proximally and for the most part' *Dasein* is inauthentic within the social context. This does not mean, however, that it cannot be raised from this fallen state into authentic-Being-in-the-world, especially when the call to authenticity is amplified by Heidegger's enticing presentation.

But Heidegger goes further, claiming that owing to the necessary interaction among Beings-in-the-world, any individual's authenticity functions as a call to others to strive to become authentic as well: 'When Dasein is resolute, it can become the "conscience" of Others. Only by authentically Being-their-Selves in resoluteness can people authentically be with one another' (ibid., p. 344). By uniting the fragmented self into one authentic whole, *Dasein* inspires others to follow its example.

Heidegger's ontology of authenticity has yet another function: it tries to show that guilt, and hence authenticity, are fundamental presuppositions for the existence of any morality at all. Heidegger dissolves the clash between authenticity and ethics by making authenticity a necessary condition for morality via the phenomenon of guilt. The primordial search for self becomes the basis for responsibility and guilt and, hence, for moral standards: 'only because Dasein is guilty in the basis of its Being . . . is conscience possible' (ibid., p. 332). Here Heidegger differs from Nietzsche, who tried to anchor the phenomenon of *Schuld* (guilt or debt) in socio-economic relations, and Freud, for whom guilt resulted from breaching the moral code of 'totem and taboo'. Nietzsche and Freud thus consider the moral context prior to the emergence of guilt. Heidegger reverses this approach,[16] claiming that 'the idea of guilt must . . . be detached from relationship to any law or "ought" ' (ibid., p. 328) since 'Being-guilty does not first result from an indebtedness (*Verschuldung*), but on the contrary, indebtedness becomes possible only "on the basis" of a primordial Being-guilty' (ibid., p. 329). Here Heidegger is not suggesting a kind of secularized doctrine of original sin. His conception of guilt, intimately connected with his notion of primordial authentic selfhood, is ontological in nature. To be authentic is to be guilty, because it is to own one's self and to be responsible for its mode of existence, including falling. Feeling guilty attests one's potential for authenticity and one's responsibility for recovering one's sense of self should it be lost.

'Being-guilty' is 'being responsible for' one's self, 'being the author of' one's self as well as 'being the occasion for' the authenticity of other selves (ibid., p. 327). The ideal of authenticity 'can regulate the very manner in which we are with one other publicly'. Thus authenticity is not just a regulative ideal, but the constitutive ideal for a morality according to which each of us is responsible for our own sense of selfhood and for the well-being, that is, the authentic Being, of others. This ethic could be realized in a social framework of 'authentically bound' relations wherein public betrayal of individual selves would be minimal. Just as the ideal of psychoanalysis is a society in which instincts are repressed as little as possible, yielding relatively few intensively guilty and neurotic persons, Heidegger's ideal of an authentically orientated society is one that will minimize damage to its members' authenticity.

But if authentic Being-towards-death is the climax of *Dasein*'s authenticity, how can it serve as the basis for an authentic society? Is it not over-individualistic? The same is true of one's personal sense of guilt. Anticipating such questions, and his above-mentioned critics, Heidegger stresses that authentic 'anticipatory resoluteness' in the face of death is not 'a kind of seclusion in which one flees the world' (ibid., pp. 357-8); it is not confined to one's resoluteness towards one's own Being and self. On the contrary, it enables one to cope with the world firmly and positively. 'Individualization' is that 'authentic Being-one's-Self' (ibid., pp. 369-70) which enables one to take a significant stand. A genuine morality is the province of individuals who have managed to acquire '*power* over [their] *existence*' (ibid., p. 357). Slaves do not need morality, which presupposes the freedom of the self to Be, authentically and responsibly. Since Being-towards-death individualizes, making possible authenticity and freedom, it brings about the conditions fundamental to ethics. Insofar as anticipatory resoluteness in the face of death leads to the 'dispersing' of 'all fugitive Self-concealments', it makes possible authentic individuals who can establish an ethic of authenticity which promotes, secures and enhances that very basis for a genuine morality.

VI

Authenticity does not consist solely of courageous resoluteness in the face of death, for it also entails a special relationship with one's individual past and historical heritage. An authentic Being must appropriate its tradition in an authentic 'coming-back' which secures its authentic looking-forward. One must accommodate one's past to have a present. The discussion of time and history that concludes the treatment of authenticity in *Being and Time* highlights the primacy of this ideal in Heidegger's thought. Indeed, the issue of temporality is raised precisely (*BT*, p. 424) to further the discussion of authenticity and resolve its problems.

The introduction of the notion of temporality provides a more complete explanation of the call to authenticity from inauthentic everydayness. The call does not stem solely from the irrepressible, authentic part of *Dasein*, but also emerges from its past and history: 'the call is from afar unto afar' (ibid., p. 316). One hears and responds to the call because it comes from within one's Being and is amplified by one's past and history. But to hear and understand this call from the past, one must already be authentic. Moreover, one's past and history must be authentic to deliver such a call. To break out of this vicious circle, Heidegger spoke, after *Being and Time*, of 'Grace' from above (not just from 'afar') and of 'God' as uniquely able to 'save' us from inauthenticity.

Here, however, the concept of the individual's historicality is intended to emphasize the active dimensions of authentic Being. This balances the weight accorded to moods and such states of mind as anxiety and guilt. For moods are passive and uncontrollable – to base authentic life exclusively upon them would clearly undermine the whole project. By introducing temporality, essential to the ongoing struggle to secure one's sense of ownness, including the ownness of one's past and history, Heidegger counters the passive and emotive elements of authenticity discussed thus far. The struggle between authentic and inauthentic modes of Being as future possibilities of *Dasein* takes place in time. The idea that one has to win one's past in order to win one's future, that one must actively appropriate one's heritage, making it one's own, highlights the active *Dasein*. For *Dasein* inherits its past not only by 'accident' but also with authentic 'resolve'; it 'choose[s] it' freely (ibid., p. 435). One's heritage is not passively handed from generation to generation, but has potential for willingly chosen reinterpretation and appropriation. This active element in *Dasein*'s authentic resoluteness contrasts with the essential passivity of inauthentic modes of existing: 'Everydayness determines Dasein even when it has not chosen the "anyone" for its "hero"' (*SZ*; p. 371, my translation). For the most part we resolutely choose neither our selves nor the heritage into which we are thrown. Consequently, inauthenticity ensures the rarity of the authentic present, that 'moment of vision' when existence gains mastery over the everyday but can 'never extinguish it' (ibid.). The victory of authenticity is never final and may be limited to a moment (*BT*, p. 387), but it is always possible, because to be is to be in time, to create and recreate one's past, heritage and future in an 'active ecstasis' and in 'resolute rapture' (ibid.). Temporality is the source of *Dasein*'s self-constancy. 'The "who" of Dasein' (ibid., p. 427) lies in its past and future as well as in the past and future of its community.

The issue of historicality and temporality makes it even clearer that Heidegger sees *Dasein* as essentially existing with others, and hence as being able to be, and not just to die, authentically within its community. *Dasein* cannot achieve individual authenticity apart from the community. The heritage which *Dasein* authentically appropriates is not merely its individual history but rather the heritage of the entire people, folk or 'generation' it belongs to (ibid., p. 436). By firmly fixing authenticity in *Dasein*'s wider socio-historical context, Heidegger adds an important dimension to the more personal focus of authentic dying.

Any ethos has its own history. By appropriating its values and accepting its responsibilities, I make this particular ethos into my own, becoming an authentic Being within its framework. This appropriation of a given ethos leads from so-called objective history, constituted by a uniform succession of events in objective/chronological time, to the historicality of authentically existing *Dasein* in-the-world. Authentic time of one's own making is constituted by *Dasein*'s 'leaping' from and into moments of authenticity: it is time created and freely recreated. This move from history to historicality parallels the shift from the ethos of objectivity to authenticity.

To be authentic is to own one's self. But one cannot do so completely without also owning one's past and one's heritage, because one's self is an integral part of the history of one's community. Alienated self which is estranged from its community cannot become fully authentic. The view held by Kierkegaard and Nietzsche that any given ethic and society are potential enemies of authentic life is diametrically opposed to Heidegger's intuition of what it means to be authentic. Ethos, history and society are the constitutive elements of authenticity.

It follows from Heidegger's discussion of historicality that any ethic authentically appropriated by one's self is constitutive of one's authenticity. This, however, is qualified by his distinction between 'inauthentic historicality' and 'authentic historicality' (ibid., pp. 433ff.). The former combines an 'evasion' of choice and resoluteness regarding one's future as Being-towards-death with 'forgetfulness' of one's folk past and heritage. Authentic historicality is indifferent to specific content or values of one's past or present, and relates to the mode of referring to them. Each *Dasein*, by its own acts of appropriation, by 'revering the repeatable possibilities of existence' (ibid., p. 443) recreates and owns its historical ethos, which becomes the 'sole authority' for its authentic Being. Here we are reminded of Kierkegaard's notion of authenticity as the passionate commitment to an authority which becomes sole author of one's biography. But instead of Kierkegaard's authoritative God, Heidegger's authority is the historical dimension of the people in which one is rooted. One is historically authentic when one creates one's own history by utilizing and recreating one's past and the past of one's people, projecting them with anticipatory resoluteness towards one's future. If 'resoluteness constitutes the *loyalty* of existence to its own Self' (ibid.), authenticity is the loyalty of one's self to its own past, heritage and ethos. The sum of the many authentic resolutenesses of individual *Dasein*s in their personal lives, and the whole network of such authentically bound individual *Dasein*s in-the-world, constitutes the authentic historicality of one's self and one's society, folk or people: in short, of one's authentic ethos.

Does this mean that all moralities are equally valid as far as authenticity is concerned? No, for any ethic that militantly suppresses authenticity, which levels the living *Dasein* into a present-to-hand observable entity, a ready-to-hand object for the anyone's manipulations and domination, is unacceptable. For example, a militaristic ethos which advocates subjugating other countries and eradicating their cultural heritage by suppressing their history would be an anti-authentic ethos, since it prevents the inhabitants of the conquered land from owning and appropriating their historicality and heritage. But even within the militaristic society itself there is no possibility of authenticity. Authentically bound relations within such an aggressively task-orientated society are almost a factical impossibility, because of the intrusion of the state into virtually every social unit. The state will aggressively attempt to own each *Dasein*'s Being, regarding it as an object to be used, instead of allowing each *Dasein* to realize its individual aim of owning its own Being. In spite of Heidegger's personal affinity with Nazism, there is nothing in his notion of authenticity that provides sound philosophical underpinnings for regarding the Nazi attitude as authentic. Indeed, Heidegger's own teachings on authenticity work against his support for the Nazi regime. In any event, because of the purely a-political character of the ideal of authenticity as presented in *Being and Time*, Heidegger did not use it in speeches he made in support of Hitler when he was a rector of the University of Freiburg.[17]

The voluntaristic nature of Heidegger's notion of authentic Being is underlined by the primacy of the future for the possibility of authenticity: 'The primary meaning of existentiality is the future' (ibid., p. 376). The distinction between the actively authentic mode of Being and passive inauthenticity is poignantly expressed by the language Heidegger uses to distinguish the two modes in reference to the future: anticipating (*Vorlaufen*) the future as opposed to waiting for or expecting (*Erwarten*) it. One actively looks forward to and goes towards one's authentic future by anticipating it in the present, but passively, even fatalistically, waits for the inauthentic future to draw near, letting it happen, as it were. Anticipation of the future has an element of decisive resoluteness about it which makes *Dasein* into agent and author of its self to come: '*anticipation* indicates that Dasein, existing authentically, lets itself come towards itself as its ownmost potentiality-for-Being – that the future itself must first win itself' (ibid., p. 386).

The primacy of the future for authenticity is also reflected in the Heideggerean concept of care (*Sorge*). Only *Dasein* can ask: 'How should I Be? How should I exist: should I own my Being or let it be expropriated by everydayness? What is the meaning of this Being as compared with inauthentic Being?' These questions attest my genuine concern for my Being. In asking myself what I am, I am authentic *Dasein*. But these questions have meaning only when my future is visible in my present. Anticipatory resoluteness directed towards the future attests the profound significance of the future in the pursuit of authenticity. One owns, creates and realizes one's self in terms of its possibilities for the future.

The primacy of the future also comes to the fore when we recall that authenticity reaches its culmination in authentic Being-*towards*-death which is always ahead of us. Moreover, anxiety in the face of one's eventual death, which is constitutive of one's individuality, and hence also of one's potential for appropriating one's Being, 'springs from the *future* of resoluteness' (ibid., p. 395). Heidegger's doctrine that possibility is ontologically prior to actuality is the key here. Authenticity reigns in the realm of possibilities not yet realized. The roots of authentic Being are in the future, because possibilities are never in the actual present. In other words, to Be is to be in time and history; it is to comport one's self to one's own Being in a time-consuming process of realizing one's potential for authenticity.

Being moves towards authenticity in the future. Is Heidegger proposing a kind of biological model for authenticity? In saying that 'origin always comes to meet us from the future',[18] is he asserting that our inborn potential for authentic Being is realized just as genes are actualized in an organic entity?

In support of this interpretation is the fact that Heidegger regards authenticity as ontologically prior to inauthentic modes of Being (*BT*, p. 68). Consistent with his assertion of the primacy of authenticity he states that 'proximally and for the most part Dasein is *not* itself but is lost in the they-self, which is an existentiell modification of the authentic Self' (ibid., p. 365). Every *Dasein* can be ontologically authentic; inauthenticity is only a modification of this primordial possibility. One must own one's Being to be able to lose it in everyday concerns. Applying Young's aphorism to Heidegger, we can say that 'we are born original, but proximally and for the most part die as copies'. Furthermore, because the authentic mode is always grounded in possibility, which is ontologically prior to actuality, authenticity is always prior to inauthentic actuality. Thus authenticity cannot be reduced to inauthenticity; it cannot be described in terms of, or as a function of, inauthenticity.

Nevertheless, a simplistic biological interpretation of Heidegger's notion of authenticity is unacceptable, because we refuse to 'be seduced (*verführen*) into an intolerable and quite unphenomenological construction' (ibid., p. 349). A bio-developmental model of authenticity posits the self as a kind of substance-soul which persists as an unchanging entity through the course of events on its way to self-realization. But *Dasein* is not a substantial Cartesian self: in inauthentic modes of Being we lose the self, cover it up, which would hardly be the case if it were an already-made substance or present-to-hand entity. The concept of substantial subject is limited to the ontic level and has no place in the ontological analysis of *Dasein*. *Dasein* is not an isolated subject in relation to an object but is that relation itself. It is the intentional activity that constitutes subject-object relations, making them transcendentally possible. In biology we witness the growth of a substance which is a certain kind of entity: an embryo or seed. A biological model implies a metaphysical sense of 'essence' as something that can be fully actualized. However, in 'The Letter on Humanism', arguing against Sartre's slogan 'Existence precedes essence', Heidegger says that his notion of 'Being' has nothing in common with this phrase, because it is prior to this distinction of potentiality and actuality.

So should we interpret Heidegger's idea of authenticity in terms of the artistic–creative model? His notion of authenticity calls upon us to comport ourselves to Being. Here the creative activity of every *Dasein* proves helpful. When one is creating, one concentrates on one's own work, ideas, projects, etc. Only as a *homo faber* does one feel at home; one is concerned about one's work. To create is to reflect upon one's own ideas, which presupposes a distancing from everydayness and its inauthentic 'hubbub'. Yet, any kind of creation requires a social and cultural context. It is as a creator that one can be an authentic Being-in-the-world. Moreover, by temporalizing itself *Dasein* creates itself towards its death. The coming to Be of *Dasein*'s ownness, as ontologically temporal, does not take place in time, which always refers to the ontic world. *Dasein* creates a time saturated with significance.

Actually, the biological and the artistic models for authenticity are synthesized in Heidegger. From the ontological perspective, authenticity is a creative self-and-world-referential, intentional activity; ontically, authentic Dasein actualizes its possibilities in-the-world and within its 'situation' (ibid., pp. 346–7) in accordance with a biological model. However, even these ontic possibilities are of one's making '*through* resoluteness and in it' (ibid., p. 346). Thus authenticity is the fundamental starting-point and, in the rare cases of authentic Being-towards-death, also the end-point. It is the dynamic activity of making one's Being one's own, by a process in which one may also lose it through an inauthentic modification. The tension between Nietzsche's two prescriptions for authentic life, 'Be what you are' and 'Create your own self', is resolved by Heidegger's ontological synthesis, rephrased by me as follows:

> Own your Being by creating your self and by appropriating your heritage. Return to your self and its historicality and accept them anxiously by overcoming the temptation to lose them in the distraction of everydayness.

It would be a mistake to hold, with some interpreters,[19] that the authentic individual is principally concerned with such morbid and intimately personal issues as guilt, death, disillusionment and sober anxiety. Possessing one's self within the social context in which 'Dasein becomes free' brings 'an unshakable joy' (ibid., p. 358). In this passage of *Being and Time* we find a rare instance of strong emotion colouring Heidegger's ordinarily stern pedantic teaching. He clearly intends to evoke joy and a sense of authentic liberation in his readers.

This 'joyous' mode is rooted in voluntarism.[20] But free employment of creative will presupposes the agency that exercises it – the subject. Hence *Dasein*, in resolutely creating or recreating its own authenticity, is actually a subject 'taking action' towards its own self and death within the world, where it can enjoy genuine relations of being authentically bound with others. Yet from the ontological perspective, *Dasein* cannot be an active subject or self, but only an intentional 'relation of subject to object' (*LH*, p. 229) underlying (*sub-jectum*) the possibility of any experience of a self. This self, we are told, is not a thing or a subject, but a way in which *Dasein* exists (cf. *BT*, p. 312). It seems that Heidegger's ontological approach clashes with authenticity in the sense of the courageous will to own one's Being, to relate resolutely to one's death and to appropriate one's historicality.

Adequate ontological investigation requires validity, certainty and 'assurance' (ibid., p. 69), that is, it needs accepted criteria of truth. Furthermore, to articulate the findings of phenomenologically oriented ontology one needs language and thus must rely on its referential reliability. This is especially so from the point of view of the human *Dasein*, who attempts to gain authenticity by adopting an articulated notion of authenticity. Yet all conventional and objective accounts of truth are irrelevant to authenticity understood as a primordial and pre-verbal state of mind or of Being. Heidegger voiced this insight in *Being and Time*, speaking of the existential import of silence. The voice of conscience or the call to authenticity 'discourses solely and constantly in the mode of keeping silent' (ibid., p. 318). Authenticity cannot 'be tied up with an expectation of anything like a communication' (ibid.). Ordinary language is immersed in 'idle talk' which binds *Dasein* to the crowd, conveying inauthentic meanings and covering up authentic ones. Hence, an 'authentic *Being*-one's Self' must remain '*silent*' (ibid., p. 370). It seems that one may live authentically in-the-world but cannot communicate to others this ownness. But if so what about Heidegger's own writing? Is not his ontological interpretation, coming from within ontic everydayness and necessarily using the language of the anyone, suspect, as is its adequacy for disclosing authenticity? Heidegger asks himself this question, rephrasing it as follows:

If historicality belongs to the Being of Dasein, then even inauthentic existing must be historical. What if it is Dasein's *inauthentic* historicality that has directed our questioning . . . and has blocked off our access to authentic historicality?

(ibid., p. 439)

121

Clearly, this query can be applied to Heidegger's entire ontological enterprise of explicating authentic Being, pursued as it is by a philosopher dwelling concretely within the world, in the inauthentic realm of the anyone. Nietzsche acknowledged such an unavoidable circularity, saying that his entire explicative philosophy of power might well be thoroughly subjective, an expression of his *own* will to power; 'well, so much the better', he concluded.[21] However, Nietzsche did not aspire to providing a valid fundamental ontology. As a philosophizing human using everyday language Heidegger cannot function as an a-temporal, God's-eye-view observer. Hence he should keep silent, following the advice he gave the authentic *Dasein*.

Underlying the whole problem is the distinction between pure ontology and everyday ontic facticity. The correspondence between the two levels is ambiguous. Heidegger claims that all pre-ontological, ordinary experiences have exact counterparts in ontological phenomena and interpretations. But what exactly is the nature of the relations between the 'objectivity of an ontological analysis' and the 'everyday understanding'? Heidegger provides no concrete answer and is 'satisfied with alluding to the essential problems' (ibid., p. 336) generated by the distinction between the methodological and the ontological level.

Even on the strictly ontological level, it is far from clear, as I argued above, that the authentic mode of Being is fundamental and primordial and that it alone is essential to *Dasein*. For there are places where Heidegger claims that falling into inauthenticity is 'an *essential* ontological structure of Dasein itself' (ibid., p. 224; cf. p. 78) no less than the authentic mode, and even hints that the latter is a derived mode of the former (ibid., p. 168). Yet Heidegger's basic exposition is in terms of such concepts as being lost, thrownness and fall, which presuppose an original fundamental state of affairs from which one has fallen. Hence I prefer to regard authenticity as the *primordial* existential of Being, and inauthenticity as 'an existentiell modification of the authentic Self' (ibid., p. 365). Moreover, if inauthentic Being is as ontologically mine as authentic Being, there is no real difference, in this respect, between authentic and inauthentic Beings, and thus no criterion to distinguish between them. Furthermore, should we endorse the interpretation that inauthenticity is an essential phenomenon, it would follow that each of us is doomed by ontology to be an inauthentic self within-the-world. If inauthenticity is 'structurally' or essentially innate in *Dasein*, as Heidegger sometimes implies, (e.g. at *BT*,

p. 70), how can *Dasein* become fully authentic? And if it cannot, how can Heidegger explicate its meaning phenomenologically as opposed to regarding it as a purely theoretical construct – a stand he categorically rejects? If inauthenticity and authenticity are *both* essential structures of *Dasein*, the transition within-the-world from one to the other remains inexplicable. Finally, if *Dasein* is doomed to inauthenticity, why does it not realize this potentiality at once, rather than starting from authentic Being, which it must lose?

My solution to these problems is to regard authenticity as the only fundamental, a priori and ontological mode of *Dasein*'s Being-in-the-world. At the ontological level *Dasein* is essentially authentic; it becomes inauthentic (though not completely or necessarily so) only at the ontic level. In other words, as long as we are concerned with the fundamental explication of *Dasein*, we remain in the realm of authenticity, but at the ontic level 'proximally and for the most part' we encounter inauthentic manifestations of *Dasein*. This interpretation is preferred by Heidegger himself,[22] who, in several passages, maintains that 'everydayness' is not a 'distinctive possibility of Dasein's existence' but only an 'average way of existing, which has nothing conspicuous about it' (ibid., p. 421). That is, everydayness, being a neutral, descriptive notion, is not identical with inauthenticity, which is a narrower phenomenon. Here we seem to have an ontological solution to the problem of authenticity unsolved by Kierkegaard and Nietzsche. Inauthenticity is not a necessary mode of Being within the social context. Thus authenticity is ontically possible, as Heidegger implies in saying that 'Everydayness is determinative for Dasein even when it has not chosen the "anyone" for its "hero" ' (ibid., p. 422). Resoluteness towards authenticity is not solipsistic and does not exempt the individual from social responsibility. On the contrary, as we saw, authentic resoluteness pushes one into a solicitous Being with others. Heidegger's view is communitarian, and even in his Marburg lectures he claims that authenticity is fully actualized only in community. For 'in choosing itself Dasein really chooses precisely its Being-with-Others'.[23]

Alas, the above-mentioned shortcomings subsequently led Heidegger to abandon the voluntaristic elements of authenticity, to the point where the very concept of human *Dasein* was engulfed in the wider notion of Being, with its theological undertones. He began to avoid such concepts as 'phenomenology' and '*Dasein*' in favour of the less anthropocentric and more cosmic idea of *Ereignis*. He described authenticity in terms of passivity, regarding it as a gift, as something which befell an individual unexpectedly, as an outcome of grace from above, etc.[24] This amounts to abandonment of the intuitions about authenticity he previously shared with earlier thinkers.

Authenticity is not a mode of Being in general but of Being a human. Thus, without *Dasein* there can be no authenticity as a mode of Being of human beings. Hence close analysis of Heidegger's later writings is not germane to our discussion. To be authentic is to be a struggling agent trying resolutely to overcome passivity in her or his life. It is the project of winning self-possession, of creating and owning one's self within the situation as interpreted by the human agent. Passivity and authenticity are incompatible. From Heidegger's later perspective, authenticity is no longer human failure or achievement but destiny or fate (*Geschick, moira*). This Protestant attitude to authenticity severely diminishes the active and spontaneous freedom of creation which characterized the earlier ideal of authenticity. It also denies all human and ethical import. Yet even before this abandonment of authenticity as an attainable ideal, as an ethical standard to be aspired to, Heidegger's attempt at ontologizing authenticity was of little help in fostering its implementation. It was fraught with problems, problems Jean-Paul Sartre tried to overcome by turning away from a phenomenological ontology of authenticity to politics. Was Sartre's version more amenable to implementation?

Notes

1   *Being and Time*, trans. J. Macquarrie and E. Robinson (New York: Harper & Row, 1962), p. 35. Most page references will be to this English translation (henceforth *BT*), although revisions have been made where necessary. Occasionally the German edition is consulted: *Sein und Zeit* (Tübingen: Max Niemeyer, 1963) (henceforth *SZ*).
2   Heidegger's Preface to W. J. Richardson's *Heidegger: Through Phenomenology to Thought* (The Hague: Martinus Nijhoff, 1963), p. xx.
3   'The Word of Nietzsche: "God is Dead" ', in *The Question concerning Technology, and Other Essays*, trans. W. Lovitt (New York: Garland, 1977), p. 58.
4   Cf., e.g., *BT*, p. 348, where Heidegger claims that the phenomenon of authenticity is the bridge to the general ontological question of the meaning of Being. In what follows I use the customary translations, 'authenticity' and 'authentic', for Heidegger's *Eigentlichkeit* and *eigentlich*. This helps bring Heidegger closer to thinkers on authenticity with

whom his philosophy is intimately connected. Moreover, other English (and perhaps more literal) translations of these terms, such as 'ownedness', 'self-possessedness' and 'appropriation' either do not make for smooth English or do not cover the range of meanings associated with Heidegger's use of these notions. As to *Dasein* (literally 'Being-there'), Heidegger follows more or less the everyday usage of this term, denoting that kind of Being that belongs to persons (cf. *SZ*, p. 12). Since no satisfactory English equivalent is commonly accepted, and since this term is quite familiar to English-speaking readers of Heidegger, I leave it untranslated.

5   As, e.g., M. Grene, who writes that 'the investigation of personal existence is ancillary to the search for Being itself': *Martin Heidegger* (London: Bowes & Bowes, 1957), p. 12.

6   *What Is Called Thinking?*, trans. Fred D. Wieck and G. J. Gray (New York: Harper & Row, 1968), p. 79.

7   'Letter on Humanism', in Martin Heidegger, *Basic Writings*, ed. D. F. Krell (London: Routledge & Kegan Paul, 1978), trans. F. A. Capuzzi (henceforth *LH*), pp. 193, 205.

8   *The Piety of Thinking: Essays by Martin Heidegger*, trans. J. G. Hart and J. C. Maraldo (Bloomington: Indiana University Press, 1976), p. 20; cf. 'ontology functions only as a corrective formally pointing out the ontic' (ibid., p. 19).

9   *An Introduction to Metaphysics*, trans. R. Manheim (New York: Doubleday, 1961), pp. 9, 10.

10 K. Harries, 'Heidegger as a Political Thinker', in *Heidegger and Modern Philosophy*, ed. M. Murray (New Haven, Conn.: Yale University Press, 1978), p. 307, and R. Rorty, *Contingency, Irony, and Solidarity* (Cambridge: Cambridge University Press, 1989), p. 113. Thus Heidegger's statement in his essay 'Thinker as Poet' that 'what is spoken is never, and in no language, what is said' (*Poetry, Language, Thought*, trans. and ed. A. Hofstadter (New York: Harper & Row, 1975), p. 11) also applies to *Being and Time*.

11 Concrete examples abound in his writings; see e.g., *LH*, where we find an ironic admonition against the 'inevitable misinterpretations' of his doctrine which attribute to it anti-humanistic, anti-logical, anti-moral, anti-transcendental and nihilistic connotations: 'Because . . . we everywhere speak against all that humanity deems high and holy our philosophy teaches an irresponsible and destructive "nihilism". For what is more "logical" than that . . . mirroring . . . what one believes he knows already before he reads' (*LH*, pp. 225–6).

12 *The Basic Problems of Phenomenology*, trans. A. Hofstadter

(Bloomington: Indiana University Press, 1982) (henceforth *BPP*), p. 170.

13 Grene, *Martin Heidegger*, p. 14 *et passim*.

14 *BT*, pp. 164, 166, 220. Here and elsewhere I have retranslated *das Man* as 'the anyone' which also includes myself. I thus reject the Robinson and Macquarrie translation of *das Man* as 'the they', which implies 'their' inauthenticity in contrast to my seemingly authentic sense of selfhood.

15 *BT*, pp. 303–4; my emphasis. This and other passages prevent me from endorsing Zimmerman's claim that everydayness, 'our usual tendency to conceal things, to regard them superficially . . . is intrinsic to us; it cannot be escaped' (M. Zimmerman, *Eclipse of the Self: The Development of Heidegger's Concept of Authenticity* (Athens: Ohio University Press, 1981), p. 44).

16 See Golomb, *Nietzsche's Enticing Psychology of Power*, pp. 304–21.

17 Cf. Harries, 'Heidegger as a Political Thinker', a balanced and concise analysis of the relations between Heidegger's philosophy and his 'brief aberration' – his warm embrace of National Socialism. Cf. V. Farias, *Heidegger and Nazism* (Philadelphia, Pa: Temple University Press, 1987), who claims that no connection is evident between Heidegger's theoretical philosophy and his political involvement.

18 'A Dialogue on Language', p. 10.

19 Grene, for example, claims that ' "being to death" is the sole content and meaning of existential authenticity, as Heidegger makes it' ('Authenticity: An Existential Virtue', *Ethics*, 62 (1952), 266–74. E. Levinas also seems to hold such a view, saying that 'the fundamental relation with being, in Heidegger, is not the relationship with the Other, but with death, where everything that is non-authentic in the relationship with the Other is denounced, since one dies alone' (*Ethics and Infinity*, trans. R. A. Cohen (Pittsburgh, Pa: Duquesne University Press, 1985), p. 58).

20 Thus Zimmerman is right in claiming that '*Being and Time* uses voluntaristic language to describe Dasein's resolve [and] courageous will' (*Eclipse of the Self*, p. 40; cf. pp. 19, 129). For an opposing view, see C. B. Guignon, 'Heidegger's "Authenticity" Revisited', *Review of Metaphysics*, 38 (1984), 321–39.

21 *BGE*, sec. 22.

22 And by some interpreters. W. J. Richardson, for example, maintains that, at least in the second division of *Being and Time*, Heidegger definitely 'refers to authenticity as the "more primordial" phenomenon' (*Existential Epistemology* (Oxford: Clarendon Press, 1986), p. 44; cf. pp. 152–4). For a lucid analysis of the question, see Joan Stambaugh, 'An Inquiry into Authenticity and Inauthenticity in *Being and Time*', in

Radical Phenomenology: Essays in Honor of Martin Heidegger, ed. J. Sallis (Atlantic Highlands, NJ: Humanities Press, 1978), pp. 153–61. Stambaugh concludes, as I do, that 'the authentic is the fundamental level of Dasein and the inauthentic is simply a flight from authenticity, however prevalent that inauthenticity might be' (p. 160). Richardson denies this, claiming that 'both authenticity and inauthenticity are fundamental modes of Being' (*Existential Epistemology*, p. 50).

23 *The Metaphysical Foundations of Logic* (1928) (Bloomington: Indiana University Press, 1984), p. 190.

24 See, e.g., 'Letter on Humanism', where Heidegger states that *Dasein* can exist only by the grace of Being; cf. 'A Dialogue on Language', p. 45. Zimmerman points out that as early as his 1930s essay 'On the Essence of Truth' Heidegger began the shift from the active notion of authenticity as 'self-appropriation to the notion of authenticity as being appropriated' (*Eclipse of the Self*, p. 231). For a lucid exposition of 'The Mature Concept of Authenticity' and the idea of *Ereignis*, see chapter 8 of Zimmerman's book.

6

Sartre: from phenomenological ontology to psychoanalysis and politics

Jean-Paul Sartre is the first thinker to supplement his philosophy of authenticity and bad faith[1] with a call to direct political action. Ironically, the philosopher most intimately associated with the notion of authenticity and considered its most influential proponent was deeply pessimistic about its viability. At one point in his conversations with Benny Lévy, Sartre asserted that his work was 'a failure', seeing that it led to the 'contradiction in *Being and Nothingness*'.[2] He is referring to the unbridgeable gap between the authenticity he aspired to and the disappointing ontological conclusions that follow from his theoretical premises.

When he realized that an ontological approach to authenticity could not bring about its social implementation, Sartre turned from phenomenological ontology to political action directed against the social conditions responsible for life-patterns manifesting bad faith. As he admits to Lévy,[3] both his debate with Marxism and his political action aim at bringing about a society free of oppression in which there are no structural incentives for people to act in bad faith and to relate to each other as objects.

Using explicitly Kantian language, Sartre explains that his ultimate objective is to promote a 'kingdom of ends', where human beings 'forbid themselves to use men as matter or as a means to an end';[4] a society of social 'fusion', whose members are both objects and subjects for each other. In his *Notebooks*, Sartre describes the ideal of authenticity as viable 'within the city of ends' (p. 500). Anticipating his later political writings, he designates as 'the Apocalypse' (ibid., pp. 1, 374, 413-14) the 'moment' at which a society of authentic individuals bonded into a harmonious group would emerge. Nonetheless, unlike Heidegger, Sartre rarely uses the term 'authenticity' in his published writings, preferring the more anthropological notion of 'bad faith'. But 'bad faith' and 'good faith' are not simply synonymous with the opposition between inauthenticity and authenticity, since they are also used to signify, among other things, our attitudes towards the ontological predicaments that make authenticity an unattainable ideal.

Sartre read *Sein und Zeit* both carefully and critically, then embarked on a kind of Kantian revolution against Heidegger. Just as Kant, with his critique of reason, 'found it necessary to deny *knowledge*, in order to make room for *faith*',[5] Sartre proffered a critique of the search for authenticity aimed at redirecting human effort from this 'useless passion' (I take this to also mean the wish to become as authentic as humanly possible) to politics.[6] If Kant's critique of absolute truth led to the ideal of personal truthfulness, Sartre's ontology, in demonstrating the uselessness of the individual search for authenticity, encourages us to take part in political action aimed at 'a morality of revolution, in the sense that there is a revolution in . . . Kant'.[7]

Sartre's 'Copernican revolution' against Heidegger starts with the fact that Heidegger denied that any particular ethic could be incompatible with authenticity. For Heidegger, authenticity functions as a prerequisite for morality. Sartre, however, sees moral systems, especially unjust and oppressive ones, as enemies of authenticity. While for Heidegger the 'fall' is engendered by finality, for Sartre, as for Rousseau, it is brought about by sociability.

Initially, however, Sartre accepted Heidegger's view of the primacy of authenticity over any specific moral system. In *The War Diaries* he claimed: 'I can't really see anything but a moral code based on authenticity.' At this stage, Heidegger's influence 'has . . . struck me as providential, since it supervened to teach me authenticity and historicity just at the very moment when war was about to make these notions indispensable to me'. With regard to authenticity, he wrote, he could not but strongly '*feel* our inconsistency, as beings without a God, yet not authors of ourselves'.[8] After his political conversion, though, he reversed this priority of authenticity over morality, arguing that only a just and non-oppressive society, whose members are no longer instruments for each other or mere means for the attainment of lofty goals, could foster free and authentic individuals who are 'authors' of their lives. Such a society would make it possible to overcome the universal tendency to bad faith: 'One cannot be converted alone . . . ethics is not possible unless everyone is ethical' (*Notebooks*, p. 9).

At the end of his life, in an interview with Michel Sicard in 1978, he spoke of a new ontology of consciousness that would leave 'nothing of *Being and Nothingness* and even of the *Critique of Dialectical Reason* standing', but would lead to an ethic of 'we' in contrast to the individual 'I'.[9]

In spite of his promise at the very end of *Being and Nothingness* to compose an ethical treatise, Sartre refrained from doing so because he realized that a purely intellectual appeal to solitary readers was useless. Indeed, this explains why the term 'authenticity' appears so infrequently in *Being and Nothingness*. One of the very few instances of it is Sartre's statement about the 'conversion to authenticity' (*BN*, p. 246) as a 'self-recovery of being'. This 'radical conversion'

> does not mean that we cannot radically escape bad faith. But this supposes a self-recovery of being which was previously corrupted. This self-recovery we shall call authenticity, the description of which has no place here. . . . These considerations do not exclude the possibility of an ethics of deliverance and salvation. But this can be achieved only after a radical conversion which we cannot discuss here.
>
> (*BN*, pp. 70n.; 412)

Hence *Being and Nothingness* is 'the idetic imagery of bad faith'[10] before the authenticating political 'conversion'.

Sartre's last political works, especially the *Critique of Dialectical Reason*,[11] portray a state of social alienation. As he relates in conversation with Lévy, he was seeking 'the deepest relation between men . . . which binds them together beyond the relations to production' (Lévy, pp. 169–70). He mentions 'a certain primary relationship, which is the relationship of brotherhood' found in 'a single family'; 'a true brotherhood', sharing 'a common end or goal' (ibid., pp. 170–1).

Authenticity rooted in the ontology of 'human reality' can be attained neither by intellectual means nor by social revolution, but the impulse to act in bad faith can be subdued in appropriate social frameworks. Sartre provides an anthropological analysis of the mechanisms that impel us to bad faith. His descriptions of the 'hell' that others are for us serve to counter the seductive charm of bad faith that abounds in society. Sartre emphasizes the negative as a foil to the positive patterns of justice and equality, which, though unable in themselves to guarantee authenticity, at least provide genuine morality and dignity. The direct political action Sartre envisages is aimed at reforming society to such a degree that bad faith is no longer rewarded and hence loses its appeal.

Interestingly, the two thinkers who adopted an ontological approach to authenticity both went through a kind of midlife *Umkehr* or 'conversion': Heidegger, from the phenomenological ontology of *Dasein* to the poetry and mysticism of Being, and Sartre, from phenomenological ontology to politics. These changes manifest their dissatisfaction with the meagre progress their respective ontologies had made in terms of implementing social authenticity.

In Sartre, as in Heidegger, we find a gap between ontology and anthropology. But in Sartre's case the resonance between the ontological impossibility of authenticity and the anthropological version of 'existential psychoanalysis' – according to which some analysed figures, such as Genet, indeed managed to attain authenticity on the Nietzschean aesthetic model – is the force that incites us to take responsibility for the creation of our selves: 'the moral problem which has preoccupied me till now is basically [that] of relations between art and life' (*WD*, p. 72).

I

As long as he remained under Heidegger's influence, Sartre believed that phenomenological ontology could establish authenticity as a viable moral ideal. His phenomenology of the emotions, for example, aimed at purging consciousness of all content until it emerged as pure transparency and spontaneity. This creatively uninhibited consciousness becomes the author, or origin, of self. Sartre's aim here is the same as that of Nietzsche's purification of nature into a cosmic *tabula rasa* – to make way for the aesthetic model of authenticity by making possible spontaneous creativity, unrestrained by any transcendental principle.

Sartre does not speak of authenticity in his early essay *The Transcendence of the Ego*.[12] Retrospectively, however, he can be seen to have addressed the issue in reflecting on how consciousness can generate spontaneous creativity. In effect, he is inquiring into the transcendental conditions for authenticity.

Using a revised phenomenological framework, Sartre argues for a non-egological intentional theory of consciousness. He maintains that anything considered to be part of consciousness or an immanent content of consciousness is really an object towards which consciousness directs itself. Images, emotions, motives, values and the ego itself are produced by this consciousness, yet by virtue of its intentionality it is always transcendent to the objects it has created. The self, for example, does not disclose itself to immediate intuition in its entirety and thus, as an object transcending consciousness, belongs to the world. The world is constituted by intentional acts of pure consciousness; hence the self is the result of a synthetic act of organization rather than its agent. Sartre uses Husserl's notion of *konstituieren* as the ordering of our images and representations of things, and the establishing of the meaning of the object as certain order, to help bridge the gap between passive immanent content and spontaneous activity.

For Sartre, the self is an object constituted within the phenomenal field: 'The ego is not the owner of consciousness; it is the object of consciousness' (*TE*, p. 97). Consciousness is a kind of pure transparency, a mere openness to a world to which it adds nothing of its own. This enables it to be a truly spontaneous and creative force unimpeded by such inner obstacles as 'psychic dispositions' (ibid., p. 70), inhibiting emotions, or traits of character. Character is not a predetermined set of innate traits, but merely a set of dispositions. 'Potentiality' is a fiction, otherwise 'the *I*, with its personality, would be a sort of center of opacity' (ibid., p. 41). The purification of consciousness maximizes creativity, enabling the individual to attain authenticity modelled on God's own.

Sartre, like Heidegger, uses his phenomenology to attack the Cartesian *Cogito ergo sum*. There is no 'I' that thinks, but only thought and reflection upon this thought. With Sartre, the dissolution of the Cartesian egological self initiated by Nietzsche reaches its climax. Sartre's phenomenological reading of consciousness leads him to believe that there is no entity that is an original, authentic self or ego, as Rousseau tended to believe. Authenticity lies in the created products of consciousness – it is the creative process itself.

Sartre favours a 'realistic' interpretation of Husserl's concept of intentionality, which he considers 'fruitful' (ibid., p. 41) and utilizes to introduce authenticity into the world. On Sartre's more pragmatic reading, phenomenology is redefined as a 'science of *fact*', not 'essences' (ibid., pp. 35, 113 n. 3). Sartre rejects the Husserlian technique of reduction along with Husserl's notion of the transcendental ego. While Heidegger abandoned the concept of the transcendental ego in order to radicalize ontology, Sartre gives it up to radicalize consciousness. Even so, however, his account of the ego here is much like Heidegger's concept of 'Being-in-the-world'. The ego is not discrete and isolated but 'is outside, *in the world*. It is a being of the world, like the ego of another' (ibid., p. 31; cf. p. 75, where Sartre explicitly cites Heidegger). Sartre's application of the phenomenological method to the realm of facts and things, as opposed to essences, is motivated by the desire to avoid the solipsism (ibid., p. 103) implicit in Husserl's doctrine of the transcendental ego: 'Solipsism becomes unthinkable from the moment that the *I* no longer has a privileged status' (ibid., p. 104).

Sartre, taking literally Husserl's call to return 'to the things themselves', looks upon phenomenology as a triumph over subjectivism. He interprets Heidegger's 'Being-in-the-world' as movement: 'To be is to fly out into the world . . . in order suddenly to burst out as consciousness-in-the-world.'[13] Authenticity is rooted in this flight, this refusal to exist as substance, this life-long attempt to fight facticity. The purification of consciousness has broad moral implications: 'No more is needed in the way of philosophical foundation for an ethics and politics which are absolutely positive' (*TE*, p. 106). Thus, early in his career, Sartre attributed moral significance to his phenomenological explications of consciousness (ibid., p. 94). Purified consciousness, as creator of self, is like Spinoza's notion of substance as the absolute cause of itself (*causa sui*), introduced in his *Ethics* and referred to by Sartre (ibid., pp. 39, 82). Consciousness for Sartre is a continual self-creation *ex nihilo* at each successive instant in time. Hence, consciousness is endowed with a God-like status.

Consciousness is intentional activity directed at what is not itself. Hence authenticity does not imply the self-referential 'ownness' of the self, as it does for Heidegger, but refers to a creative process which produces transcendent contents (including our own selves) 'outside, in the world, among others' (Int.). Sartre places authenticity squarely in the human, all-too-human, intersubjective world: 'It is not in some hiding-place that we will discover ourselves; it is on the road, in the town, in the midst of the crowd, a thing among things, a man among men' (ibid.).

Now if consciousness is defined by intentionality (*TE*, p. 38), and if authenticity is the outcome of intentional acts, then authenticity is defined by consciousness. Sartre is arguing that consciousness cannot be directly influenced by the external world, and that, given its unlimited spontaneity, it alone is responsible for its own escape from this freedom. Freedom is the relation of consciousness to the world and not that of the ego to the world. The attributes Nietzsche uses to describe the authentic *Übermensch*, and Heidegger, the ontological *Dasein*, are bestowed by Sartre on this relationship between consciousness and the world. Every intentional act is self-originating, self-determining and absolutely free. As Sartre's thought develops, these features become the defining characteristics of authenticity.

Like Nietzsche, Sartre does not believe that introspection into one's inner self can lead to knowledge of one's authenticity or lack thereof (ibid., pp. 86–7). One cannot introspectively access one's self if there is no self to introspect and no immanent content of consciousness. This has important implications for Sartre's teachings on authenticity. The whole problem of recognizing one's own, and the other's, authenticity, must be shifted to the domain of concrete social and political action. This transition is further mandated by Sartre's thesis that we have no privileged access to our own ego over and above 'the ego of another'. My ego no longer belongs exclusively to myself. This helps explain why Sartre, unlike other thinkers, is comfortable assuming the role of omniscient judge when speaking of his, and others', authenticity. Again and again, in his *War Diaries*, biographies and autobiographies, we come across assessments of the authenticity or inauthenticity of individuals.[14] For if one is completely transparent to others as well as to oneself, and if 'man is nothing else but that which he makes of himself', as Sartre asserts in his post-war lecture *Existentialism and Humanism*, then given that this self-making usually occurs in public, one can certainly judge others and be judged by them with respect to authenticity or the lack thereof.

Sartre's distinction between reflecting and reflected consciousness is relevant here. Reflecting consciousness is consciousness whose object is itself. Reflected consciousness is consciousness as the object of reflecting consciousness. Sartre's contention that 'there is no *I* on the unreflected level' (*TE*, p. 48) helps explain Heidegger's account of the loss of self in the world of objects. The intentional act of directing one's consciousness towards the world of objects is in itself an unreflective noetic act. Reflection upon it produces a new object which did not exist before the act was grasped – the ego. Hence the reflected consciousness generates the 'I' which becomes the transcendent object of the reflective act but is not in itself a part of that act. Thus reflection not only discloses objects, but produces and constitutes them.

Authenticity is another product of our reflection. If I direct myself unreflectively towards the world of objects, if 'I run after a streetcar', if 'I am absorbed in contemplating a portrait . . . I am plunged into the world of objects. . . . I have disappeared. . . . There is no place for *me* on this level' (ibid., p. 49). Authenticity requires reflection as well as action. It should be noted, however, that Sartre emphasizes the discrete and autonomous nature of each intentional act – the 'ego' or 'me' produced by reflection is only a fleeting moment. Authentic states are 'instantaneous', not permanent (ibid., p. 62). Like Nietzsche, Sartre seems to limit himself to the momentary pathos of the 'now'. It is the present and not the future that determines authenticity, for in the present one has no potentiality but is completely exteriorized – one is only what one reflects upon now. Yet one is always more, since one never actually reflects upon all that is present.

This also follows from Sartre's contention that the 'I' which reflective intuition confronts is 'an object grasped with neither apodictic nor adequate evidence. . . . It is not adequate, for the *I* is presented as an opaque reality whose content would have to be unfolded' (ibid., p. 51). The 'I' appears veiled, indistinct and 'deceptive from the start since we know that nothing but consciousness can be the source of consciousness' (ibid., p. 52). When I use the word 'I', I may be in a state of what Sartre later calls 'bad faith'. To regard the 'I' as a rigid entity with permanent features beyond the instantaneous moment or pathos of 'me' is an act of bad faith: 'I may deceive myself in thinking that I have *such* a *me*' (ibid., p. 75). Bad faith is thus inherent in the epistemological features of consciousness. Sartre sees the genuine ego as 'dubitable' (ibid., p. 76), as comprised of 'the infinite totality of states and of actions . . . never reducible to an action or to a state' (ibid., p. 74).

If there is no way to talk about authenticity without a 'me', intentionality, by making possible the emergence of 'me', also makes possible my authenticity. However, this 'me', as the product of reflection, is dubitable and deceptive. To summarize, since all objects of consciousness, including the 'me', are outside consciousness, and since only consciousness possesses absolute 'certitude' (ibid., p. 44), all states, and hence all authentic states, transcend consciousness, and are thus dubitable (ibid., p. 64). Sartre is introducing a rational and Cartesian element into the genesis of authenticity, an element absent from previous accounts. Sartre implies that the more intense the reflection on one's consciousness, the clearer the sense of 'me', 'I' or 'self' that emerges. Hence the more reflective one is, the more authentic one becomes. But how can reflection produce authenticity? Does not the reflective attitude give rise to a feeling of alienation from one's 'reflected' self that prevents one from spontaneously feeling one's authenticity? Sartre alludes to this problem, saying that 'reflection "poisons" desire' (ibid., p. 59). Thus, in radical contrast to Kierkegaard, whose notion of authenticity involves intense, immediate passion, Sartre opts for a passionless authenticity. Yet Sartre later came to agree with Kierkegaard that reflection kills action, thereby destroying authenticity as well. This led to his desperate existential move to concrete political action, undertaken to extricate himself from this epistemic trap, a trap in which some of his literary heroes, such as Mathieu in *Roads to Freedom*, were also deeply entangled.

It could, of course, be argued that reflection on our conscious processes, along with intentionality as directedness towards objects which are not part of consciousness, helps maintain a healthy distance from, and objectivity with respect to, our selves and our actions. This in turn may foster awareness of our transcendent ego, and in particular, our authenticity or lack of it. In this sense, it could be claimed not only that one constitutes one's self (ego), but that one is also free to check, control and judge it. This defence is unsatisfactory, however, since even at the phenomenological level of exposition, before ontology is introduced, human authenticity emerges as a 'useless passion'. As a 'passion', as an immediate pathos, it must be attained unreflectively, but this precludes the emergence of an ego. The spontaneity of the unreflected consciousness cannot be co-opted into the authenticity of the reflected 'I'; hence the precarious and dubious nature of authenticity. Indeed, given these epistemological considerations, Sartre absolves us, at one point, of any responsibility for these consequences of reflection, citing the very un-existential 'essence': 'it is not my fault if my reflective life poisons "by its very essence" my spontaneous life' (ibid., p. 59).

It could be argued that if consciousness is *necessarily* spontaneous and absolute, one is either fully responsible for one's authenticity or not responsible at all. If my phenomenological make-up is such that I am not responsible for this self-generating self, how can I become a free and authentic being? If the reverse is true, I seem to be 'condemned' to be authentic in the same way as 'I am condemned to be free'. But how, then, is it possible to act in bad faith? Sartre wrestles with these questions in the anthropological sections of *Being and Nothingness*. Indeed, even after writing that book, Sartre held the view that there was a serious problem here: 'authenticity will unveil to us that we are condemned to create and that at the same time we have to be this creation to which we are condemned' (*Notebooks*, p. 515). For if bad faith is epistemologically necessary, how can political conversion overcome these pervasive features of consciousness? Thus tension between Sartre's early ontological phenomenology and his later anthropology can be traced to his earliest writings.

Be that as it may, if authenticity has an inherently public character, it becomes one's duty to strive to attain it, and thus one hears what Heidegger refers to as 'the call of conscience'. The categorical imperative is implicit in several of Sartre's unpublished statements: 'Authenticity is a duty that comes to us from outside and inside at once, because our "inside" is an "outside" ' (*WD*, pp. 53–4); one 'can and must in authenticity assume the objective transformation of [one]self' (*Notebooks*, p. 418).

Every consciousness is continually creating an ego that can, in principle, be known to everyone else. This exposure of the transcendent ego to public scrutiny and the constant awareness that one is being watched by the 'other' (*le regard d'autrui*, as Sartre calls it in *Being and Nothingness*), impels us to escape this judgemental 'hell'.[15] We turn to disguises and acts of bad faith. While Sartre's phenomenology establishes our authentic being in the world, it also accounts for the pervasive tendency to circumvent this mode of being by escaping into inauthenticity.

Sartre argues that the transcendent ego is comparable to a melody. Just as separate notes constitute a melody, so an individual's intentional acts, states and dispositions, over time, form a pattern which we perceive as personality or character. We compose our selves and our characters much as a musician composes music: originally and authentically, or imitatively and in bad faith.

Sartre's *Sketch for a Theory of the Emotions*[16] is an '*experiment* in phenomenological psychology' (*STE*, p. 31) in the tradition of Husserl's attempts to establish an alternative to the positivistic psychology then in vogue. Why did Sartre choose the study of the emotions to spearhead this attempt? His aesthetic approach to authenticity was a decisive factor. By using the emotions as the first subject of his phenomenological explication, Sartre hoped not only to defend his thesis of the transparency of consciousness, but also to prove that there is nothing '*accidental*' (ibid., p. 19) or passive in either consciousness or life. Even what are generally regarded as the most opaque, unconscious and involuntary aspects of our mental life are actively and intentionally created. We 'ourselves', or, rather, 'the human-reality', as Sartre refers to Heidegger's *Dasein*, deliberately anthropologizing it, are the sole authors of our lives and emotions, and thus wholly 'responsible' for them (ibid., pp. 23-4). I constitute myself freely as an emotional human in choosing this particular 'organized type of consciousness' (ibid., p. 23). But I could have chosen differently, depending on my particular aim or 'finality' (ibid., p. 48). One is always free to shape and create one's own pathos. The familiar excuse for inertia, passivity, impotence and unwillingness to take in hand our lives and selves – our emotions – is no longer available to us.

As sole author of my emotional states, I understand them perfectly, though I may not always have the means to account for them verbally. In *Sketch for a Theory of the Emotions*, as in Sartre's earlier essay, self-awareness is a key element in what gradually becomes an explicit pattern of authenticity. Sartre introduces the concept of intentionality into the realm of emotion. Displaying almost Cartesian rationalism, he claims that 'the human reality which is myself assumes its own being by understanding it' (p. 24). Yet introspection is not the way to understanding, since 'my comprehension of the human reality is dim and inauthentic' (ibid.). To attain authenticity, to gain a genuine understanding of my self as self-created, this obscure and opaque reality 'has to be made explicit and corrected' through phenomenological analysis of the undeniably obscure realm of the emotions.

Note that of all the thinkers on authenticity we have considered, Sartre comes closest to the traditional equation between truth and authenticity, which essentially makes the whole notion of authenticity redundant – a redundancy analogous, in Sartre's opinion, to that of Husserlian transcendental self. What saves Sartre's notion of authenticity from being swallowed up by the traditional model of objectively valid truth is his adaptation of the phenomenological exhortation to go 'back to the things themselves' (ibid., p. 31). By this Sartre refers not to cognitive encounters with pure phenomena as such, but, rather, to direct experiences with the real world and with the authentic creations of our consciousness – our egos, emotions and imaginations,[17] whether admirable or not.

For it is the function of the emotions to paint our confrontation with the complexities of the world in colours that make this confrontation bearable, or make it possible for us 'magically' to escape it altogether. Preoccupation with feelings and inner pathos gives rise to inertia: one feels in place of doing. The emotional states thus function as escape routes, and we alone are responsible for their construction. Unlike Kierkegaard, who blamed our reflective tendencies for rationalizing away action and suppressing authentic passionate faith, Sartre contends that it is the emotions that are at fault. Constructed by our consciousness to escape active commitment and responsibility, states like 'passive sadness', 'melancholy', etc. (ibid., pp. 68ff.) are intentionally organized pathological behaviours (note that this term comes from *pathos*): 'Lacking both the ability and the will to carry out the projects I formerly entertained, I behave in such a manner that the universe requires nothing more from me' (ibid., p. 69). Since 'emotion is play-acting' (ibid., p. 65) it becomes clear that Sartre's presentation of our emotional life here anticipates the notion of bad faith in *Being and Nothingness*.

Sartre's reluctance to 'give up the Cartesian *cogito*' (ibid., p. 52), and his notion of authenticity as spontaneous creativity, play a crucial role in his attack on psychoanalysis (developed in *BN*: see, e.g., pp. 50–4). The postulation of unconscious emotional causes not only compromises the ideal of immanent, self-sufficient and lucid consciousness by introducing alien and '*passive* . . . causal relation[s]' (*STE*, p. 52); it also undermines spontaneous self-creation, since we cannot control that which is not part of our consciousness. We cannot be responsible for that to which we cannot respond. Because of its anti-Cartesian premises, Sartre denies that psychoanalytic therapy, by helping us becoming aware of our unconscious life, can lead to authenticity.

Nonetheless, though Sartre rejected the causal-deterministic Freudian approach to mental life, he was influenced by the psychoanalytic notion of wishful thinking and the Freudian thesis that even in the irrational and chaotic realm of the emotions, 'functional' order prevails (ibid., p. 74). He saw the emotions as intentionally seeking 'transformation of the world' when 'all ways are barred and nevertheless we must act' (ibid., p. 63). Emotions attempt to overcome the facticity and determination of the world 'by magic' (ibid.) when direct and realistic courses of action are unavailable owing to weakness of will or fear.

Despite Sartre's insistence on the active and creative essence of the emotions, however, he cannot deny that, to the extent that they are a reaction to something in the world, they are passive. Instead of changing the world or transforming 'the object' (for example, by political action), consciousness acts upon itself and transforms itself 'in order to transform the object' (ibid., p. 63). This passive component of emotion contributes, along with the active element, to the generation of bad faith. The emotions, as self-manipulative acts of consciousness, in which consciousness plays at being other than it is, become expressions of bad faith.

Using his phenomenology to reveal the magical and debased nature of the emotions, Sartre seeks to undermine our faith in this magic and clear the way for a lucid, Cartesian understanding of the situation, and a genuine struggle to cope with it: 'Liberation can come only from a purifying reflection or from the total disappearance of the emotional situation' (ibid., p. 81). The authentic frame of mind can only be attained by a lucid, unemotional and completely sober appraisal of one's situation and one's place in it, since only this sober assessment can bring about a 'conversion' of one's self within that situation. This effect can be enhanced by transforming the situation in such a way that magic is no longer needed to mask its unbearableness. If emotion is a 'fall of consciousness into magic' (ibid., p. 90) which makes the whole 'social world' into one which is 'primarily magical' (ibid., p. 85), the most realistic way to deliverance lies in exploding this magic and removing emotion from the sphere of authenticity.

Sartre's characterization of consciousness as free spontaneity reflectively positing its own transcendent objects, as active rather than reactive, as neither caused by nor causing external objects and as transparent to itself, calls to mind the attributes of authenticity: spontaneity, lucidity, activity, reflectiveness, self-sufficiency and originality. Sartre felt that this characterization of consciousness sufficed to secure the phenomenological viability of the aesthetic model of authenticity, though not, of course, its ontological and social viability.

Nevertheless, the phenomenological studies make it clear that we cannot create our selves by looking inward into our seemingly given selves, by indulging in emotions or by imagining. Only by action, by changing the world, can the self be created. Sartre's political turn is thus in no way incompatible with his early phenomenology and its implications for authenticity. Later, Sartre will claim that it is the individual choices we make that define us and constitute our identity. He draws a parallel between the phenomenological unity of conscious-ness, which creates the ego, and the ego's acts, which create an auth-entic author of the ego.

But can we imagine a being that feels nothing? Sartre's ideal sounds like a cold-blooded machine, calculating its way to freedom but avoid-ing feeling anything on the way. Is this picture accurate? Below, I try to answer this question by analysing two heroes of Sartre's early fiction: one who exemplifies the genuine seeker of authenticity, and one who escapes into the security of bad faith.

Sartre's discussion of freedom, authenticity and bad faith began not with *Being and Nothingness*, but, rather, in two works of fiction I consider good introductions to the theoretical examination of these subjects in *Being and Nothingness*. Roquentin in *Nausea* desperately seeks his freedom: 'all I have ever wanted was to be free'.[18] Lucien, the hero of 'The Childhood of a Leader', is just as determined not to exercise his freedom. The two are thus literary prototypes of the two basic attitudes to authenticity.

The writer Sartre emulates in his first philosophical novel, *Nausea*, is Kierkegaard. He borrows the device of the fictive diary used in *Either/ Or* and assumes the role of 'editor'. Sartre tries to blur any distinction between art and life. Roquentin's past is kept sketchy and indefinite. There are only short references to it, since the past, in keeping with Sartre's phenomenology of approximately the same period, does not determine the present or the future. Roquentin claims: 'now my past is nothing but a huge hole' (*N*, p. 95) and 'I can no longer distinguish the present from the future' (ibid., p. 50). Both literature and life are forms of created art. Indeed, the theme of melody, yet another form of art, recurs in the novel at significant moments of the hero's inner life and becomes a metaphor for the authenticity Roquentin is trying to create from a shabby and fragmented life.

Sartre writes on two parallel levels to stress his rejection of the distinction between literary fiction and life: in real life each of us creates himself much as the author creates his characters. Thus Roquentin identifies with the subject of his historical research, the Marquis de Rollebon, whose 'documents' and 'diary' (ibid., p. 25) he edits and analyses, just as Sartre 'edits' the diary of Roquentin. By researching Rollebon and seeking out pieces of 'testimony' which 'don't agree with one another' (ibid.), Roquentin tries to mould him into a consistent individual with a substantial identity, just as Sartre shapes Roquentin and we all create our lives. It is no coincidence that, after writing on Nietzsche in his youth, Sartre's first literary hero is a biographer who attempts to prove that self-creation is possible. Roquentin, at the beginning of the novel, is in a state of 'limbo' (ibid., p. 28); he is about to embark on an uncertain existential project, the creation of the self by the self alone.

Nausea is a phenomenological novel about the hero's internal states, which are created through Roquentin's reflection; there is almost no external action or plot. The diary format is thus highly appropriate. However, in addition to the novel's phenomenological thrust, it also makes some subtle ontological distinctions, elaborated later.

Why is Roquentin 'disgusted' by 'the flat pebble' (ibid., p. 10), by 'a lined page' (ibid., p. 22), by 'the dessert knife' (ibid., p. 176) and, later, by 'the chestnut tree' (ibid., pp. 182–93)? Is it because, unlike himself, they are always what they are, or because he wishes to become like them, knowing that this is impossible – that he will never have such a well-defined essence, solid as a rock or a chestnut tree? The disgust and the feeling of nausea are not directed at the objects, at the opaque facticity proper, but, rather, at the 'useless passion', namely, at his own unattainable wish 'to be sure' (ibid., p. 10). Roquentin is fascinated by a 'cold object' (ibid., p. 13), which acts as a foil to his own self-transformation. After intense scrutiny of these objects, Roquentin claims 'it's I who have changed' (ibid., p. 14). The changelessness of material objects highlights internal changes and makes awareness of them possible. My intentional directedness towards other objects shows me that, as pure consciousness, I am fluid and lack definition.

In addition to the ontological distinction between consciousness (*être-pour-soi*, Being-for-itself in later terminology) and material thing (*être-en-soi*, Being-in-itself), we also find the Heideggerian category of the 'they' – the 'people' or the 'crowd' which envelop one's 'solitude' (ibid., pp. 18–19). The search for the pathos of authenticity is thus interrupted by occasional flights to the 'regular world' (ibid., p. 11), to a kind of Heideggerian 'everydayness'.

Sartre's first fictional hero is encountered in the midst of loneliness and reflection, but he is not devoid of feelings and emotions. He expresses a variety of intense emotions throughout the novel: 'disgust', 'thrill', 'fear', 'melancholy'. All are self-created states, but this does not detract from their vivacity and intensity. The search for authenticity, far from being a mechanical adventure, is laden with emotional pathos, crises and feelings. Despite Sartre's attempt to balance Heidegger's emphasis on 'moods' with a sober Cartesian attitude, the emotions still play a significant role in the pathos of authenticity. Moreover, it should be noted that the search for authenticity is not a clear and explicit intention, but a kind of dreamlike, 'misty' state that cannot 'fix anything' (ibid., p. 17).

Nausea, however, does not belong to the category of feelings. Like Heidegger's *Angst*, it is a necessary existential (i.e. ontological) structure of human beings that 'seizes' us 'in its grip' (ibid., p. 33). It is a symptom of the fact that we are free to pursue authentic self-creation, that there is indeed no escape. Thus nausea is the predicament of anyone immersed in the search for authenticity. Sartre portrays the search as undertaken alone by an individual with no meaningful social relationships. Others cannot help; one must act on one's own. Roquentin's long-standing relationship with his girlfriend Anny, who also aims at personal 'transformation' (ibid., p. 205) independently of Roquentin and more or less in complete isolation, illustrates this point. Only in this way is attaining authenticity a truly spontaneous achievement. The other people around Roquentin make him 'a little sick', and he feels them 'so far away' from him (ibid., p. 155). This solipsistic search follows logically from Sartre's phenomenology, which discloses that consciousness is self-sufficient and self-generated, and cannot be influenced by others. Unlike Heidegger's authentic *Dasein*, who appropriates his history and heritage, Sartre's hero cannot avail himself of his past and history: 'all the past history of the world is of no use' (ibid., p. 103). He is completely alone in his search.

Sartre describes Roquentin's attack of nausea when facing the chestnut tree as a kind of 'revelation' (ibid., p. 182). This nauseating experience reveals the meaning of one's 'existence', namely, its 'absolute contingency' (ibid., p. 188). Sartre explicitly employs Heidegger's term *Dasein* when he states that 'to exist is simply to *be there*' (ibid., p. 188). Nausea is the piercing awareness of one's contingency that engenders the need to justify one's existence: to make it seem necessary. However, lucidity dictates that we accept this contingency and '*play* with the absurdity of the world' (ibid., p. 186). Sartre, like Nietzsche and Camus, seems to hint that it is this contingency that makes authenticity possible in a completely immanent world. Immanence and contingency are synonymous. We come to terms with our estrangement from the world of objects which are also contingent by creating other contingent things. As creators we feel ourselves necessary rather than contingent.

One of the contingent aspects of our existence is the manner and date of our death. In this novel, death is presented as something basic. Echoing the Heideggerian approach, Sartre claims that death enters our lives to define them. In Sartre's words, 'an adventure . . . achieves significance only through [one's] death. Towards this death, which may also be my own, I am drawn irrevocably' (ibid., p. 59). *Nausea*, however, does not fully replicate Heidegger's 'Being-towards-death'; indeed, Sartre plays down the role of death in achieving authenticity, and it is not really a central motif in his writings. In Sartre's preface to Sarraute's *Portrait of a Man Unknown*, however, he claims that authenticity 'is the real connection with others, with oneself and with death'.[19]

It is interesting that, aside from his occasional attacks of nausea, there are no significant events in Roquentin's life. His constant struggle with bad faith does not require extreme or extraordinary circumstances. In contrast to the heroic models of authenticity in Kierkegaard and Nietzsche, he is a new type of hero: the anti-hero whose life is devoid of any extraordinary events, whom we would pass on the street without noticing. Behind this mundane anti-hero is Sartre's ontology, which emphasizes that all human beings are in the same ontological predicaments: we all are contingent beings encountering other things and trying to define our selves. The ontologization of the clash between the lonely individual and the 'crowd', which began with Heidegger, reaches a climax in the early Sartre. Roquentin was 'free . . . in the midst of this tragic crowd taking its rest' (ibid., pp. 78-80). The search for authenticity in these circumstances dooms Roquentin and other twentieth-century heroes to feel themselves estranged from the 'they': 'it was their Sunday and not mine' (ibid., p. 81). This is, in the early Sartre, the basic condition for the search for one's authenticity, which takes place not necessarily in the 'heart of darkness', but in the heart of everydayness, in the crush of the contemporary throng, in the glut of material objects. The elitist tone of the nineteenth-century thinkers on authenticity is drowned out by the noise of everydayness.

Rather simplistically, however, Sartre identifies the bad faith of the 'they' with the bourgeois ethic of 'self-important people' (ibid., p. 101) who regard their selves as serious and solid 'objects' (*en-soi*) and who die as copies. Roquentin clashes with this 'bourgeois élite' (ibid.,

p. 128) and with their ethos, which emphasizes such values as God, the family, wealth, authority, respect, rights and duties, tradition, etc. (ibid., pp. 128ff.). This clash necessitates that Roquentin remain lonely as a shelter against what Heidegger called 'the domination of the they'. The lonely seeker after authenticity can often feel 'weak' (ibid., p. 150). This sensation of weakness also stems from the vulnerability of the individual who, devoid of a firm and definitive self, is trying to create one.

It is difficult to evaluate the results of the process of self-creation. In reference to his biography of the Marquis de Rollebon, Roquentin asks himself a basic question about this: 'How on earth can I . . . save the past of somebody else?' (ibid., p. 139). This question can be para-phrased as 'How can one judge the authenticity of someone else's life?' Here, before the conception of Sartre's existential psychoanalysis, the problem remains open. Roquentin gives up his project of evaluating the authenticity or lack thereof in the lives of others and 'stop[s] writing . . . about Rollebon' (ibid., p. 138).

Instead of creating Rollebon as a work of art, Roquentin becomes immersed in creating his own self along the lines of the musical-aes-thetic model, which creates a 'melody' out of 'a host of little jolts' (ibid., p. 37; cf. p. 59). This process of self-creation allows one to overcome nausea or Heideggerian *Angst* and to cope with the contin-gency, nothingness and meaninglessness of our existence. Authentic creation can add 'a little order' to one's lonely life and give it meaning. Hence Roquentin's exclamation: 'What summits would I not reach if my *own life* were the subject of the melody?' (ibid., p. 60). Whether or not this goal is attainable is unimportant, since the very act of pursuing it fosters the will to affirm and accept one's life. It is significant that at this decisive moment Roquentin expresses the Nietzschean idea of authentic *amor fati*, a notion Nietzsche ties to the concept of the 'eternal recurrence of the same'. Roquentin cries: 'To live it all over again, in the same circumstances, from beginning to end' (*N*, p. 60). At the end of this novel, Roquentin feels he 'might succeed . . . in accept-ing [him]self' authentically (ibid., p. 253).

At this stage, Sartre's conclusion is that one is 'saved' (ibid., p. 251) by music, more generally, by art. In creating one's self, one may become both a genuine artist and a work of art. By becoming and living like 'a saxophone note' (ibid., p. 248), like a 'melody' (ibid., p. 249), one can achieve 'justification of one's existence'. The metaphor of music and the aesthetic model of authenticity transform this gloomy and nauseating novel into an optimistic literary manifesto of the viability of the search for authenticity within the anonymous crowd.

It is also true, however, that another type of hero can emerge, one who shuns aesthetic authenticity, preferring the easy convenience of a life of bad faith.

In *Nausea*, the hero's search for authenticity is undertaken and narrated in earnest. By contrast, Lucien's escape from such a search into adventures conducted in bad faith is narrated in an increasingly ironic tone, reaching its parodic climax in the last sentence, where 'he decided' to 'grow a moustache'.[20] The irony that Sartre employs to describe Lucien's flights from freedom to bad faith is highlighted by the very name of the story, 'The Childhood of a Leader' (or, in the original, *L'Enfance d'un chef*). The word *chef* in French connotes not just a leader or boss, but one who belongs to the social elite, who owns considerable property and is a patron of his or her country's heritage and culture. However, when we follow the hero's spiritual adventures and his recurrent endeavours to synthesize personal identity from people and literary figures he encounters, we begin to see that Lucien is a weak and frightened person, a true anti-hero who runs away from the freedom to create an identity for himself and by himself. Indeed, he prefers to concoct an identity from ready-made formulas, from the hackneyed traditions and demands of his ancestors, his homeland, his religion and his past. And thus, in contrast to the sympathy one feels towards Roquentin in *Nausea*, one now feels utter contempt towards the figure of the 'leader' of the French nation, the embodiment of the ethos of its social elite.

Why is Lucien so repulsive? It is because, as this anti-hero goes through the various stages of the 'search' for authenticity, he manifests virtually every one of the modes of bad faith classified by Sartre in *Being and Nothingness*. In 'The Childhood of a Leader', Sartre emphasizes reflection and introspection rather than action and plot, in line with his phenomenological thesis that we create our selves through reflective, intentional acts of consciousness. Lucien is preoccupied with such acts throughout the story; though he seems intent on finding his personal identity and his 'genuine' self, he is actually using this absorption to escape genuine creation of his authentic self.

At one point in Lucien's search he experiences a brief homosexual adventure. Despite the tempting permanent identity that homosexuality offers, Lucien rejects it because he feels that this identity will not be welcomed by respectable society or fit in with the role and image of the factory-owner. And thus we sense, as we follow further Lucien's ruminations about and adventures with surrealism, psychoanalysis, etc., that Lucien has already decided what he is and what he wants to become, that from the beginning of his search he has accepted the role his family and heritage have imposed on him: to be a *chef*, a pillar of his community. Lucien knows all along that owning a factory is his predestined fate, his life's 'natural' destination, and that he was born into the role of *chef* and all it demands of him. Hence, though it looks as if Lucien rejects all kinds of scenarios for his life because of dissatisfaction with them, he actually rejects them a priori since he has already decided to become what others have destined him to be: a leader of his nation. Lucien plays the part of one choosing his life, but he really chooses nothing and becomes what he already is. In deluding himself into believing that he is freely creating and choosing, Lucien is playing a sophisticated game rather than actually proceeding towards authenticity.

Only when he arrives at the last stage of his search for identity – his adventures with the fascist youth – and begins to hate foreigners and everything not French, does the game end. The mix of anti-Semitism and nationalism fits in well with his predestined mission – to become a *chef* who demands the veneration of those who surround him, especially the non-French populace. This last exploit becomes Lucien's permanent identity since it does not require the painful reflection on his life that was an integral part of his previous adventures. Psychoanalysis and surrealism force Lucien to think rather than to do. Only 'healthy' and steady nationalism emphasizes and encourages deeds. The exteriorization of Lucien from consciousness to 'moustache' reaches its peak during his activities as an anti-Semitic thug and a fighter for the sacred values of traditional France.

Notwithstanding the fact that views found in Sartre's later essay on *Anti-Semite and Jew*, where he presents the anti-Semite as embodying bad faith, are also present in this early story, here Sartre does not directly fault Lucien for becoming an anti-Semite and does not explicitly criticize the ethic of the 'master' (CL, p. 218) who is actually a slave. Sartre's tactic is ironic throughout, as even the use of the word *chef* in the French title of this story attests. This word alludes to right-wing politics, and its very use is a marker of ironic distance. Sartre's readers reject Lucien's character not because of any specific content, but because of the manner in which he acquires it. Specific attributes are in any event not the focus of Sartre's irony; rather, it is Lucien's fundamental bad faith in creating this persona that Sartre despises. Lucien's final identity is rooted not in his free choice, but in the land of France, its tradition, its 'owners' and its rulers. Values which are simply the products of arbitrary circumstances are not values at all, according to Sartre, who views morality and authenticity from an aesthetic perspective: morality is not what is found, but something created spontaneously.

The end of the story does not leave any doubt as to Lucien's bad faith. He is determined to end his journey of self-creation, to stop reflecting on his life and its meaning and to start doing: to possess 'a virgin' (ibid., p. 219), to become the legitimate owner of his father's factory and a pillar of his community - its *chef*. Lucien's resolution is particularly conspicuous against the background of Roquentin's continuing hesitation at the end of *Nausea*, where the outcome is left open. Here Lucien's final decision leaves no room for authenticity. In opposition to Roquentin, who tries hesitantly to become what he is, Lucien decisively becomes what he is not and never can be: solely the product of his education, heritage, tradition and nation (*CL*, pp. 217-19).

It should be noted, however, that in this parody of a *Bildungsroman* Sartre does not distinguish between two types of what he later calls *facticité* (facticity). The first is physical or biological facticity, examples of which would be the characteristic of being 'tall' (e.g. Lucien's height, which earns him the nickname 'beanpole') and characteristics that have to do with one's 'situation' in the world, such as class, family or tradition. In reference to the second type of facticity, the freedom of others is a relevant factor. For example, one must accept the rights of one's forefathers to have their own traditional values and to wish to share them with their sons. This is thus a kind of cultural/historical facticity. Only in the first volume of the *Critique of Dialectical Reason* does Sartre begin to address this issue, by trying to examine how and under what conditions our creations become forces beyond our control, shaping the *praxis* which created them.

Both stories attest Sartre's belief that authenticity is 'useless passion': when one seeks it sincerely, as did Roquentin, it is elusive; when one escapes it, it disappears. To account for this disappointing state of affairs, Sartre articulates an ontological account of human reality.

II

Sartre does not supply his readers with a precise definition of authenticity, but is content to remark generally that it 'consists in having a true and lucid consciousness of the situation, in assuming the responsibilities and risks that it involves, in accepting it in pride or humiliation, sometimes in horror and hate'.[21] But what exactly is the 'situation' in question? One possible answer is that authenticity, as creation of the self, is actually an ongoing project. Sartre's conclusion is grounded in this ontology: 'Man is not what he is' implies that man cannot *be* authentic, however he tries to *become* authentic.

On Sartre's reading, to wish to be authentic is to wish to become God. God has no secret self. He is totally self-identical and self-caused. Sartre accepts Spinoza's formulation: God is the only *causa sui* – the only entity that is the necessary foundation of its being. In the original Greek sense of authenticity as 'having *auctoritas*', as possessing inherent authority over one's self, and as being the sole source of one's own being, only God is wholly and absolutely authentic. God is always just 'what he is'. On this divine model of authenticity, to become authentic in the world of people and objects is to be God – to be a being in whom objectivity (authenticity as a social value) and subjectivity (authenticity of the individual) coincide. Unfortunately, we are not God; thus for us to aspire to be authentic is a form of bad faith. The quest for authenticity presupposes salvation where none is available, and one who goes ahead with this project is thus disregarding what he knows full well to be the case. Thus Sartre accuses Heidegger of 'bad faith' in speaking of the 'moral' drive or 'ethics' of authenticity (*BN*, pp. 80, 531).

By contrast to his ambivalence towards Heidegger, Sartre's attitude to Nietzsche is unmistakably positive.[22] He agrees with Nietzsche that 'we have killed God', but qualifies Nietzsche's claim that to overcome this loss we ourselves must 'become gods' (*GS*, sec. 125). We must be God, Sartre agrees, but, owing to our ontological limitations, we cannot. We must try, within our limited 'situation', 'human reality' or 'facticity' to overcome our tendency to be what we cannot and instead be what we are, not as God but like God. We must maximally create our own selves within the factual limitations of our heredity, history and traditions. Sartre is telling us we have no choice but lucidly to face our real situation rather than fantasize about 'useless' alternatives. Like Nietzsche, Sartre anthropologized the concept of God and chose atheism in his quest for authenticity. Significantly, the very first pages of *Being and Nothingness* introduce the concept of the immanence of the world as it appears to us. Sartre claims that appearances do not point to a 'hidden reality' (*BN*, p. xlv). The first philosophical teaching he refers to in *Being and Nothingness* is Nietzsche's 'illusion of worlds-behind-the-scenes' (ibid., p. xlvi).

Sartre claims that the analysis of the structure of consciousness yields two ontologically primitive types of being: being-for-itself, or conscious being; and being-in-itself, which, having no consciousness of its own, is an object for consciousness. One of Sartre's main ontological contentions is that nothing can be, or have, both sorts of being at once: nothing can be 'being-for-and-in-itself'. This is the impossible sort of being to which our consciousness unremittingly aspires. We are condemned to be free because from the moment we exist we are, and cannot escape being, makers of choices. This in fact follows even from Sartre's earlier phenomenology, according to which consciousness is characterized by spontaneity. The claim that 'existence precedes essence'[23] is the claim that one is what one does – how one attempts to fulfil one's goals and projects – and what one is going to do. Since one's consciousness is completely independent, its essence cannot be given beforehand as a substantial form waiting to realize its nature.

This helps elucidate Sartre's infuriating formulation: 'human reality is a being which is what it is not and is not what it is' (*BN*, p. 58). 'I am what I am not' in the sense that I cannot *be* a human being with the positive ontological completeness that a tree *is* a tree. Since there is no self to speak of, and no one is what she is, it follows that we cannot speak of authenticity in the Nietzschean manner of 'becoming what one is', or romantically, as did Rousseau, in terms of an inner essence to which one must remain true. According to Sartre, one can never attain self-identity, only the identity of selfless becoming – never being. Note, however, that Sartre asserts that 'human reality is a being'. This self-contradiction is an inevitable consequence of Sartre's ontology. It indicates the impossibility of imposing a rationalistic logic of identity on his notions. In this, Sartre resembles Kierkegaard. In any event, authenticity is not an essence of consciousness or of human reality; one strives to attain authenticity not as essence, but as freedom. Authenticity cannot be predicated of either the individual consciousness or humanity as a whole. To attribute authenticity to someone is to acknowledge the 'nothingness' (the consciousness) in that person's being and the fact that she does not try to disguise it in bad faith.

Unlike sincerity, 'the grasping of the authentic self is not based on being, it is a willing directed to a willing: it is a project that loses itself in order to save itself' (*Notebooks*, pp. 479–80). It is a willing *not* to will to be authentic in the sense that God is authentic. In contrast to Kant, whose morality emphasizes intentions, Sartre stresses actions that originate spontaneously and 'gratuitously' (ibid., p. 481). 'In authenticity ... I reduce the internalized objective quality to a sequence of behaviour' (ibid., p. 475). Consequently, one can attain authenticity only when acting, and not through reflection. More exactly, using the language of Sartre's earlier phenomenology, we can say that actions are not actions of the self; rather, the self is a product of a series of actions. Hence it is more correct to speak of 'actions generating me', some of them generating me authentically, than to speak of 'my actions'. One's authenticity is, then, the sum-total of authentic self-generating actions. Moreover, Sartre claims that there is rarely a single significant act which is not part of some 'original projection of myself which stands as my choice of myself in the world' (*BN*, p. 39). Authenticity is not one notable action, as it is not the self or a predicate; rather, it is from this fundamental project of self-choice that all other predicates of authenticity and authentic actions derive their meaning.

Criticism of Kant's categorical imperative is implicit here. Kant urged us to be moral for the sake of morality *per se*. Sartre, on the other hand, claims that to behave authentically for the sake of authenticity or of being hailed as an authentic person is not to behave authentically at all: 'if you seek authenticity for authenticity's sake, you are no longer authentic' (*Notebooks*, p. 4). Thus to will authenticity for its own sake is to will to be defined as being-for-itself-in-itself, as a conscious thing-in-the-world, which is not possible. As a predicate of human reality, authenticity is unattainable, because authenticity is nothing. The project of becoming as God is enmeshed in bad faith. But what about the more modest project of becoming *like* God by adopting the aesthetic model of authenticity? Sartre's ontology seems compatible with spontaneous activity which generates authenticity. Indeed, this is the conclusion Sartre reaches in his *Notebooks*: 'authenticity will unveil to us that we are condemned to create and that at the same time we have to be this creation to which we are condemned' (p. 515). Yet what sense of authenticity can Sartre grant to the aesthetic model of 'creating the self' if one can never be a complete self or wholly at one with the created self, as prescribed by Heidegger?

Being and Nothingness introduces another conception of authen-

151

ticity, one which focuses on the seeker's attitude to this ideal. The authentic stance is in fact the sober realization that one's search for authenticity cannot be realized because one never owns one's 'transcendent' self. I am not what I am, and I pursue this realization by overcoming the seductive invitations to bad faith I encounter everywhere, with their offers of a self I can never have. Thus I must relate to my self as something which cannot be God. One cannot *be* authentic, but one can act authentically by trying not to make the search for authenticity into one's 'fundamental project' in life.

This conclusion also follows from Sartre's conception of the free *être-pour-soi*. Were our consciousness not free of any external determination, were it unable to create its values, it would simply be an object. But consciousness cannot be a 'being-in-itself', since it cannot escape its freedom: we are free even when we try to renounce our freedom. However we act, we are always responsible for ourselves and for what becomes of us. The awareness of this 'dreadful freedom' is anguish. Referring repeatedly to Kierkegaard and Heidegger, Sartre claims that 'it is in anguish that man gets the consciousness of his freedom' (*BN*, p. 29).

Sartre assumes that it is difficult to live with freedom and responsibility, and that people commonly try to cast off the burden – to live as though they were inanimate objects, to make excuses for their conduct in a world they themselves created and are responsible for. They live in perpetual anguish, for they can neither bear their freedom nor renounce it; they can neither bear being conscious nor exist as things. To exist in this perpetual quandary is to affirm anguish and to live authentically.

Since Sartre cannot describe authenticity in a positive way, he provides lengthy descriptions of patterns of bad faith to discourage us from adopting them in our daily lives. Significantly, at the beginning of his discussion of bad faith, Sartre refers to 'irony' as something that 'annihilates' what has been posited 'within one and the same act. . . . [It] affirms to deny and denies to affirm' (ibid., p. 47). Sartre's discussion of bad faith, however, far from adopting a subtle ironic tone, is actually a clear example of how his whole ontology is deliberately imbued with moral evaluation. From the start, his explication of the phenomenon of bad faith voices strong disapproval of these 'negative attitudes' (ibid., p. 47).

Because human reality is freedom, the possibility of bad faith is an inherent feature of being human. The obsessive pursuit of substance by the 'for-itself' inauthenticates the human consciousness, since originally and genuinely consciousness is pure intentionality, that is, pure nothingness. Here, however, we find one of Sartre's notorious contradictions: if consciousness is not a substance and thus cannot have essential properties, how can the 'passion' for being *en-soi* be inherent in it? How can consciousness tend to bad faith if it is entirely dispositionless? If the desire to be God is a universal phenomenon, as Sartre argues, making it a central feature of his ontology, must it not be rooted in consciousness?

Sartre claims that bad faith is the refusal to recognize the self as both facticity and transcendence. Three basic negative attitudes toward the self are possible:

1   The individual may regard himself as pure transcendence, as forever beyond his 'situation', as neither part of nor responsible for choices he has made, since he is, as it were, beyond choosing (for example, Lucien). Such an individual sees himself not as possessing a *situated* freedom, but as having a ghostly, dislocated freedom that glides through the world untouched and untouching. This posture is one of extreme alienation, like that which characterizes Kierkegaard's 'aesthetic sphere'.

2   One may choose to deny one's transcendence completely, viewing oneself as a thing and one's values as determinate consequences of this objective existence. Sartre describes this as the 'spirit of seriousness' (*l'esprit de sérieux*) in which one regards all values and the very meaning of the world as constituted prior to and independently of one's own existence.

3   A third sort of bad faith consists in treating oneself as an *other* instead of treating oneself as one's self. This pattern of bad faith is distinct from, though parallel to, the second pattern. To treat oneself as an other is to deny transcendence and turn one's self not into a thing, but into pure facticity. This pattern occurs through being-with-others and is the most fundamental of the three.

We can now comprehend Sartre's attack on the ideal of sincerity (*BN*, pp. 58–9, 64–7; cf. *Notebooks*, pp. 474–5), which puts him squarely within the tradition of the other philosophers of authenticity. Sartre repudiates this ideal, namely, the view that one is and ought to be for oneself only what one is for others. He regards this as a sophisticated form of bad faith, one which is based on the objective attitude and derived from the rationalist ideal of correspondence. It reduces human reality solely to the ontology of 'in-itself', and has meaning only in a world of objectified subjects – a world where patterns of bad faith dominate human relationships: 'in order for bad faith to be possible, sincerity itself must be in bad faith' (*BN*, p. 67). One can even claim that according to Sartre all rationalist philosophies embracing objective 'norms and criteria of truth' manifest a *'Weltanschauung* of bad faith' (ibid., p. 68). Moreover, if 'inauthenticity' is, to use Sartre's later formulation, 'to comprehend oneself in terms of the world' or 'nature' (*Notebooks*, pp. 468, 6), then the biological model of authenticity is itself in bad faith. If the aesthetic model of authenticity is also thwarted by social facticity and intersubjective 'hell' – the socially rooted structures of bad faith – then what remains is to confront the primary obstacle to authenticity in the political realm. Yet the illusion that politics will bring about authenticity must be abandoned, since society will simply turn the authentic individual into a fact of the social world, a being *en-soi*.

Nevertheless, love (in which consciousness interacts as a freedom with another freedom), artistic creation, play and philosophic reflection are examples of acts which seek not the impossible synthesis of the in-itself-for-itself, but the intentional relations between consciousness and the world (i.e. between for-itself and in-itself).

Only things-in-themselves are wholly subject to the law of identity. For humans, identity is always something yet to be achieved. To try and escape the endless search for identity by embracing ready-made 'identities' is to adopt a *persona*, literally a mask and a role, with set speeches and patterns of behaviour. The genuinely free 'master', on the other hand, will experience continual striving and will always be in the process of becoming, never of being. She is dynamic, fluid and ever creative, never ceasing to search for greater self-knowledge and self-transparency. She will always strive to become what she chooses to become, regardless of what others expect, demand or invite her to be. The 'slave' (*BN*, p. 47), Sartre says, referring deliberately not only to Hegelian metaphor but also to Nietzsche's distinction between moralities of masters and slaves, tries ceaselessly and in bad faith to become something fixed and affirmative. Yet this is impossible: one is encompassed by one's existence, and 'there is no exit'.

Sartre intends his ontological explication of human Being as creative but limited consciousness to restrain our desire to persist in the impossible 'project' of becoming authentic by becoming God. Attentive reading of *Being and Nothingness*, he hopes, will inspire the reader to let go of the impossible dream of becoming an ideally authentic being and embrace the more realistic goal of living authentically in a humanly possible manner. This alternative settles for keeping one's freedom intact and using it within the limits of one's situation without escaping to bad faith.

Sartre adopts Nietzsche's idea that one becomes what one is by overcoming the wish to be that which one is not. Like Nietzsche, Sartre wants to provide us with salvation from our need for salvation. However, here Sartre includes also salvation from the Nietzschean ideal of authentic life.

Sartre thus works himself into a corner with respect to the social viability of authenticity. Ironically, his philosophy of engagement and personal commitment seems impossible to implement. Yet this irony discloses the limits of ontology in reference to authenticity and points to a solution – political activism. Thus in spite of Sartre's claim that it is 'not possible to derive imperatives from ontology's indicatives' (ibid., p. 625) and the fact that he never published his long-awaited ethical treatise, it would be more accurate to conclude that *Being and Nothingness* itself contains the long-awaited ethical imperatives. In *Being and Nothingness* two ethical conclusions with respect to authenticity are reached. The first is that we must accept the ontological fact that human Being is an ambiguous fusion of immanence ('in-itself') and transcendence ('for-itself'), and that bad faith is the flight from this ambiguity. Consequently, one's authenticity consists in 'lucid' recognition of the impossibility of becoming a Godlike authentic creature. The second ethical implication is that our efforts must shift from theory to concrete political action. If social authenticity is not viable, let us at least proceed to political reform.

The 'useless passion' cannot be expunged, but it can be frozen out by ontological explication, which reveals its futility, and by literature, which depicts this graphically. An example is Sartre's play *In Camera*. Sartre's attempts to influence readers thus point in a direction entirely different from that of earlier promoters of authenticity. He encourages readers to give up their futile desire for unconditional authenticity and instead commit themselves to the more practical aim of bringing about political and social change that will ultimately lead to freedom, equality and justice. Sartre warmly endorses edifying literature; indeed, he demands that writers engage in socio-political dialogue and confront moral issues. He calls for committed writers to persuade their readers and 'move' them 'to action'.[24]

In *Being and Nothingness* the notion of authenticity is left dangling: like other values, it is neither justified nor 'unjustified' (*BN*, p. 38), though Sartre claims it is a 'useless passion'. Nevertheless, Sartre did not despair of trying to make authenticity a viable moral-social value. In a 1946 lecture, *L'Existentialisme est un humanisme*, Sartre tried to attract listeners and readers by speaking, as it were, their language, as Kierkegaard did in his aesthetic writings.[25]

Sartre used the lecture to consider two basic problems that had haunted his ontology. (1) If freedom is solely a form, and if authenticity as a value is absolutely unjustified – why not embrace, say, fascism? To justify freedom for all and to defend himself against this critique, Sartre turns to Kant. (2) How is it possible to make the transition from the general theoretical realm of ontology to the ontic sphere of everyday existence and concrete action?

If Sartre could objectively ground value-judgements and provide for their concrete application, he would be able to give positive content to authentic existence. Moreover, justification of the moral superiority of authenticity to bad faith, and explication of the relation between authenticity and social morality, would enable him to move on to political philosophy and socio-political freedom, without having to recant his ontology. The lecture attempts to steer the search for authenticity onto a more viable path than that of ontology proper. While Sartre never did write his treatise on ethics, this lecture on the objectivity of freedom covers the same ground.

Sartre failed in this endeavour. Recognizing his failure, he came to regret publication of the essay and plunged into intense political activity. Nevertheless, while proclaiming himself a Marxist at this stage, Sartre did not repudiate his earlier ontology and its theoretical prognosis as to the viability of the ideal of authenticity. Nor did he repudiate his earlier aesthetic model of the free creation of the self despite the obvious difficulties that would face anyone who tried to adopt it. However, Sartre acknowledged that 'the possibilities of any individual were strictly limited by his situation' (*FC*, pp. 209–10). To come to grips with the limited freedom of actual life, particularly as regards social constraints, that social situation itself must be changed.

In his later writings Sartre sets aside ontology in order to concentrate on his aesthetic model. He argues for two main developments: (1)

maximization of individual freedom through 'radical' change in the nature of society, which is possible given that the social order is contingent and hence changeable; and (2) inspiring the individual's will to self-creation by providing role models in his existential-psychoanalytic biographies. These biographies demonstrate that authenticity is viable even in the most taxing circumstances. Sartre's book on Jean Genet analyses a potential hero of authenticity in relation to his social context. At the end he concludes: 'Genet holds the mirror up to us: we must look at it and see ourselves.'[26]

III

The ontological impasse over authenticity prompted Sartre to explore the method of existential psychoanalysis.[27] It was devised to assist us in rethinking our life-patterns, which have become moulded in the 'spirit of seriousness' that views us as objects subordinated to the world. For Sartre, 'conversion' is fostering a new version of our selves and our surroundings within the given ontological framework. Sartre's existential psychoanalysis attempts to induce readers to change, transform or accept their original choices. We can change these projects only when we know what they are and how we came to create them. Sartre tries to provide us with the means for examining our lives so that we can decide whether to go on with them or 'radically' change them.

As de Beauvoir attests, Sartre wrote his biography of Flaubert 'to prove that any man is perfectly knowable so long as one uses the right method and possesses the necessary documents'.[28] Sartre's 'existential psychoanalysis' is based on the intentional structure of consciousness he explicated earlier. However, he now introduces the notion of the 'person', and develops the idea of 'situated freedom' by bringing concrete examples – examples of free creations of consciousness itself within the facticity of a given 'situation' and its concomitant social relationships.

In his biography of Flaubert, Sartre examines his anthropological thesis about authenticity as self-creation in agonizing detail. He tests his thesis under the most severe conditions, picking the most unfavourable circumstances for the initial factical 'situation'. Sartre deals with Flaubert's life in order 'to understand this scandalous occurrence: an idiot who becomes a genius'.[29] In another study he examines a thief, 'ragamuffin' and 'bastard' who, nonetheless, 'not for a moment has wanted to believe that there was no way out of the situation' and became a brilliant playwright 'by forging his destiny' (*Genet*, pp. 15, 16). Unlike Lucien, Genet had no 'natural right' to anything and was deprived of everything; nevertheless, by dint of suffering and turmoil, he managed to emerge 'a triumphant hero' (ibid., p. 137).

Both Flaubert and Genet exemplify extreme cases where severe 'facticity', the manner in which consciousness is necessarily embedded in the world, in materiality and in one's past, harshly limits our freedom to shape our lives. But, precisely because of this, these cases can reveal to us the hard-fought liberation of a particular freedom from the grip of a destiny to which one does not yield. These cases show that the only facticity of freedom is that freedom is not free not to create freely.

Sartre regards his psychoanalytic-anthropological tests of aesthetic authenticity as successful. He therefore claims that we ourselves have created all the 'passive' factors that supposedly constrain our freedom to become spontaneous authors of our selves. At the very least, our response to them is wholly of our making: 'passivity *does not simply exist;* it must continually create itself or little by little lose its force' (*FI*, p. 42). In other words, everything depends on how one deals with the hand one is dealt, as exemplified in Genet's case of homosexuality and criminality – imparted not genetically, socially or divinely, but by Genet alone.

The chief aim of Sartre's existential psychoanalysis is to illuminate the concrete formation of aesthetic authenticity by individual choices as to one's 'fundamental project', one's conscious choice of a style or walk of life. One's 'original choice' (*Genet*, pp. 187, 250) shapes the total meaning of one's life and makes one into what one becomes. Sartre makes it clear that these existential-psychoanalytic examinations of 'fundamental projects' are based on the phenomenology of totally vacant consciousness. But if the nature of consciousness, which Sartre must paradoxically posit, is genuinely the same for all, and fundamentally empty, how can one validly make any value-judgements of, or distinctions between, different 'fundamental projects'? At one stage, Genet's revolt against the Kantian universal 'objective Good' involves choosing to yield to 'the temptation of Evil', where 'freedom tempts itself' (ibid., pp. 158-9). Could we not claim that even the Nazis were tempted by their own freedom? Less dramatically, why is the project of making a lot of money grasped as inferior to and less significant than the project of creating an authentic life? While Sartre speaks of 'a naked, undifferentiated existence which was capable of being everything and which, depending on circumstances, became a murderer or a public prosecutor; in short, human existence' (ibid., p. 588), surely we recognize that we must also take into consideration the forces that formed the individual's historical, social and existential situation.

These problems arise from Sartre's failure to set aside his phenomenology of bad faith and stick to analysis of concrete acts of bad faith. The incompatibility between Sartre's ontological conclusions as to the impossibility of authenticity and his anthropological theories of its viability remains despite the positive results of his existential-psychoanalytic case studies. Moreover, there are difficulties even on the anthropological level. Clearly, in carrying out the project of authentic creation of one's self, one may have no choice but to relate to others as means (given the individualistic nature of the 'project'), and, hence, to relate to them in bad faith. Likewise, the others, by submitting to the situation, are also active participants in encouraging bad faith. The social problem of authenticity is highlighted rather than resolved by Sartre's anthropology.

Still, the ideal of aesthetic authenticity remains the 'real morality' (ibid., p. 186) for Sartre. Yet by picking up the figure of Genet the 'thief' who, nonetheless, pursues 'his original will to assume himself entirely' (ibid., pp. 350, 353), Sartre tries to tell us that an ethic of authenticity 'is impossible today' (ibid., p. 186n.). He quotes Genet's saying that 'a philosophy, with its politics and ethics, cannot be derived from theft' (ibid., p. 185) several times. Sartre adduces this example to demonstrate that on the basis of Nietzsche's formula for authenticity – one wills one's self to become what one is – a person, like Genet, who 'wants to make himself what he is' (ibid., p. 350) is outside the sphere of ethics because 'he attains moral solipsism' (ibid., p. 166).

Ultimately, the relationship between ethics and authenticity as revealed by existential psychoanalysis is highly complex: 'aesthetic values must . . . contain and reveal the values of ethics' (ibid., p. 578). While describing Genet's degradation and his humiliation by others, Sartre emphasizes Genet's salvation by his 'major decision . . . to take the leap and perform . . . [a] creative *act* . . . in public' (ibid., p. 426). Freedom and aesthetic authenticity require self-overcoming of bad faith. Sartre's notion of authenticity is ultimately negative, despite its creative aspect, because it has no meaning apart from society – it has no meaning for the individual *per se*. It requires the liberation of society from bad faith. Yet although there is no ethic of authenticity, authenticity can be introduced into society by means of the free transformation of the 'objective' and alienated object (human reality as *en-soi*) into the 'subjective', free and creative person (ibid., p. 599). Bad faith can be transformed into a 'freedom grasping itself in its absolute gratuitousness' (ibid., p. 582) and into a state of genuine 'generosity' (ibid., pp. 578, 579, 582). To breed generosity in society, our attitude towards 'the principle of property' (ibid., p. 579) must be changed, and there must be a 'radical conversion' of our social and political systems and fundamental values. In the final chapter of *Saint Genet*, Sartre delivers a moralistic sermon about our potential freedom to be anything and to invent everything pending the socialization of authentic self-creation.

IV

We cannot change the ontological impossibility of authenticity, but we can do our best to weaken the social forces that perpetuate our tendency to live in bad faith. We can try to secure 'for *everyone* a margin of *real* freedom'. Only then can 'Marxism' be replaced by 'a philosophy of freedom'.[30] The ontological impasse over the viability of authenticity, far from discouraging Sartre from trying to 'improve' human conditions politically, in fact has the opposite effect.[31] The 'radical conversion' to the ethic of 'salvation' is the shift from ontology to political activism.

Sartre's political 'conversion' is bi-directional, encompassing the channelling of our passions into more viable directions – inner conversion, and transformation of society at large from its present state to egalitarianism – external conversion. The two goals are complementary. By inner conversion we learn to desist from trying to become what we are not and cannot be, from seeking the impossible in-itself-for-itself, the abstract being-for-itself, and the material being-in-itself.

The societal transformation to egalitarianism enables us to overcome our tendency to be reduced to being *en-soi*, abused masochistic objects or sadistic subjects who objectify others to satisfy unrealistic needs (*BN*, pp. 361–412). Masochistic tendencies lead to an alienation from one's own subjectivity and freedom. 'Sadism and masochism are the revelation of the Other. They only make sense . . . before conversion' (*Notebooks*, p. 20).

In his later political writings Sartre links social exploitation and political oppression to alienation and regards the latter as an 'objectification' of one's self by other selves or vice versa. To overcome the socio-political ramifications of this alienation, a new society, free of oppression, must be created. In the *Critique*, Sartre describes how the collectivity of individuals with common interests, values and goals is a means of attaining greater individual freedom and, therefore, of increasing authentic social interaction as opposed to objectification.

Of course, even a successful 'radical' political conversion cannot change our basic ontological predicament. Nevertheless, Sartre attempts to socialize authenticity through the socialist movement, which he defines in terms of the creative model of authenticity: 'It is the movement of man in the process of creating himself; the other parties believe that man is already created.'[32] That is, the opponents of socialism are described as exemplifying bad faith.

Sartre's political activity aims at creating a social fabric which will encourage and assist each individual to engage in self-creation. He envisages a just and free society that overcomes hunger and scarcity. Such a society will greatly lessen the appeal of acts of bad faith. Once the need to exploit each other for the sake of survival is gone, relationships will become subject-to-subject interactions. Sartre contends that economic scarcity and unjust conditions force human beings to treat one another as instruments, and make the failure of the search for authenticity almost a foregone conclusion.

But Sartre was realistic about his radical politics. Despite his optimism in the Lévy interviews, he appreciated the impossibility of the Kantian ideal morality: 'The idea of a kingdom of man becomes the dream of an idea' (*Genet*, p. 188). Referring to his descriptions of human relationships in *Being and Nothingness*, he delineates three scenarios where authentic human interaction might be viable:

> If we could all be, simultaneously and reciprocally, both object and subject for each other and by each other, or if we could all sink together into an objective totality, or if, as in the Kantian city of ends, we were never anything but subjects recognizing themselves as subjects. . . . But we cannot carry matters to an extreme in either direction: we cannot all be objects unless it be for a transcendent subject, nor can we all be subjects unless we first undertake the impossible liquidation of all objectivity. As for absolute reciprocity, it is concealed by the historical conditions of class and race, by nationalities, by the social hierarchy.
>
> (*Genet*, p. 590)

The factors mentioned at the end of the passage obstruct the path to authentic 'reciprocity' of 'human reality . . . in-society'; yet they can be changed by political conversion. There is 'one' course which 'is open to us', Sartre asserts, and he promises, at the end of his existential psychoanalysis of Genet, to discuss it 'elsewhere' (ibid., pp. 598–9).

Thus in Sartre's later work we can discern a kind of dialectical orientation: first his existentialist anthropology will modify Marxism from within by imbuing it with a thirst for authenticity; then, after the 'radical conversion' of society, this search will be carried out spontaneously within the political framework of existentialistic Marxism. It is unclear to what extent this programme succeeded.

In his later, 'Hegelian' political writings, Sartre argues that the personal authenticity of one individual can come together with that of another, until this 'fusion' ultimately creates a shared social consciousness and solid social fabric. It seems as if his later political thought, like his early phenomenology, is intended, among other things, to demonstrate the viability of the aesthetic model of authenticity in society as a whole. The first volume of the *Critique*, for example, is a diagnostic treatise on how 'practico-inert' social institutions destroy personal authenticity. This diagnosis underlines the need to cure such social sicknesses by active political action. This attempt to prove that individual 'conversion' to authenticity is possible only within a transformed society can be seen as a corrective to *Being and Nothingness*.

I cannot enter into a detailed analysis of Sartre's political writings here;[33] it may not be warranted in any event, since he considered them a 'failure'. Indeed, he later said the *Critique of Dialectical Reason* seemed not to have 'ripened within him' (Lévy, p. 170). And the venture he planned with Lévy – a re-examination of the fundamental questions of politics and ethics, to be entitled *Pouvoir et Liberté* (*Power and Freedom*) remained unexecuted.

By way of summary, I want to consider whether Sartre's pessimism about authenticity is in fact warranted.

'We are beings whose being is perpetually in question' (*Genet*, p. 60). Hence not to try to answer the question of authenticity, let alone not to raise it, indicates bad faith and one's reduction to the status of an object whose 'being *is not in question*, it is stable and fixed, like that of objects. In short, it is a being *in itself* and *for others*, but it is not a being-for-itself' (ibid.). Ultimate failure to achieve authenticity is irrelevant because it is the striving, the overcoming of difficulties and the acceptance of defeats that endows life with structure, unity and meaning. As Sartre puts it, 'to create oneself and to kill oneself come to the same thing. Existence is no longer anything but an interminable death-agony which has been willed' (ibid., p. 167). Thus authenticity as self-creation is on a par with authenticity as self-destruction. To become author of one's own self is *ipso facto* to be author of one's death. One who looks forward to achieving authenticity 'pursues [one's] own nothingness', and therefore 'an entire life dooms itself to failure' (ibid., p. 183). One of the main reasons why failure is imminent is that an individual like Genet 'wants to derive his being from himself and to derive all his acts from his being' (ibid., p. 187). Genet's mistake was that at one point he wanted to be *causa sui*, to *be* God, but the most he, like everyone else, could achieve, was to be *like* God, namely, a freely creative person. And, indeed, in the case of Genet, who saved himself through art and liberated himself by writing, 'the *loser wins*' (ibid., pp. 184, 585). In both *Nausea* and the study of Genet, Sartre describes the artist as an authentic self, liberated from the 'good' objective ethos and from the 'evil' of nothingness (*Genet*, p. 422). By making the *pour-soi-en-soi* 'only the object of . . . art', Genet overcame the pull of this impossible fusion. From that moment on, for Genet 'to compose is to re-create *himself*' (ibid., p. 543).

Unquestionably, even in his later years, Sartre's assessment was not entirely pessimistic, and he did express some guarded optimism regarding authenticity: 'it suffices to *will* the failure [to become God] for it to change into a success [for one to become like God]' (*Genet*, p. 187). The 'useless passion' is not completely useless: the art of authenticity is to achieve authenticity by art or creative activity. Sartre construes creativity broadly: in the second of the two *Notebooks* he characterizes the rearranging of household furniture as creative.

To create or write 'is to communicate' and to enter into 'relations with others' (*Notebooks*, p. 423). There and elsewhere a positive tone creeps into Sartre's discussion of authentic relationships. He refers to 'authenticity' several times as 'a double source of joy' (ibid., p. 491), speaks of authentic '*loving*' (ibid., p. 501) and increasingly refers to such notions as 'gratuitousness', 'reciprocity', 'gift' and 'generosity' as characterizing authentic relations wherein each person regards the other as an end-in-itself and not just as a means of furthering her own projects and whims. Such authentic relationships are already implied in Sartre's earlier discussion of 'the look' (*BN*, pp. 252–302) in the context of his thesis that in inauthentic relationships, one party is a living 'hell' who objectifies the other. Sartre's phenomenology of consciousness seems to presuppose an intuitive recognition of the other as a person 'for-herself'. As Sartre argued in *Being and Nothingness*, objects do not mirror other objects; therefore the fact that I do indeed see myself reflected or mirrored as an object in the 'look of the other' necessarily implies that I see the other, not as an object, but as a subject. Hence, at least epistemologically, authentic (i.e. subject-object to object-subject) relationships were countenanced as early in Sartre's thought as *Being and Nothingness*.

Authenticity in the sense of spontaneous activity in freely creating one's self does not necessarily entail the Kantian moral kingdom of ends. I relate to my self as an end in itself (for example, in my fundamental project of seeking authenticity) and regard others as potential partners who may help me in carrying out my project. However, if this is all there is to it, then conflict between myself and others is inevitable, for I will prevent them from expressing their own selves spontaneously. A reciprocal situation, in which two or more individuals enter into meaningful relationships with each other, though rare, is nonetheless not impossible, and it is conceivable that each of them can become an essential element in creating and expressing the other's authentic self. Mutual generosity, respect and genuine feelings cement such relations. I choose to help the other become authentic by not trying to dominate her and by regarding her as an autonomous person who can act simultaneously as object and subject in relation to myself. The other's otherness is accommodated but not assimilated in my self and my life.

Creativity, generosity, unselfish love, etc., are not esoteric values never encountered in the real world. They have been popular in different cultures and periods. Nevertheless, from the perspective of authenticity, they acquire new meaning, for they connote the genuine spontaneity of the process of self-determination and of creation of the authentic self.

Sartre realized that the authentic Nietzschean *Übermensch* 'can appear only at the conclusion of a *social* evolution' (*Genet*, p. 245). To encourage such evolution he advocated his own brand of socio-political revolution. By the very end, however, Sartre regarded his politics as a total failure. In the next chapter, we shall see whether Camus was any more successful in developing a socially viable ethic of authenticity.

Notes

1   *Mauvaise foi.* I render this notion literally as 'bad faith' to avoid the problematic issue of 'self-deception', which has been the subject of much discussion, and to distinguish it from the notions of 'good faith' (*bonne foi*) and 'inauthenticity'. I do not use 'inauthenticity', since if authenticity is not ontologically viable this is also true of its negation.

2   B. Lévy, 'Today's hope: conversations with Sartre', *Telos* (1980), 155-81 (henceforth Lévy).

3   When Lévy asks Sartre whether this 'exhausting debate with Marxism' was prompted by a desire to overcome the inevitability of 'bad faith' as expressed in *Being and Nothingness*, Sartre answers, 'Without a doubt' (Lévy, p. 158).

4   Ibid., p. 162. The notion of *le regne des fins* was used by Sartre in *Cahiers pour une morale* (Paris: Gallimard, 1983) (see, e.g., p. 17); trans. D. Pellauer as *Notebooks for an Ethics* (Chicago, Ill.: University of Chicago Press, 1992) (henceforth *Notebooks*), p. 10. In these notebooks, which date from 1947/8, Sartre, referring to the 'Kantian ideal', calls it 'the city of ends' (p. 161; cf. pp. 168-9). We must bear in mind, though, that Sartre valued his published works over his unpublished manuscripts, which I only quote here if they do not contradict his published writings.

5   Immanuel Kant, *Critique of Pure Reason*, trans. N. Kemp Smith (New York: St Martin's Press, 1965), p. 29.

6   *Being and Nothingness: An Essay on Phenomenological Ontology*, trans. H. E. Barnes (London: Methuen, 1957) (henceforth *BN*), p. 615.

7   'Consciousness of Self and Knowledge of Self' (1948), in *Readings in Existential Phenomenology*, ed. N. Lawrence and D. O'Connor (Englewood Cliffs, NJ: Prentice-Hall, 1967), pp. 113-42.

8   *The War Diaries*, trans. Q. Hoare (New York: Pantheon, 1984) (henceforth *WD*), pp. 94, 182, 95.

9   Translated in H. Spiegelberg, 'Sartre's Last Word on Ethics in Phenomenological Perspective', *Research in Phenomenology*, 11 (1981), 90-107.

10   *Situations*, trans. B. Eisler (London: Hamish Hamilton, 1965), p. 234 n.

11   *Critique of Dialectical Reason*, volume I: *Theory of Practical Ensembles*, trans. A. Sheridan-Smith, ed. J. Rée (London: New Left Books, 1976) (henceforth *CDR*); volume II: *The Intelligibility of History*, trans. Q. Hoare, ed. A. Elkaïm-Sartre (London: Verso, 1991).

12   *The Transcendence of the Ego*, trans. F. Williams and R. Kirkpatrick (New York: Noonday, 1957) (henceforth *TE*).

13   'Intentionality: A Fundamental Idea of Husserl's Phenomenology', trans.

J. P. Fell, *Journal of the British Society for Phenomenology*, 1 (1970), 4-5 (henceforth Int.).

14 See, e.g., *WD*, pp. 11, 336; note Sartre's resigned tone at pp. 51, 61, and other places.

15 The motif of watching and judging others is salient in Sartre's 1944 play *In Camera*, where he proclaims: 'Hell is . . . other people!' (*In Camera, and Other Plays*, trans. S. Gilbert (Harmondsworth: Penguin, 1982), p. 223). One character expresses the transparency of our consciousness and the public status of our egos as follows: 'I'm watching you, everybody's watching, I'm a crowd all by myself. . . . It's no use trying to escape' (ibid., p. 222). In another play, *Lucifer and the Lord*, from 1951, we find the same idea: 'No way of escaping men' (ibid., p. 169).

16 Translated by P. Mairet (London: Methuen, 1962) (henceforth *STE*).

17 See Sartre's phenomenological account in *The Psychology of Imagination* (London: Methuen, 1972).

18 *Nausea*, trans. R. Baldick (Harmondsworth: Penguin, 1965) (henceforth *N*), p. 97.

19 Preface to N. Sarraute, *Portrait of a Man Unknown*, trans. M. Jolas (New York: George Braziller, 1958), p. xi.

20 'The Childhood of a Leader', in *Intimacy*, trans. L. Alexander (London: Panther, 1960) (henceforth CL), p. 220; cf. M. Brinker, 'A Double Clearing of the Fog: Sartre's "The Childhood of a Leader" and its Relation to his Philosophy', in *Commitment in Reflection: Essays in Literature and Moral Philosophy*, ed., L. Toker (New York: Garland, 1994), pp. 101-19.

21 *Anti-Semite and Jew*, trans. G. J. Becker (New York: Schocken, 1965), p. 90.

22 Indeed, in his youthful first novel, 'A Defeat', he identified with the figure of 'Frederic', as he later testified: 'my first novel . . . was the story of Nietzsche and Wagner, with me in the role of Nietzsche. . . . a novel that would express my particular way of feeling and my conception of the world', quoted in Simone de Beauvoir, *Adieux: A Farewell to Sartre*, trans. P. O'Brien (Harmondsworth: Penguin, 1985), pp. 136, 151. Cf. ibid., p. 157, and *WD*, p. 156.

23 *BN*, p. 25, and *Existentialism and Humanism*, trans. P. Mairet, (London: Methuen, 1973) (henceforth *EH*).

24 De Beauvoir, *Adieux*, p. 169. In 'What is Literature?' Sartre writes: 'the literary object has no other substance than the reader's subjectivity. . . . But on the other hand, the words are there like traps to arouse our feelings and to reflect them toward us' (*Literature and Existentialism*, trans. B. Frechtman, (Secaucus, NJ: Citadel, 1949), p. 45). In an unpublished note he admits that 'What is Literature?' led to his being a co-

founder of *Rassemblement Democratique Revolutionnaire* (an international socialist organization), much like Mathieu in *The Roads to Freedom*, who, on tiring of being free to no end, decides in favour of action in the last unfinished volume, *La dernière chance*.

25 Cf. Simone de Beauvoir, who claims in *Force of Circumstance*, trans. R. Howard (Harmondsworth: Penguin, 1968) (henceforth *FC*) that in *EH* 'Sartre seduced them by maintaining the rights of morality' (p. 47).

26 *Saint Genet: Actor and Martyr*, trans. B. Frechtman (London: Heinemann, 1988) (henceforth *Genet*), p. 599.

27 See *BN*, pp. 557–75.

28 De Beauvoir, *Adieux*, p. 64.

29 *The Family Idiot*, trans. C. Cosman (Chicago, Ill.: University of Chicago Press, 1981) (henceforth *FI*), p. 41.

30 Jean-Paul Sartre, *Search for a Method*, trans. H. E. Barnes (New York: Vintage Books, 1968), p. 34.

31 He declares in an interview: 'First, all men must be able to become men by the improvement of their conditions of existence, so that a universal morality can be created' (*Encounter* (London), June 1964, p. 62). In another interview (*Le Monde*, 18 April 1964) he admits: 'alienation, the exploitation of men by other men, undernourishment . . . make metaphysical unhappiness a luxury and relegate it to second place. Hunger – now that *is* an evil' (trans. H. Barnes in *Existentialist Ethics* (New York: Alfred A. Knopf, 1967), p. 31).

32 R. Howard's translation (*FC*, p. 210) is more accurate than that found in Jean-Paul Sartre, *The Spectre of Stalin*, trans. I. Clephane (London: Hamish Hamilton, 1969).

33 But see W. L. McBride, *Sartre's Political Theory* (Bloomington: Indiana University Press, 1991), which also claims that Sartre's political writings 'continue to capture the *spirit* of "ethics" ' and that with reference to such phenomena as bad faith and authenticity 'one can discern a considerable continuity of concerns on Sartre's part' (p. 5).

7

Camus's return to authentic human morality

Of the few scholars still interested in Camus, most esteem his literary genius but denigrate his importance as a philosopher.[1] Camus himself was to some degree responsible for this attitude, on account of his declaration that he was not an existentialist.[2] From the current perspective, however, it is clear that he is very much a part of philosophy. Though, like Kierkegaard and Nietzsche, not a philosopher in the technical or academic sense, Camus expresses ideas and dilemmas that are intimately related to the ideal of authenticity.

Chronologically and thematically, Camus is the last thinker on authenticity. Ironically, in his later writings we find regression to an essentialist position that re-introduces a quasi-biological humanistic essence, reminiscent of Rousseau's human nature, and thus undermines the great revolt of authenticity against the notion of objectivity. Unlike Kierkegaard, who entices us to take an absurd leap of faith, Camus rejects transcendence, adopts a position of strict immanence[3] and invites us to live out a rebellious acceptance of our absurd fate. He encourages us to win authenticity by 'an act of lucidity as one makes an act of faith' (*LACE*, p. 81). This illuminates the dilemma that confronted all the thinkers we have considered: the singularity and the spontaneity of the ideal of authenticity imply a clash with the prevailing ethic; yet to resolve this impasse by granting authenticity a recognized social meaning in turn neutralizes this spontaneity by forcing it into a fixed ontological yoke. In any event, however, Camus rejects this solution since ontology is meaningless in an absurd world. To deal with the problem, Camus returns to one of the classic teachers of authenticity, Nietzsche.

Camus has great respect for Nietzsche and acknowledges his debt to him.[4] His idea that authenticity – 'this desire for unity . . . this need for clarity and cohesion'[5] – should embrace the absurd echoes Nietzsche's claim that inner harmony and the courage to accept the contradictions as well as the immanence of our world are characteristic of the authentic *Übermensch*. The 'passionate world of indifference' in which Camus's heroes are immersed (*MS*, p. 89) is a result not of weakness, but of strong personalities that courageously overcome the never-satisfied need for salvation. This power enables me to adopt a Nietzschean *amor fati* stance and to 'accept *what* is when once I have admitted that I cannot change it'.[6] This 'indifference' seems incompatible with the deep emotional involvement of Abraham, the 'knight of faith'. But, like Kierkegaard's heroes, Camus's heroes of absurd authenticity, 'obeying the flame', commit 'the existential leap' (*MS*, pp. 55-6) into the pathos of authenticity. However, while Kierkegaard's authenticity still retains some positive content, Camus invites us to accept the immanently absurd world – in the original sense of *absurdus:* i.e. an incongruous universe devoid of the harmony and meaning that ordinarily dwell in things through the power of an ordering principle allegedly external to our world. Kierkegaard sought to endow life with authentic experience which to some degree transcends it. Like Nietzsche, however, Camus rejects this transcendence and tries to entice us to shape our lives without seeking such external meaning. Sisyphian life in the face of the absurd is the only authentic attitude available to mortals who reject suicide and proudly affirm their lives.

Camus's two major philosophical essays, *The Myth of Sisyphus* and *The Rebel*, are philosophical commentaries on his understanding of authenticity as it is portrayed in his novels, short stories and plays. Camus's early perspective is found in *The Outsider* (*L'Etranger*); that of his transitional period in *Caligula;* and his later perspective in *The Plague* and 'The Guest'. Camus understood that since the ideal of authentic life goes beyond rational discourse it is best evoked by literature rather than exposition. By generating in us deep existential anguish, Camus's fiction offers us a chance to overcome it by being true to ourselves for the sake of humanity. 'This is why any authentic creation is a gift to the future' (*MS*, p. 169).

Camus uses metaphors to entice us into self-change by plunging us without comment into the stark climate of authenticity. Only when we begin to feel it can we proceed to the philosophical essay, which neither explains nor justifies, but merely describes authentic living and its consequences. This medium is more abstract and therefore less effective for arousing our pathos than the concrete images in Camus's fiction.[7]

Would it be true to say that Camus's, and for that matter the other philosophers', works of fiction are really just treatises in literary garb? Can such literary works be reduced to philosophy? Camus himself juxtaposes literature and philosophy in his treatment of Dostoevsky, Proust and Kafka, commenting that 'the great novelists are philosophical novelists' (ibid., p. 82). He goes on to explain that

> the preference they have shown for writing in images rather than in reasoned arguments is revelatory of a certain thought that is common to them all, convinced of the uselessness of any principle of explanation and sure of the educative message of perceptible appearance.

In this respect the novel is an 'instrument' (ibid., pp. 82–3).

In a 1938 review of Sartre's *Nausea*, Camus maintains that 'a novel is never anything but a philosophy put into images. And, in a good novel, the whole of the philosophy has passed into the images'.[8] But if so, why was Camus not satisfied with his literary works? Why did he feel he also had to express his views in the more abstract form of philosophical essays, given his belief that no 'reasoned arguments' can be adduced for the ideal of authentic life? In his Nobel Prize speech in 1957, Camus states that art, by providing a concrete, though imaginary, description of authentic life in an immanent world, is the best means for awakening the greatest number of people. Camus uses fiction to overcome 'the current nihilism' and entice readers into adopting the 'art of living' in its place.[9] He encourages them to fashion their lives into works of art. Why, then, does he find it necessary to provide a philosophical commentary on his literary masterpieces?

Camus provides a clue, saying that 'the work of art . . . is complete only through the implications of that philosophy' (MS, p. 83). The consummation of a literary work mobilized for a moral-didactic goal is not necessarily inherent in the work, which, as an aesthetic product, is always complete in its own right. However, in such a work, it is relevant to ascertain what the author intends to effect in creating it, i.e. to what end it is an instrument. Hence the moral-didactic purpose must be clarified. The theoretical essays of Camus and other exponents of authenticity explicate the messages implicit in their fiction. Fiction, with its rhetoric and irony, shakes us, opens us to change and entices us to pursue change. But only the philosophical essay makes clear the purpose of this enticement and thereby removes any hesitation we may experience in following the traumatic adventures of the heroes of authenticity. The pathos of absurdity does not suffice to make us fully aware of the sometimes dangerous consequences facing those who try to hold on to it. After completing *The Outsider*, with its emotional 'climate' of a hero who lives and dies absurdly, Camus delineates for us its terminological map and consequences:

> The climate of absurdity is in the beginning. The end is the absurd universe and that attitude of mind which lights the world with its true colours to bring out the privileged and implacable visage which that attitude has discerned in it.
>
> (ibid., p. 17)

By 'universe' Camus means 'a metaphysic' of 'all those irrational feelings' (ibid., p. 16). He describes these feelings 'by gathering together the sum of their consequences in the domain of the intelligence, by seizing and noting all their aspects, by outlining their universe' (ibid., pp. 16–17). Thus Camus moves from literature depicting the 'feeling of the absurd' to the phenomenology of the 'notion of the absurd'.[10]

I

> All those lives maintained in the rarefied air of the absurd could not persevere without some profound and constant thought to infuse its strength into them. Right here, it can be only a strange feeling of fidelity.
>
> (*MS*, p. 77)

Unlike the ontologists, Camus rarely uses the term 'authenticity'. Nonetheless, the concept of authenticity pervades everything he wrote. In the above passage, for example, he speaks of the 'strange feeling of fidelity' without which it is almost impossible to live authentically. His fascination with the mythological hero Sisyphus, who attained happiness through courageous determination to create his own self and remain loyal to it, despite a life of meaningless torment, is a good example of his preoccupation with authenticity. Up to the Second

World War, a Nietzschean motif is clearly evident in Camus's thought, and the aesthetic model of authenticity reaches its culmination: 'the absurd joy *par excellence* is creation. "Art and nothing but art", said Nietzsche; "we have art in order not to die of the truth" ' (ibid., p. 77) – or of the spirit of objectivity which stifles personal truthfulness.

Camus approaches the absurd from a personal perspective. He describes the pathos of one who is seized by a penetrating feeling of absurdity and asks himself the cardinal question of 'whether or not life had to have a meaning to be lived' (ibid., p. 47). In his preface to the English edition, Camus speaks of the personal nature of *The Myth of Sisyphus*, stressing the appeal of suicide to anyone who experiences the immanence of our world:

> This book is . . . the most personal of those I have published in English . . . it attempts to resolve the problem of suicide . . . without the aid of eternal values which, temporarily perhaps, are absent or distorted in contemporary Europe. The fundamental subject . . . is this: it is legitimate and necessary to wonder whether life has a meaning; therefore it is legitimate to meet the problem of suicide face to face. The answer . . . is this: even if one does not believe in God, suicide is not legitimate . . . even within the limits of nihilism it is possible to find the means to proceed beyond nihilism. . . . *The Myth of Sisyphus* . . . sums itself up for me as a lucid invitation to live and to create, in the very midst of the desert.

The protagonists of absurd authenticity live in a world in which all their actions, including those which lead to suicide, are devoid of reason or meaning. They keenly feel the lack of any correspondence between their 'longing for happiness and for reason' and 'the unreasonable silence of the world' (ibid., p. 29). Camus soberly depicts this 'intellectual malady' and does not explain it away with reference to some 'metaphysic' (ibid., p. 10). The personal pathos of such individuals rises above the objectivist-normative ethic grounded in reason or in some higher or lower powers such as God or Nature.

This pathos, which is not a logical 'conclusion' of any argument, is Camus's 'starting point' (ibid.). Camus has advanced beyond Dostoevsky's nineteenth-century hero, Ivan Karamazov, who concluded that if there is no God 'everything is permitted' (ibid., p. 57) and no act is of any importance. Camus declares that his hero feels that everything is unconditionally permitted, owing to the 'deadly climate' (ibid., p. 29) which lures him into destructive nihilism.

Before proceeding further, it will be useful to distinguish between several types of nihilism. (1) *Metaphysical nihilism* asserts that our world is absolute chaos devoid of any order, so that no objective, valid knowledge of it is attainable. (2) *Epistemological nihilism*, ordinarily called scepticism, claims that we are incapable of attaining such knowledge of our world, our perceptions and cognitions. (3) *Ethical nihilism* denies any possibility of objectively valid justification of our fundamental values. (4) The type of nihilism most relevant to Camus is *practical nihilism*, which can provoke one to annihilate one's self by suicide or another's life by murder. Now ethical nihilism, as just defined, can certainly be ascribed to Camus. Yet this ethical-theoretical nihilism does not necessarily imply practical nihilism. On the contrary, as Camus tries to show, creative acceptance of the absurd deters us from turning in this fatal direction.

Indeed, Camus does not write on suicide because it follows from one of the types of theoretical nihilism mentioned above. He maintains no particular metaphysical thesis as to the nature of reality and therefore is not committed to any kind of theoretical nihilism. Rather, Camus limits himself to providing quasi-phenomenological descriptions of 'pathos', the 'elusive feeling of absurdity': it appears as 'weariness', 'anxiety', 'strangeness', 'nausea', etc. (*MS*, pp. 17-19). Camus insists that the crisis that brings on the 'feeling of the absurd' when 'one day the "why" arises' (ibid., p. 18) is utterly arbitrary, and hence beyond argument and justification. The 'feeling of the absurd' can have no philosophical justification. However, the crisis it induces is a crisis of justification.

'The stage-sets collapse' abruptly and our 'mechanical life' (ibid., p. 18) demands justification and meaning. Nevertheless, this demand cannot be satisfied:

> I don't know whether this world has a meaning that transcends it. But I know that I do not know that meaning and that it is impossible for me just now to know it. What can a meaning outside my condition mean to me?
>
> (ibid., p. 45)

The theoretical position taken here by Camus is simply acknowledgement that there can be no answer. The pathos of the absurd stems directly from the acute realization that there is an unbridgeable gap between our need for meaning and happiness, and reality, which is unresponsive to this need. We cannot overcome this feeling of absurdity by trying to find some existential *raison d'être*, since it is precisely our doubts about the power of our reason to do so that cause the crisis in the first place. The philosophical attempt to overcome the feeling of absurdity brings us to the point of 'philosophical suicide', since by indulging us and providing us with an illusory 'reason for living' it also provides us with an 'excellent reason for dying' (ibid., p. 11). One who requires reasoned arguments for living and finds them in a particular ideology, endangers his life when that ideology collapses. This collapse can be the impetus to turn to practical nihilism and physical suicide.

Hence Camus recommends acceptance and affirmation of life even if it lacks transcendent meaning. The solution to absurdity is not to escape to philosophy or suicide, but, rather, to accept it as a given. The sober and creative life is the authentic solution and indicates an authentic overcoming. To Camus's generation the war had given little reason to be hopeful; Camus, like Nietzsche before him, offers hope without reason as the authentic reaction to the absurdity of immanence embodied in the myth of Sisyphus.

Like the Nietzschean *Übermensch*, who adopts the existential formula of *amor fati*, 'the absurd man says yes' (ibid., p. 99). In the effort to shape an authentic life in a world of immanence, the way is the goal, for there is no goal at the end of the way. In spite of the fact that his efforts lack purpose, and there is no chance he will fulfil his longings, 'one must imagine Sisyphus happy' (ibid., p. 99); otherwise one would have to commit suicide. Admittedly this is not happiness generated by transcendental values or the logical outcome of the feeling of absurdity; still, this happiness allows one to function creatively and vitally. Thus the feeling of absurdity enables one to attain happiness and secular, 'godless holiness': 'I conclude that all is well', says the Sisyphian authentic hero, 'and [this] remark is sacred' (ibid., p. 98).

Nonetheless, it could be argued that if the world is devoid of meaning and unable to sustain any absolute moral norms, then this fact about the world cannot, in itself, generate any values. If Camus claims that Sisyphian efforts in a meaningless world are a meaningful value enabling one to overcome practical nihilism, he is guilty of this fallacy.[11] However, a close reading of Camus reveals that he can defend himself against this charge. The concept and the experience of absurdity originate in the intrinsic intentional relation between the individual and the world. Camus refers to Husserl and 'the phenomenologists' in examining 'the theme of the "Intention" ' (ibid., p. 39). He claims that 'the Absurd is not in man . . . nor in the world, but in their presence together', that is, in their 'confrontation' (ibid., p. 30). Anticipating the above critique, he elaborates:

> I said that the world is absurd but I was too hasty. . . . What is absurd is the confrontation of the irrational and the wild longing for clarity whose call echoes in the human heart. The absurd depends as much on man as on the world.
>
> (ibid., p. 24)

Emphasizing that 'there can be no absurd outside the human mind' (ibid., p. 31) Camus makes it clear that the absurd is rooted in the subjective human perception of the world's immanence. Therefore, quite apart from the metaphysical question of whether the world in itself is in some way transcendent, divine or rational, humans can always express their unrequited 'nostalgia' (ibid., pp. 29, 39, 43, 44) for order and meaning by endowing it with reason, God and virtue. Thus, Camus does not intend to derive any 'value' from facts about the world in itself, as the critic claims, but seeks to make us resilient within the immanent sphere of our perceptions, notions and longings.

Camus champions the subjective authentic stance that refuses to give in to promises of 'salvation'. Like Nietzsche, he demands that we liberate ourselves from the yearning for salvation by overcoming our nostalgia for it. Camus's determination to withhold from us any 'metaphysics of consolation' (ibid., p. 42) makes authenticity all the more vital since in his eyes it is the only solution capable of withstanding the feeling of absurdity. Because it can never be eliminated, one must, despite the enormous difficulty, accept it and go on living. The way to live with the absurd on the verge of the abyss is not to seek external salvation but to turn to self-creation or creation in general.

But why should we not commit suicide and disentangle ourselves from the stifling, ever-present feeling of absurdity? Camus acknowledges the legitimacy of this question and tries to answer it. His discussion of the issue is illuminating in that it gives us a better understanding of authenticity as the only value in our subjective immanent world. 'The absurd does not liberate; it binds' – it binds us to this immanence. One can avoid the bond only by 'philosophical suicide', that is, by grabbing on to something transcendent but illusory. However, since there is nothing there to hold on to, this stance is untenable and ultimately collapses when we recognize that it is absurd in itself. Granted this, however, one can indeed escape the absurd by its utter destruction, namely, by physical suicide.

If 'the absurd merely confers an equivalence on the consequences of . . . actions' and if in a world devoid of any hierarchy of values 'all experiences are indifferent', then 'that of duty is as legitimate as any other'. But suicide, then, also becomes a legitimate option. Just as one can adopt an objectivist ethic and 'be virtuous through whim' (ibid., p. 58), one can also commit suicide out of sheer whim. And even if suicide indicates passive 'acceptance' (ibid., p. 48) it is difficult to argue with the wish to destroy the central component of the intentionality between man and his world that constitutes the absurd. Indeed, Camus admits that 'in its way, suicide settles the absurd. It engulfs the absurd in the same death' (ibid.). Admittedly, this is a personal solution which cannot solve the question of absurdity for others, but in any case the feeling of absurdity is a private concern of each individual. Even if suicide merely indicates resigned acceptance of the harsh implications of the relationship between the individual and the world and not the overcoming of this absurd – so what?

It might be claimed that physical suicide is not the solution, since it creates a hierarchy of values within which there is one sort of action of ultimate value. In other words, to commit suicide can be seen as preferring one course of action over all others. But if our existence is sheer absurdity, why would suicide be any more valuable than Dr Rieux's useless efforts to cure his patients in *The Plague*?

Camus knows that he has no valid argument against suicide. Suicide is an issue subject to the discretion of each individual who confronts the feeling of absurdity. Camus claims that we can 'escape suicide' to the extent that we are 'simultaneously awareness and rejection of death' (ibid., p. 60). The latter attitude is the 'revolt' that gives life its 'value' (ibid.) – its authenticity, the only possible value given the absurd. This 'majestic' revolt has 'something exceptional' about it, for, Camus feels, it displays 'human pride' (ibid., p. 48). It is not coincidental that at that point in his essay Camus begins to use first-person sentences such as 'I must carry . . . the weight of my own life . . . alone' (ibid.).

One possible response to the charge that his solution lacks objective validity is poignantly expressed by Nietzsche's hero of authenticity, Zarathustra: ' "This is my way; where is yours?" – thus I answered those who asked me "the way". For *the* way – that does not exist.' In my own way I can find pride and sublimely express my will to live authentically. To do so I will continue struggling and overcoming everything in me and my surroundings that tries to humiliate me and reduce me to suicide. Camus, following Nietzsche, declares: I embrace a lucid and sober attitude, since I want to attain authenticity, to live intensely but without 'stage-sets' that distort my selfhood; hence I turn away from suicide which will prevent me from engaging in revolt, the practical embodiment of authenticity.

Thus the feeling and notion of absurdity and the constant struggle against their nihilistic implications are necessary conditions of authenticity. 'I am authentic *ergo* it is absurd' is Camus's existential version of the Cartesian *Cogito*. 'Only from chaos is a star born', Nietzsche claims; and Camus develops this idea, maintaining that only from the feeling of absurdity and from the complex sensations that constitute its pathos is the aspiration to authenticity born. This happens when the 'stage-sets' of normative ethics 'collapse' and the question of where to go – 'suicide or recovery' (ibid., p. 18) – becomes inescapable.

Absurdity is an extreme existential pathos which reveals inauthentic being. The revolt against this feeling, together with resistance to taking shelter under the 'stage-sets' of alleged paths to salvation, makes a sober and authentic attitude possible. Physical suicide precludes adoption of this steadfast stance in the face of the absurd; one must, therefore, 'preserve' (ibid., p. 46) the spirit of revolt and the Sisyphian relation to the world without yielding to it (suicide) or getting lost on its account (selling out to transcendence). In itself the revolt is of no value, but the impact of the rebellious attitude on the rebel generates authenticity, the free and courageous determination to go on living creatively despite everything.

But in a world devoid of value why grant any meaning at all to authenticity? This is, of course, an arbitrary and free personal choice with no objective or logical validity. In making this choice Camus affirms something stressed by other philosophers of authenticity: the search for authenticity is a personal wager in a world where other outcomes are no more probable. But if this unique gamble succeeds, our prize is optimal: authentic selfhood.

In 'this hell of the present' the hero of absurdity 'has forgotten how to hope' (ibid., p. 46). She prefers life without hope to belief in a transcendent world, and takes upon herself 'the heartrending and marvellous wager of the absurd' (ibid.). In contrast to Pascal's famous bet on the eternal survival of the soul, this is a bet on the authenticity of our life. What point is there in such a wager in a Godless world of immanence where arbitrary probabilities unknown to and uncontrollable by the gambler determine the outcome? Unlike Pascal, whom he admires,[12] but like Kierkegaard, Camus believes that to bet against all logic is the supremely absurd wager which can help us authentically to defy our absurd life. In his own words, 'at last man will again find there the wine of the absurd and the bread of indifference on which he feeds his greatness' (ibid.). Camus is inverting the Christian ritual of the Eucharist to bind us to our immanent world. The hero of the absurd needs 'indifference' since he is always 'tempted' by 'religions or prophets, even without gods' who seduce him to 'leap' (ibid., p. 47). Camus uses the concept of negative enticement, which may have been inspired by Nietzsche, to describe the approach of organized religions, Christianity in particular, which aim at diverting us from the path to empowering authenticity.[13] Faced with these temptations, one can only choose the given world of immanence. The strength of this persistence will increase as we learn to enjoy the given. Though it is limited in principle, there are countless ways to savour its treasures, for example, the 'Don Juanism' which Camus describes as choosing an 'ethic of quantity' over that of 'quality' (ibid., p. 61).

At this point, however, it is not easy to accept Camus's approach on the strength of its inner logic, which denies any logic. If 'all experiences are indifferent' (ibid., p. 58), and devoid of any value, then the maximization of these experiences still adds up to nothing. Camus himself says that Don Juan, who, in the wake of Kierkegaard's description of the aesthetic, serves as a model of authenticity in the midst of absurdity, 'exhausts . . . his chances of life' to the point where he 'has chosen to be nothing' (ibid., p. 62). In what way is this different from choosing suicide? Since Camus has rejected Kierkegaard's teachings regarding the religious sphere of existence and the 'quality' of the authentic 'knight of faith', and since he regards the ethical-objective sphere as merely a stage-set, all that remains for him is the aesthetic dimension of life. Indeed, Camus sees the realm of the aesthetic as the main source of authenticity in the face of the absurd. Again, this is Camus's arbitrary personal preference and does not constitute an argument for adopting this position. Thus if others are to be persuaded, there remains only literary inducement to authenticity through fiction and poetic essays.

Camus is in many ways an inverted Kierkegaard. For him, as for Kierkegaard, the notion of intentionality that sustains the authentic

178

attitude retains a vestige of rational correspondence between the subjective world of human pathos and the absurd world which controls its intensity. 'Purity of heart is to will one thing', Kierkegaard claims and leaps into absurd faith. Camus too wants but one thing – to preserve the tension of the absurd in order to continue to rebel against it and to struggle authentically with its practical implications. Kierkegaard's absurd under the wing of God resembles Camus's absurd in the Godless world of immanence. In Camus, too, we 'leap' to the dogma of the absurd.

It is also illuminating to compare Camus's stand to that of Nietzsche. In Nietzsche's philosophy, everything is open, including this very openness. For Camus, everything is open except for this openness. However, in Camus, as in Nietzsche, authenticity has much to do with the relation between the absurd authentic individual and society. According to Camus, no ethical rule can be sustained in an absurd world. 'What rule, then, could emanate from that unreasonable order?' (ibid., p. 58) asks Camus, and answers: 'There can be no question of holding forth on ethics. I have seen people behave badly with great morality and I note every day that integrity has no need of rules' (ibid., p. 57). Here Camus alludes to the many self-proclaimed moralists who preach at the city's gates while themselves eschewing morality. He describes them as having 'clean' consciences, because they never use them. For Camus, the ideal of integrity, or, in Nietzschean language, truthfulness in life, stands above the objective ethical norms of honesty and sincerity. Authenticity reigns 'beyond good and evil'; it does not require, nor can it have, ethical rules for the rational justification of actions. Authenticity is a personal, intuitive morality that springs from freedom and spontaneity without any external a priori dictates of Reason, God or History. The authority of authenticity lies in itself. Thus Camus's authentic hero 'can be virtuous through a whim' (ibid., p. 58), can experience an inner 'duty', can shield his action 'from any judgment but his own' (ibid., p. 57). Judgements as to authenticity, for both Nietzsche and Camus, cannot be the subject of any normative ethics. Only the individual can put herself on trial – a trial in which she is both judge and defendant. Clearly, this leaves open the possibility that this individual will be not just a judge, but also a murderer, like Meursault in *The Outsider*.

Camus's arsenal for fighting evil-doing is limited – conventional normative ethics is barred, of course. His claim that 'everything is permitted does not mean that nothing is forbidden' (*MS*, p. 58) is not grounded in any argument but is simply an expression of his innermost wishes. It is true that the absurd 'does not recommend crime' (ibid.), since it lacks any authority to do so, but it neither punishes nor restrains criminal atrocities and cannot even recommend that they be shunned. If 'duty is as legitimate as any other experience', (ibid.) the murder of the Arab on the Algerian beach is no less legitimate. Nor is authenticity responsible for crime. Furthermore, it too does not protect the victim. Thus the real test of authenticity is whether, without cosmic or social police, without any fear of transcendental punishment or legal sanction, one chooses not to commit crimes against others. The authentic hero of the absurd displaces normative ethics onto the realm of personal, intuitive and spontaneous morality.

Having chosen to live in society – that is, having decided against suicide – the authentic hero is obliged to pay the ethical price for his desire to live authentically, which may generate conflict with the public ethic. Cases of conflict are frequent, since the authentic posture constitutes an incessant affront to anything which attempts to control the subjective pathos of authenticity. Yet this conflict is essential. The Sisyphian struggle in the face of the absurd paradoxically demands that the individual act within society and its boundaries, even if this entails rebellion. Often the revolt fails, since there is no transcendental guarantee of its final success, and even Sisyphus tires of endlessly climbing his mountain. Like Zarathustra, who left the cave where his authenticity was formed but which lacked any human-practical content, so too Sisyphus, despite the fact that 'his fate belongs to him', will stop his struggle 'towards the heights' and return 'towards his rock' (ibid., pp. 98–9). For there to be any value in Sisyphus' authenticity, wrested with so much effort from the rock of absurdity, someone must assert it as a value that has significance for society, if only at its margins. But is authenticity viable in society? This question has not yet been addressed, though it has been strikingly articulated. There are some clues as to its answer in *The Outsider*.

II

In the 1956 preface to the American edition of *The Outsider*, Camus writes:

Meursault doesn't play the game . . . he refuses to lie. To lie is not only to say what isn't true. It is also and above all to say *more* than is true, and, as far as the human heart is concerned, to express more than one feels. . . . He says what he is, he refuses to hide feelings, and immediately society feels threatened.

(*LACE*, p. 336)

These remarks have led several commentators to claim that Meursault is an earnest hero of total sincerity, and a model of honesty who shuns any lie.[14] Camus probably had such commentators in mind when, in 1959, he answered the question 'Is there a theme in your work that you think is important and has been neglected by your commentators?' with one word: 'Humor' (ibid., p. 362). He was referring to the genre of humour most appropriate to the discussion of authenticity - irony, to which Camus dedicated a whole essay in a collection that bears a Kierkegaardian title, 'The Wrong Side and the Right Side'.[15]

For Camus, immanence and irony are closely connected on many levels. For example, there is an inherent tension between the means of expression and the meanings expressed, a tension which invokes the ironic posture. Camus's key moral terms, such as justice and happiness, are never defined or rigorously examined. Camus's irony and indirect style of communicating have much in common with Kierkegaard.

In *The Outsider*, until the moment he is sentenced to death, Meursault represents the honest and sincere hero who acts *ad absurdum* according to the prevailing ethos, exploding it from within. This gives rise to a pathos of authenticity which gradually asserts itself as he awaits the guillotine. Recall how Kierkegaard, using irony and indirect tactics, exploded the aesthetic sphere of existence from within. Camus similarly radicalizes the honest type, who lives the ethic of sincerity without any compromise, to the point where his society finds him unbearable and rejects him for embodying this impossible ideal.

As noted in the first chapter, sincerity and honesty are attributes of one who lives according to the ethic of objectivity and implicitly adopts the correspondence theory of truth. Sincerity and honesty are found where there is a correlation between feelings, words and acts; when one does not hide anything from the public eye. This is exactly how Meursault lives - by strictly applying the correspondence theory to his life. He does not 'say *more* than is true . . . he says what he is, he refuses to hide his feelings'. Camus demonstrates that society, which upholds the ethic of objectivity, sincerity and honesty, is not prepared to allow in its midst one who embodies the spirit of this ethic perfectly.

A society built on double standards, hypocrisy and worn-out slogans cannot tolerate a hero who demonstrates that virtually all its members are 'strangers' to its ethic, 'outsiders' who cannot live up to its demands. This is the real danger Meursault represents and the reason why the prosecutor proclaims him 'a menace to society'.[16]

The prosecutor asks for 'the capital sentence' because 'This man has . . . no place in a community whose basic principles he flouts without compunction' (*Outsider*, p. 102). Meursault is punished not for the murder, base as it is, but because of his utter sincerity, which calls into question the most 'honest' citizens in his community. Indeed, as Camus stresses in his commentary on *The Outsider:* 'In our society any man who does not weep at his mother's funeral runs the risk of being sentenced to death' (*LACE*, p. 335).

Like Kierkegaard's Don Juan, Meursault serves as a Trojan horse which threatens to attack from within the fundamental moral values of its society. The real Meursault, behind the ironic screen, is 'outside' this ethic, alienated from its double standards. Recall that absurdity is the lack of harmony between one's expectations and behaviour on the one hand, and an indifferent world on the other. For individuals like Meursault who feel this absurdity intensely, values such as honesty and sincerity are meaningless. When Meursault acts according to these values, the result is mechanical, almost automatic behaviour, that allows no exception or compromise, as called for by Kant's categorical imperative. Indeed, Meursault acts piously, as prescribed by this ethic, but little by little begins to perceive the hypocrisy and hollowness of its watchdogs – the examining magistrate, the press, the judge, the prosecutor, the chaplain, and so on. He becomes aware of the shortcomings of this ethic, and, while in prison, turns to his own self and to an authentic pathos that emerges in the face of his impending death. He does not retreat from this new stance, in spite of the chaplain's promises of salvation and eternity.

The story is clearly divided into two parts: a first, ironic section where Meursault witnesses the collapse of the ethic of sincerity and begins to feel the absurd; and a second where he becomes conscious of the notion of the absurd and reflects upon his life. He affirms his life and authentically faces his imminent death.

The crucial question is whether Camus thinks that, without God, one is permitted to kill in the pursuit of authenticity. I do not refer to the legality of such an act, since Meursault himself admits that despite the fact that he is not 'conscious of any "sin"; all I knew was that I'd been guilty of criminal offence' (*Outsider*, p. 116). But does Camus agree with Kierkegaard that for the sake of authenticity one is permitted to 'suspend' all moral considerations and set aside ethics? Initially, it seems that Meursault indeed suspends ethics or even confronts the accepted order to form his authenticity.

This understanding of the story, however, ignores its literary structure and Camus's basic intuitions concerning personal authenticity. We must bear in mind that Meursault does not become a hero of authenticity because he kills the Arab without any reasonable motive. His authenticity is acquired only after the murder and, more precisely, after he is sentenced to death. It is impossible, on the inner logic of Camus's absurd, for Meursault to become authentic by virtue of only one act, however extreme. If all acts are devoid of meaning and value, murder too is valueless; hence it cannot bestow upon Meursault any value, and certainly not authenticity.

In *The Outsider* Camus distinguishes between the ethic of sincerity, or any other value derived from universal reason, and authenticity as an intimate pathos of the self. Meursault's authenticity does not spring from what Gide has called an *acte gratuit*, an act devoid of any purpose, reason and meaning, like the murder of the Arab in the first part of the story, but from the manner in which he faces his death. In awaiting the execution of his sentence Meursault's authenticity is tested in the most taxing way possible – it is tested by what Heidegger, whose influence on Camus here is undeniable,[17] calls 'Being-towards-death'. Meursault's integrity lies in his not lying to himself about his feelings and convictions and not compromising about what matters to him most, even in the shadow of the guillotine. Meursault goes authentically to his death, reconciled with his self and his earthly and limited happiness.

Camus thus intimates not that authenticity licenses murder, but, rather, that it asks us to die while affirming our lives: not life in general, as the highest human value, but our own individual lives. The concluding sentences of the story sound as if they were taken from Nietzsche, where 'the eternal recurrence of the same' is the loftiest criterion of personal authenticity. Echoing Nietzsche's idea, Meursault, without any resentment or remorse, pronounces: 'And I, too, felt ready to start life all over again . . . I laid my heart open to the benign indifference of the universe. . . . I'd been happy, and . . . was happy still' (ibid., p. 120). To be happy while awaiting death at the guillotine? Is this the happiness of a masochist? Of course not. Meursault loves his life and enjoys the small pleasures it offers him, but his roots in this earthly life grow yet deeper as he approaches death. At that moment Meursault feels and perceives the harmonious bond between his feelings of absurdity and the world which, despite or because of this absurdity, is *his*. It is this insight that brings happiness to Meursault, as it does to his philosophical twin Sisyphus.

The 'outsider' is thus a hero of immanence, and the name is therefore an intentional irony. Those who believe in religions, transcendental principles, objective reason, political and messianic ideologies and the other 'isms', are the genuine outsiders in our world, which becomes, for them, merely a transitory stage, a narrow corridor to the other world or to personal or political salvation. Escape from our life here and now is nihilism *par excellence*, Camus contends, following Nietzsche. It amounts to annihilating the sole life we shall ever have. This type of escape makes us alienated strangers to our lives. Meursault is an outsider to these strangers and hence the only one who is actually at home. He affirms his life and does not flee from immanence at its end to embrace the chaplain and shield himself in God's embrace. Thus Camus is describing the inner journey of one who achieves authenticity in the face of death, but he does not justify this unjustifiable journey.

In the story, Camus never explicitly mentions 'authenticity', but its importance can be inferred from another story, where his intentions are more explicitly presented. I am referring to *A Happy Death* (*La Mort heureuse*), published posthumously, in which there is a sharp and explicit division of the story into two parts, each containing five chapters. The first part, which was actually an early experimental version of *The Outsider*, describes the inauthentic and routine pattern of Mersault's (*sic*) life. Mersault 'was ridding himself . . . of himself as well' (*HD*, p. 22). Following the murder of a rich invalid, in the second part of the story, Mersault secures a happy solitude for himself upon realizing 'that his rebellion was the only authentic thing in him, and that everything elsewhere was misery and submission' (ibid., p. 41).

In his review of *The Outsider*, Sartre stresses the link between Meursault's notion of the absurd and the literary style Camus employs to describe the climate of this absurd. He refers to the atomistic sentences in the present tense that lack any rational connection between them. They give the impression that each moment of the hero's life is completely separated from all others. No rational explanation is provided, and there is no attempt to enable the reader to understand the sometimes bizarre acts of Meursault. The sentences simply depict arbitrary facticity, providing neither softening tone nor meaningful context. This description of the intimate union between literary style and the nature of the absurd applies equally, and perhaps even more, to Camus's attempt to reduce *ad absurdum* the 'objective' ethic of complete sincerity. In his distinctively spare style, Camus builds a one-to-one correspondence between Meursault's acts and his feelings. These sentences clearly reveal that nothing is hidden, that everything is absolutely transparent and public; the hero's heart is in perfect accord with his deeds. Use of first-person language and the present tense allows us the privilege of entering into our hero's innermost life, only to discover that there is nothing to uncover: no hidden motives, no implicit feelings, only a few basic instincts such as sexuality and fear. This total disclosure is mandated so that readers will be able to track the ethic of sincerity closely, with nothing omitted – there are no secret desires or private fantasies to mystify the proceedings.

In the first part of *The Outsider* the language is terse: background is left out and descriptions lack softness. Only expressions of rejection or approval are recorded, though without justification or explanation. The narrative is so hollow it seems to parody the British empiricist 'bundle' theory of the self. This extremely harsh portrait of the objective ethic of sincerity is thus ironic, ultimately exploding to reveal the unviability of unidimensionality in the realm of human emotions and intentions. After this ethic is ravaged by the murder, Camus devotes the second part of the novel to describing Meursault's feelings, motives and world outlook. The reflective mood is especially salient in the dialogues forced on Meursault by the prison chaplain. This second part, unlike the first, is marked by a sentimental tone and a sense of happiness. In a subjective and very personal tone, it ends with affirmation of his life.

In his Nobel speech, Camus suggested that literature should disoriente us and challenge our most fundamental assumptions. In this novel Camus does exactly that – he challenges the ethos most of us consider sacred. We begin, along with Meursault, to see the preposterous in the ethic of sincerity, and we are induced, with the hero, to feel estranged from it.

Camus assumes that lucid acceptance of immanence is the only possible authentic attitude for one who feels the absurd and perceives its consequences. What constitutes acceptance of immanence? One must see that one is responsible for one's deeds and misdeeds, desires and aspirations, and say loudly: despite the worthlessness and earth-liness of my life, despite the pain and disappointment awaiting those who attempt to realize their longings, I will not forsake my legitimate will to be happy.

This attitude is expressed in the metaphor of the sun, which appears in almost all the stories and essays that preceded *The Outsider*.[18] It symbolizes awareness of the immanent nature of the world at a time when the 'stage-sets' collapse and the ethic which formerly guided our behaviour appears unreliable and empty. The sun metaphor, which is also found in the final sentences of *Thus Spoke Zarathustra*, raises the question of Camus's view on the problem Nietzsche posed regarding the viability of the authentic hero in society. Does Camus imply in this story that since authenticity is a state of mind or subjective pathos, it is necessarily individualistic and independent of society at large? Does the sun of authenticity shine exclusively for isolated individuals who, while remaining on the margins of society, are impelled to commit antisocial crimes and then die? This seems incompatible with the message at the end of *Thus Spoke Zarathustra* that the sun shines for us all, intimating that there is, indeed, communal authenticity.

At this stage Camus seems to say: 'Fine, I can do without society', an attitude personified by his psychopathic hero Caligula. However, in the play *Caligula*, written around the same time as *The Outsider*, Camus rejects the view of radical individualistic authenticity as invariably lead-ing to destructive nihilism.

III

Camus uses the figure of Caligula, the unrestrained and bloodthirsty tyrant, as a *reductio ad absurdum* argument against practical nihilism, the view that nothing is of value since '[n]o matter. It all comes to the same thing in the end. A little sooner, a little later.'[19] The 'triumph' of this destructive nihilism 'would mean the end of everything' (*Caligula*, p. 53) for 'a man can't live without some reason for living'. Inevitably, Caligula, the nihilistic hero of authenticity in the midst of absurdity, comes to a tragic end. Like Kierkegaard's Abraham, his 'purity of heart' drives him 'to follow the essential to the end' (ibid., p. 98), but this end is not the leap to absolute faith, but rather a leap to absolute nothing-ness. *Caligula* is an illustration of the failure of lonely authenticity. Caligula, who wanted to be God, determining the fates of others, declares at the end of his violent and suicidal life: 'I have chosen a wrong path, a path that leads to nothing. My freedom isn't the right one' (ibid., p. 103). The failure of negative freedom – the freedom from ethics, from the society of one's fellows and from nature (for Caligula aspires to control nature) – will inspire the audience to seek authenticity within a responsible social context.

It is intentional that Camus pursues these motifs in a play rather than a novel or philosophical essay. Well-attended performances – *Caligula* was staged hundreds of times in Paris alone – often have a powerful impact on audiences and can thus function as an effective vehicle of enticement. Around that time Sartre too was producing plays of intense existential import which focused on the ideal of authenticity. Theatre is a useful medium for conveying such messages because it enables them to be presented in an awe-inspiring manner. Viewing the horrors of nihilistic authenticity, the atrocities committed by Caligula, virtually eliminates any temptation to follow Caligula's example. The play evokes the 'climate' of the absurd and the capriciousness of its heroes, and highlights the fact that these characters have no real past and act accordingly. This is stressed by Caligula's descriptions of the present as 'an end of memories; no more masks' (ibid., p. 50). Everything is uncovered and exteriorized on the stage; everything happens and is reported in the present tense. Like the unconnected, atomistic narrative of *The Outsider*, the play consists of episodes that are unconnected with each other. Every event occurs as if *ex nihilo* and is causally unrelated to preceding incidents, a perfect mechanism for conveying the senseless climate of the absurd and its concrete horror.

Camus staged this play at the end of the Second World War, that terrible war in which nihilism reached a barbaric climax. The impact of the war on Camus was no less decisive than on Sartre, although in response to it Camus did not turn to the authenticating politics of existentialist Marxism. He did, however, manifest a decided transition from the negative freedom and authenticity of the heroic but lonely individual to the socially conscious humanism of *The Rebel* and *The Plague*. Indeed, already by 1939 – convinced that only a blind alley, the guillotine or unrestrained slaughter, awaited the hero who sought authenticity in isolation – Camus writes in the *Alger-Républicain* that 'to establish the absurdity of life cannot be an end but only a beginning'.[20] The absurd is negative, but revolt against its confines is a positive route to authentic freedom. This shift from nihilism to humanism took place before the public eye – it is manifested and even justified in *Caligula*. In contrast to Sartre's political humanism, Camus's version of authenticity is better described as immanently humanistic.

Meursault and Sisyphus are victims of society and its ethos. In *Caligula*, on the other hand, Camus explores what happens to an individual at the top of the social pyramid who can single-handedly determine the social ethos. Like Meursault, who feels only contempt for the double standards of the prevailing ethic, especially in reference to the value of sincerity, Caligula ridicules honesty and bourgeois respectability. By his words and actions Caligula manifests ironic scorn for everyday 'honesty'.[21] The play mocks the bourgeois values of the patricians who act as its tragic chorus, as the voice of the accepted ethos. This chorus of patricians stands in striking contrast to Caligula, who is desperately attempting to shape his own authenticity as well as to 'point out' to others 'the way to freedom' (*Caligula*, p. 46).

In Act I the patricians repeat the empty slogans of a moral code that has lost its credibility. Caligula, on the other hand, sums up the real state of the world's affairs lucidly and bitterly: 'Men die; and they are not happy' (ibid., p. 40). How is one to find happiness in this absurd and ephemeral world without fleeing to the illusions and deceit of the bourgeois ethic? Caligula is preoccupied with this existential dilemma until his unhappy end. He rebels absurdly against this absurd, seeking to be as a 'god on earth . . . to tamper with the scheme of things' so that 'men will die no more and at last be happy' (ibid., p. 48). Caligula's absurd revolt against the absurd intensifies its absurdity until its inevitable collapse. Caligula states that he does not 'need to make a work of art' since 'I *live* it' (ibid., p. 95), thereby becoming an authentic hero in line with the aesthetic model.

The play graphically presents us with a choice between the inauthentic bourgeois ethic of honour, sincerity and a fat bank account, and the abyss of the nihilistic jungle that swallows up Caligula, though not before he himself has slaughtered many of his fellow-citizens. Indeed, Caligula 'pushes the absurd to its logical conclusions' (ibid., pp. 82-3), demonstrating that if there is no transcendent meaning to life there is no convincing reason to subject one's actions to moral constraints. Immanence, therefore, can lead directly to the deadly embrace of practical nihilism, symbolized by Caligula's monstrousness. Caligula, like Meursault, accepts his impending death since he ultimately understands that no one can save himself on his own - that one cannot live authentically and freely at the expense of the freedom of others, or by repressing their right to their own authenticity. Only within the framework of human community is authenticity viable. Self-over-coming and creation of one's self can be performed with others but not against them. As Camus testified in a programme note to a production of *Caligula* by Hébertot:

> If his integrity consists of his denial of the gods, his fault is to be found in his denial of men. One cannot destroy everything without destroying oneself. . . . Caligula's story is that of a high-minded type of suicide. It is an account of the most human and most tragic of mistakes. Caligula is faithless towards humanity in order to keep faith with himself. He consents to die, having learned that no man can save himself alone and that one cannot be free by working against mankind.[22]

Camus understood that he had to give some content to the ideal of authentic life. This is the background to his philosophical essay *The Rebel*, and its literary parallel *The Plague*, where Camus casts the authentic hero in an active social role.

IV

Camus's second essay, written in 1951, attempts to solve the dilemma of authenticity in society. It elaborates on the central theme of *Caligula*, the difference between 'right' and 'wrong' freedom. In *The Rebel* this idea reappears as the distinction between authentic 'metaphysical rebellion' and 'historical' rebellion. The latter is political revolution engendered by ideology resorting to totalitarian regimes and mass murder to justify its particular absolutes. Camus calls such historical rebellion 'collective suicide'.[23] It arises from the nihilism that develops when individuals are 'isolated and cut off from [their] roots' (*Rebel*, p. 64); it always ends 'in chaos' (ibid., p. 65).

The shift from Camus's pre-war views to this socially oriented humanism also finds literary expression in 'Letters to a German Friend', a series of four letters written around 1943. In them Camus argues that the Nazis resorted to violence and political suppression to fill the ethical void that had opened up as feelings of absurdity spread among the masses. In a letter written to a Nazi friend, he writes:

> We both thought that this world had no ultimate meaning. . . . But I

189

came to different conclusions from the ones you used to talk about. . . . You supposed that in the absence of any human or divine code the only values were . . . violence and cunning . . . that the only pursuit for the individual was the adventure of power, and his only morality, the realism of conquests. . . . Where lay the difference? Simply that you readily accepted despair and I never yielded to it. . . . I merely wanted men to rediscover their solidarity. . . . I chose justice in order to remain faithful to the world. I continue to believe that this world has no ultimate meaning. But I know that something in it has a meaning and that is man, because he is the only creature to insist on having one.[24]

In these letters Camus tries to clarify retrospectively how the two reached such contradictory conclusions: how his friend became a zealous Nazi while Camus, as a member of the Resistance, fought the Nazis to defend 'Europe' as 'a home of the spirit' (LGF, p. 22). Like *The Rebel*, the letters teem with unequivocal value-judgements: just as Caligula's freedom was not 'right', so too the nihilistic barbaric Europe of his friend 'is not the right one' (ibid., p. 23). Camus, however, belongs to the 'free Europeans' (ibid., p. 4) who fight 'for the distinction between . . . energy and violence, between strength and cruelty' (ibid., p. 10). Yet Camus is the first to declare that in this absurd world such judgements are devoid of meaning. How then does he justify them? What distinguishes an authentic rebellion from one that is nihilistic and destructive? By what criteria is Camus's Europe preferable to the Third Reich?

Nietzsche's distinctions between the revolt of the 'slave' and that of the 'master', and between negative and positive patterns of power, are rooted in his psychological and genealogical insights, and not in any a priori ontological approach to human nature. Yet Camus does not present us with any genealogy or anthropology. Instead, his attack on practical nihilism – the road to the concentration camps and the 'isms' of the future – is based on humanism and human nature.

In 'Letters' Camus speaks of 'the truth of man', and in *The Rebel* (pp. 13-14) asserts that 'in every act of rebellion, the rebel . . . experiences . . . a complete and spontaneous loyalty to certain aspects of himself'. The rebel is one who is fed up with injustice and stands up for his dignity and for oppressed humanity. Rebellion creates values. And insofar as 'values are common to himself and to all men' (ibid., p. 16), authenticity, as a supreme value, belongs to 'a natural community' (ibid.) and is not exclusively sustained by remarkable individuals like Meursault or Caligula. 'The individual is not, in himself alone, the embodiment of the values he wishes to defend. It needs all humanity, at least, to comprise them' (ibid., p. 17). Rebellion thus makes authenticity socially viable and awakens the individual's self-respect and sense of the self as 'the supreme good' (ibid., p. 15). Camus now thinks that, in isolation from community, values are worthless, since authenticity requires 'the kind of solidarity that is born in chains' (ibid., p. 17) or in a plague, etc.

Camus addresses Sartre's claim that 'existence precedes essence', rebutting it as follows: 'analysis of rebellion leads at least to the suspicion that, contrary to the postulates of contemporary thought, a human nature does exist, as the Greeks believed. Why rebel if there is nothing permanent in oneself worth preserving?' (ibid., p. 16). Camus thus regards human rebellion in history as proof of the existence of 'a human nature' that precedes the rebellious attitude. Like Rousseau, Camus seeks to return to an authenticity rooted in this natural humanity. The 'natural humanism' he argues for in this essay starts with the rebellious posture, but uses concepts reminiscent of Rousseau's biological model to develop an authenticity capable of countering the lethal manifestations of modern nihilism. In place of the traditional cosmic police-God, Camus offers a 'metaphysical' view of 'human solidarity' (ibid., p. 17). He refers, in this context, to 'humanitarianism' as 'represented by Bentham and Rousseau' (ibid., p. 18), claiming that 'man's love for man can be born . . . in human nature' (ibid.).

Thus notwithstanding his revolt against Sartre, Camus also reverts to the objectivist-essentialist paradigm. He does not, however, unreservedly embrace Rousseau. In addition to the biological paradigm, one can also discern the aesthetic model of authenticity in the late Camus. To rebel is to create one's authentic self despite obstacles laid down by commissars of various stripes. To rebel is to create one's authenticity in a world of immanence, a world lacking any transcendental telos or rational principles. Camus contends that we can write our own life-stories only if there are no other potential authors. Thus Camus creates a sort of synthesis between the biological and the aesthetic model of authenticity: the revolt arises from human nature, but its end is to create the self.

Camus draws an analogy between his notion of the absurd and Descartes's method. Indeed, he considers himself a Cartesian rebel against the absurd: 'the real nature of the absurd . . . is an experience to be

191

lived through, a point of departure, the equivalent, in existence, of Descartes' methodical doubt' (*Rebel*, p. 8). Cartesian doubt reveals the foundation-stone upon which Descartes erected his rationalist philosophy, just as the authenticity of selfhood formed by the attempt to rebel against the absurd provides modern man with something positive to hold on to. Just as doubt is the sole guarantee of certainty, so 'the first and only evidence . . . within the terms of the absurdist experience, is rebellion' (ibid., p. 10). Given that rebellion is a collective enterprise, Camus concludes: 'I rebel – therefore we exist' (ibid., p. 22).

However, the goal of Camus's rebellion is not rational certainty but the construction of values against the background of the wreckage of rationalist metaphysical ethics. Hence Camus's aim is not cognitive but conative: actively to 'transform' (ibid., p. 10) man into the authentic creator of his selfhood. At this point Camus quotes Nietzsche: ' "My enemies," says Nietzsche, "are those who want to destroy without creating their own selves." He himself destroys but in order to create' (ibid., p. 9). In the chapter on 'Nietzsche and Nihilism' Camus stresses the positive implications of Nietzsche's teachings on authenticity, drawing a parallel between Nietzsche and Descartes: 'Instead of methodical doubt, he practiced methodological negation.' He then quotes from Nietzsche: 'To raise a new sanctuary, a sanctuary must be destroyed' (ibid., p. 66). The new sanctuary, for both thinkers, is authenticity as self-creation. This value underlies Camus's claim that every purely nihilistic revolt is basically inauthentic since it destroys but does not encourage reconstruction of positive life-patterns.

Camus emphasizes the negative power of the rebellion against what 'is' for the sake of creating authenticity – what is not. This is another Nietzschean idea: one becomes what one is when one abstains from being what one is not. Echoing *Caligula*, Camus asserts that the feeling of absurdity is only a starting-point. To move on from that point requires a positive attitude. The feeling and the notion of the absurd presume certain inherent values according to which we judge the absurd to be absurd. To feel absurdity is to say 'no' out of a spirit of rebellion, and thus to say 'yes' to something not given at present, but sought after. Hence rebellion is at the same time negation and affirmation. To say 'no' is to set limits and to indicate that within these boundaries certain values are non-negotiable. Camus mentions three interrelated values that endow us with authenticity in the face of the absurd: (1) our humanity, given our personal fates; (2) universal human nature; (3) solidarity.

Camus turns to the problem of the inauthentic solution to the dilemma of absurdity, namely, totalitarian ideologies that lead to mass murder: 'if we deny that there are reasons for suicide, we cannot claim that there are grounds for murder' (ibid., p. 7). As before, here too Camus adopts the attitude of *amor fati* in the face of immanence. Now, however, he provides a humanist-essentialist account of human nature which views life as a supreme value.'Human life is the only necessary good' (ibid., p. 6), he declares, thus rejecting suicide, murder and indifference to, or passive acceptance of, the murder of others. Life enables us to live 'the desperate encounter' between our humanity and 'the silence of the universe' (ibid.). Were we to ask Camus why such an encounter has value, he would undoubtedly reply that the confrontation moulds personal authenticity. The ideal of authenticity, then, is the force that averts suicide and murder, which threaten to cut short this vital encounter.

It is paradoxical, however, that in spite of his rejection of the 'crimes of logic' (ibid., p. 3), Camus himself uses logic to attack certain rationalizations offered to justify murder. Camus is aware that 'the only coherent attitude based on non-signification would be silence'; therefore 'the absurd in its purest form, attempts to remain dumb' (ibid., p. 8). But an authentic person creates; thus authenticity requires speech and communication. Moreover, speaking out is a pragmatic necessity if others are to be enticed to become rebels and to seek authenticity as an antidote to practical nihilism. This raises another question: what is the point of inciting to anything in this pointless world of absurdity? Camus can answer that what he is trying to do is to induce us not to be induced and led astray by alluring mirages beyond our human essence – just as Nietzsche sought to provide us with salvation from our desperate need for salvation. Camus thinks that living with contradictions is preferable to not living at all, especially as 'this basic contradiction . . . accompanied by a host of others' (ibid., p. 8) incites us to rebel, to attempt to overcome them, and to create, thereby ensuring an aesthetically authentic life.

Authentic rebellion manifests the inherent human passion for life and self-respect. The rebel attempts to reaffirm her authentic selfhood in the face of the forces that threaten to invade or subjugate it, to reaffirm her dignity as a free human being. Hence rebellion is constructive. Like Nietzsche, Camus uses various techniques of literary enticement:

metaphors (e.g. those related to 'masters' and 'slaves'), figurative speech, imagery, drama, and so on. However, unlike Nietzsche, Camus is sure that Zarathustra left his cave and returned to society to incite it to ongoing rebellion for the sake of an authentic 'sense of honour' and 'pride'.

This element of pride, central to our 'human nature', is dramatically depicted in *The Plague*. Dr Rieux, upon finding himself involved in 'an absurd situation', manages to invoke the 'pride that's needed to keep going'[25] to fight the epidemic in Oran, despite the poor results of his relentless efforts. In this allegorical story Rieux is portrayed as the Socrates of authenticity. He remains in the city to do 'the best he can' (*Plague*, p. 117) although he can flee, as many indeed do. He remains at his post 'following the dictates of his heart' (ibid., p. 272) out of sheer natural humanism that does not follow from any higher principle. To Tarrou's question

> Why do you yourself show such devotion, considering you don't believe in God?. . . . Rieux said that if he believed in an all-powerful God he would cease curing the sick and leave that to Him. But no one in the world believed in a God of that sort . . . and this was proved by the fact that no one ever threw himself on Providence completely.
>
> (ibid., p. 116)

No one, Kierkegaard would reply, but Abraham the authentic knight of faith. And Rieux is thus his atheistic counterpart. Just as Abraham's authenticity was tested and forged in an extreme existential situation, so Rieux's humanistic authenticity was acquired during the plague, which helped men to 'rise above themselves' (ibid., p. 115). But there is one significant difference: Abraham's journey was solitary, whereas Rieux was a physician who upheld the community ethic ('the law was the law, plague had broken out, and he could only do what had to be done', ibid., p. 79) and his own professional code of ethics. At the end of his ordeal Rieux 'could feel himself at one with . . . these people' (ibid., p. 278). His authentic freedom was definitely, as Camus would say, 'the right one'.

V

Our basic 'sense of honour', another integral part of our human essence according to Camus, is vividly portrayed in his short story 'The Guest'.[26] The story has a simple plot, and is written in a meticulous style similar to that of *The Outsider*. It tells of a French teacher, Daru, who lives in a remote schoolhouse on the edge of the Algerian desert. One day an old gendarme brings over an Arab who 'killed his cousin with a billhook' during a family squabble (Guest, p. 70). He hands the man to Daru, telling him that 'the order' is to deliver him to police headquarters in the nearby village. Daru does not do so, but, rather, after sleeping under the same roof and providing him with food, water and money, gives the man a choice: he can return to his tribe, or turn himself in. As Daru leaves the crossroads, he sees 'with heavy heart . . . the Arab walking slowly on the road to prison' (ibid., p. 81).

Camus does not give any explanation for Daru's act, which is the reverse of Meursault's, for 'no one in this desert, neither he nor his guest, mattered' (ibid., p. 74). Daru has no particularly warm feelings towards his guest; occasionally he even feels 'a sudden wrath against the man' (ibid., p. 70). Nor is he a chauvinist who hates all Arabs. His is simply a unique act of absurd liberation, one that is completely unjustified, as is the murder in *The Outsider*. Despite the lack of any reasonable justification, the reader feels that Daru performed a highly moral act. Outside the framework of any ethical code or transcendent value-system we recognize this as a pure expression of authentic human morality. The absurd circle that started with the absurd crime of the outsider is closed by this humane but nonetheless absurd act.

One sentence summarizes Daru's feelings about the way he ought to act: 'That man's stupid crime revolted him, but to hand him over was contrary to honour' (ibid., p. 79). Honour and dignity are values so deeply rooted in Daru that he disobeys 'the order' to uphold them. Daru does not need the categorical imperative – though Kant himself would not have acted as Daru did, as his own example of the refuge-seeker shows. In this example, pursuers ask a man who has sheltered an escapee if the escapee is in his house, putting him in an impossible bind. He must either lie to them or hand the escapee over to his pursuers: neither act can be universalized. Nor does Daru need Sartre's version of Kant's objective morality of freedom as presented in *Existentialism and Humanism*. Daru refused to obey, since no order is more valid than the ideology, ethic or regime that issues it. In a world where no historical rebellions are 'right' or authentic, according to the analysis in *The Rebel*, only the natural feelings of honour, human respect and dignity, which are prior and preferable to any ideology, remain.

Can we, however, bring the following counter-example to discredit Camus's conclusion? Suppose a war-criminal such as Eichmann happened to fall into Daru's custody: would it then also be 'right' to allow him to choose his way freely? If the answer is, even here, affirmative, where would we draw the line between 'natural' humanism and the barriers that even a humane culture must erect to defend itself against enemies who threaten to destroy it for the sake of some ideology?

There are, however, several hints that Camus is not thinking of sanctioning the Christian ethic of offering one's neck to the hangman. He himself fought to expel the Nazis from France. Referring to this chapter of his life, he writes in 'Letters to a German Friend' that he fought 'to save the idea of man'. The salient factor seems to be Daru's announcement to the gendarme that he 'won't hand him over. Fight, yes, if I have to. But not that' (Guest, p. 72). For the sake of defending cultural and social institutions, Daru is willing to fight. But when there is no imminent danger to our humanity, there is no justification for killing or turning in others.

The last pages of the story throw the contrast between Camus's atheism, and Kierkegaard's faith as portrayed in *Fear and Trembling*, into sharp relief. As Abraham led Isaac to Mount Moriah, so Daru leads the Arab. Here, however, no pillar of fire or Kantian ethics is present to provide guidance, just the desert sand and an immanent vacuum. Yet the desert is permeated by a deep sense of honour and respect for our image of man. While standing 'at the foot of the height' (ibid., p. 80) Daru listens to the authentic voice of his conscience admonishing him not to take orders from those who possess no consummately valid authority.

Alongside the implicit critique of Kierkegaard we can sense a distinctly Nietzschean idea that nicely closes the circle of heroes of authenticity we have been studying. I refer to Zarathustra's appeal to his pupils: to be loyal to his teaching and way of life they must leave him and 'go their own ways'. When Daru brings the Arab to the crossroads where he must choose, the Arab waits for Daru's instructions. He seeks some kind of order which will relieve him of the burden of choosing his own life. Following Nietzsche's Zarathustra, Camus indicates that if the student does not leave his master, the master must leave the student to choose alone. He indicates to the baffled Arab that he can choose either prison or liberty but he must choose of his own free will and assume responsibility for his own life.

This is the perspective from which we must understand the role of those whose teachings on authenticity we have examined throughout this book: like Daru, they seek to lead their readers to that crossroads where they must choose either to create their authentic selves or lose them.

Sartre puts the dilemma to a student as follows: 'You are free, therefore choose – that is to say, invent. No rule of general morality can show you what you ought to do: no signs are vouchsafed in this world' (*EH*, p. 38). Yet essentially, in this post-war lecture, Sartre returns to the Kantian paradigm of objective freedom.

The basic question, then, is whether this regression from the initial intuitions of Kierkegaard and Nietzsche regarding authenticity is inevitable if we are to make authenticity viable today. Is the flight from the earlier individualistic creative model of authenticity to some theory of human nature or some congenial ethos absolutely necessary? Is authenticity a social value that can in fact be implemented by postmodern humanity?

Notes

1   One of few books written on Camus in English claims that 'Camus can hardly be reckoned a philosopher at all' (C. C. O'Brien, *Camus* (Glasgow: Fontana, 1970), p. 60). Indeed, a British commentator who in 1954 predicted that, owing to the English 'empirical tradition' and dislike of 'the passion for morality', Camus would be considered exotic by the British, has been proved correct: see S. B. John, 'Albert Camus: A British View', in *Camus: A Collection of Critical Essays*, ed. G. Brée (Englewood Cliffs, NJ: Prentice-Hall, 1962), p. 85. To be fair, however, it should be noted that today even the French are less disposed to consider Camus a philosopher, and the popularity he once enjoyed in France has almost completely fallen off.

2   See the interview given by Camus to *Les Nouvelles Littéraires* on 15 November 1945, republished in the *Oeuvres complètes d'Albert Camus* (Paris: Gallimard 1965), vol. II, pp. 1424-5. An English translation appears in A. Camus, *Lyrical and Critical Essays*, ed. P. Thody, trans. E. C. Kennedy (New York: Vintage, 1970) (henceforth *LACE*), pp. 345-8.

3   Immanence is already a theme in Camus's earliest writings (e.g. 'Nuptials' from 1938, also found in *LACE*, p. 76). In another story, he writes:

'Between this sky and the faces turned toward it there is nothing on which to hang a mythology, a literature, an ethic, or a religion . . . no superhuman happiness, no eternity outside the curve of the days' (*LACE*, p. 90).

4 At nineteen Camus wrote 'Essay on Music', in which he examines the aesthetic import of ideas found in Nietzsche's *The Birth of Tragedy*. Camus remarks there that he is dedicating more space to Nietzsche than to Schopenhauer 'because this poet philosopher's strange personality is too magnetic not to deserve first rank' (*Youthful Writings (Cahiers II)*, trans. E. C. Kennedy (Harmondsworth: Penguin, 1980), p. 106; cf. p. 102). Camus identifies with Nietzsche's 'optimism based upon the rapture of suffering' and with his 'immense pride' (ibid., p. 110). Another youthful work, 'Intuitions' (ibid., pp. 123–34), which was 'born of great lassitude', bears a definite Nietzschean stamp and is actually a paraphrase of chapter two of the fourth part of *Thus Spoke Zarathustra*, where 'the proclaimer of the great weariness' (*Z*, p. 353) is introduced.

5 *The Myth of Sisyphus*, trans. J. O'Brien (London: Hamish Hamilton), (henceforth *MS*), p. 45.

6 'Return to Tipasa', ibid., p. 156.

7 'The feeling of the absurd is not . . . the notion of the absurd' (ibid., p. 29). Sartre also understood this, as is clear from the following remarks: '*The Myth of Sisyphus* might be said to aim at giving us this *idea* [of the absurd], and *The Outsider* at giving us the feeling. . . . *The Outsider*, the first to appear, plunges us without comment into the "climate" of the absurd; the essay then comes and illumines the landscape' ('Camus's *The Outsider*', in Jean-Paul Sartre, *Literary and Philosophical Essays*, trans. A. Michelson (New York: Criterion, 1955), p. 32).

8 '*La Nausée* by Jean-Paul Sartre', in Albert Camus, *Selected Essays and Notebooks*, ed. and trans. P. Thody (Harmondsworth: Penguin, 1967), p. 167.

9 See D. Sprintzen, *Camus: A Critical Examination*, (Philadelphia, Pa.: Temple University Press, 1988), p. viii.

10 *MS*, p. 29. It is no coincidence that Camus refers to Husserl's descriptive method several times. However, unlike Heidegger and Sartre, he did not attempt to ensure that his intuitions were grounded in a valid system and was satisfied to employ only the explicatory-descriptive side of phenomenology.

11 See F. A. Olafson's critical review of *The Myth of Sisyphus*, in *Philosophical Review*, 66 (1957), 104–7; and cf. his *Principles and Persons* (Baltimore, Md: Johns Hopkins University Press, 1967), p. 243.

12 'For us, Pascal is a great philosopher' (*LACE*, p. 234). In another essay Camus says that 'we have to choose between miracles and absurdity: there is no middle way. We know the choice Pascal made' (ibid., p. 235; cf. p. 363). Elsewhere he says: 'it's better to bet on this life than on the next' (*A Happy Death*, trans. R. Howard (Harmondsworth: Penguin, 1973) (henceforth *HD*), p. 36).

13 See Jacob Golomb, *Nietzsche's Enticing Psychology of Power* (Ames: Iowa State University Press, 1989), pp. 269-75.

14 E.g. J. Cruickshank, *Albert Camus and the Literature of Revolt* (London: Oxford University Press, 1959), p. 151; and cf. R. Solomon, who quotes other interpreters to this effect, in 'Camus's *L'Etranger* and the Truth', in his *From Hegel to Existentialism* (London: Oxford University Press, 1987), pp. 246-60.

15 'Irony' in *L'Envers et l'endroit* (*LACE*, pp. 19-29).

16 *The Outsider*, trans. S. Gilbert (Harmondsworth: Penguin, 1961), p. 101.

17 See, e.g., the penultimate sentence of 'Irony': 'Death for us all, but his own death to each' (*LACE*, p. 29).

18 See ibid., pp. 29, 59-60, 75. One of the few instances in which Camus uses the term 'authenticity' explicitly is a reference to '[an] authentic, a real light, an afternoon light, signifying life, the sort of light that makes one aware of living' (ibid., p. 46).

19 *Caligula and Other Plays*, trans. S. Gilbert (Harmondsworth: Penguin, 1984), p. 64.

20 J. Cruickshank's 'Introduction' to *Caligula*, pp. 15-16.

21 This ironic posture is also central in Camus's last novel, *The Fall*, where the 'honest' ex-judge Jean-Baptiste Clamence feels alienated from the ethic of honesty.

22 In Cruickshank's 'Introduction' to *Caligula*, p. 22.

23 *The Rebel: A Essay on Man in Revolt*, trans. A. Bower (New York: Vintage, 1956) (henceforth *Rebel*), p. 64.

24 'Letters to a German Friend' (hereafter LGF), in *Resistance, Rebellion, and Death*, trans. J. O'Brien (New York: Vintage, 1974), pp. 27-8.

25 *The Plague*, trans. S. Gilbert (New York: Random House, 1948), pp. 79, 117.

26 In *Exile and the Kingdom*, trans. J. O'Brien (Harmondsworth: Penguin, 1962), pp. 65-82.

Conclusion: Authenticity and Ethics

Most philosophical treatises end by reviewing their main arguments to show how they conclusively support certain definite 'objective' theses. This procedure, however, seems inappropriate here, given that the treatments of authenticity we have considered are unusually 'unscientific' (to use Kierkegaard's term), open-ended and tentative. Indeed, the very nature of the accounts we have examined precludes any attempt to formulate a conclusive summary.

To conclude is to reach an end together, but the authentic posture, as understood by the philosophers of authenticity, forbids me from presuming to conclude for *you* or for *us*. Each individual has to come to her *own* conclusions about authenticity. In fact, encouraging you to ponder this existential issue and to entice you into drawing your own conclusions is a central objective of this book. As Nietzsche advises us through Zarathustra, 'if you would go high, use your own legs'.

'Entice' comes from *enticier*, literally, to set on fire. I have sought, therefore, to inspire readers seriously to experiment with their lives and values, previously taken for granted. A committed search for authenticity is akin to playing with fire – the seeker may be purged and re-emerge as a genuine individual, but he may also be burned. If the attempt to become authentic does not destroy one, it can make one more genuine.

The existential question today is not whether to be or not to be, but how one can become what one truly is. Two kinds of attempt have been made to answer this question. The negative approach portrays the different routes people have taken to become what they are not; the opposite strategy is to examine literary portraits of individuals who achieve authenticity. Such concrete examples can serve as an inspiration, but cannot function as prescriptions, since there is no single exclusively valid path to authenticity; nor can there be.

From the historical perspective, however, the intuitive and individual routes to authenticity seem to be more viable and productive than the ontological-phenomenological approaches. Yet, at the same time, attaining authenticity is by no means a solitary pursuit. Indeed, what seems incontrovertible is that authenticity cannot be achieved outside a social context. The recurrent calls to strive for authenticity summon us not to embrace solipsism or nihilism, but, rather, to live a committed and active life – not in a social void or underground, but within a community.

Authenticity calls for an ongoing life of significant actions. It is actions that shape our authenticity. The thinkers we have looked at preferred action, or Heideggerian 'care', to reflection (which, Kierkegaard claims, 'freezes action') and knowledge (which 'kills action' according to Nietzsche). But meaningful activity is only possible in the context of intersubjective interaction, namely, within society.

Most accounts of authenticity are modelled on the aesthetic ideal of creativity: spontaneous creation of one's self and life. Yet no creativity is possible without the social and cultural context that provides the raw material one uses – the conventions, ideas and institutions against which one must struggle to fashion one's authentic self. Society provides the ethical norms and potential sources of self-identity that must freely and consciously be overcome, changed or assimilated into one's life if one is to become what one wants to be.

Authenticity, we saw, is best forged and revealed in 'boundary' or extreme existential situations. Yet such circumstances presuppose a social context. Even when one confronts disasters caused by nature, as, for example, Dr Rieux does in Camus's *The Plague*, these natural catastrophes require human presence and human struggle to generate existential dilemmas. On an isolated island one is measured solely according to physical criteria of survival; it would be pointless to speak of authenticity in such a situation. Authenticity does not refer to sheer factual life but to the life worth living. Even Kierkegaard, who takes the most individualistic approach to authenticity, gives, as an example of extreme circumstances which constitute an ultimate test of faith out of which authenticity can be forged, the case of Abraham's being required to sacrifice his son Isaac. Jesus too needed others – those who built the cross, and those who crucified him.

The literature on authenticity abounds in descriptions of conflicts between individuals acting on different ethical maxims. These conflicts highlight the need for resolute and authentic decisions and spontaneous actions. Nietzsche and Kierkegaard argue that one knows what one is only after realizing what one is *not*. Hence, it is essential for the individual to encounter and experiment with the various life-styles, patterns and belief-systems that arise in human society, history and ethics. Thus not only is there no theoretical incompatibility between the notions of authenticity and society; the social context is an indispensable condition of authenticity.

But can authenticity, thus understood, ever be implemented? Here too we have looked at some convincing arguments to the effect that authenticity is highly problematic at best.

The first argument has to do with the subjective nature of authenticity. If authenticity is to be embraced, it must first be desired. But it is claimed that all human values are ultimately unjustifiable, authenticity among them. There is no reason to suppose that it is any better or any more valuable to be authentic than to act inauthentically. A value that cannot be grounded and implemented by conventional (i.e. rational) means of persuasion is, by definition, not objective and therefore is devoid of ethical appeal.

The thinkers on authenticity accepted this and held that since an ethic of authenticity cannot be constructed a priori - none ever wrote a treatise on ethics, though some (Sartre, for example) promised to do so - authenticity would be manifested by willingness to embrace its subjective pathos without the crutch of a rigorous ethical code. Indeed, as a uniquely personal pathos, authenticity cannot even be argued for. Hence, its proponents lack any systematic means of demonstrating its value and must resort to indirect, mainly literary, means to induce us to become authentic. Irony is often employed to this effect. However, while irony, positive as it may be, can indeed induce subjective pathos, it cannot establish a radically new ethic. The various enticing tactics, however effective in individual cases, clearly do not suffice for widespread dissemination of authenticity and its acceptance by society as a whole. Most people, of course, do not read the 'enticing' literature; those who do and are indeed enticed by it will be unable to persuade others to follow.

Suppose we assume that authenticity can be implemented in society. This endows it with objective import. But this objective meaning undermines its standing as an individual pathos rather than a universal ethic. If authenticity succeeds in becoming an objective value, the revolt against the 'spirit of seriousness' and pompous sincerity and honesty collapses. Once it becomes an established ethic, in what way is it superior to the ethic it seeks to replace? We find ourselves where we started - with a regulative ideal comparable to those offered by Kant and Hegel! One might argue that this actually does not close the whole issue; that, on the contrary, the openness which characterizes the ideal of authenticity enables it to turn on itself in revolt.

If, on the other hand, the notion of authentic life as a personal pathos has value only within the narrow subjective realm of self-reference, why bother about whether others can be enticed into accepting it? Authenticity as a value thus seems incompatible with the motivations that inspire us to struggle to attain it.

Another argument against the viability of authenticity revolves around the problem of recognition. Since the philosophers of authenticity do not provide any criteria, however vague or subjective, for identifying instances of authenticity, for authoritatively deciding that x is authentic and y is not, how can authenticity function as an explicit value at all?

Existentially, too, the question remains open, and we are left to fulfil the expectations of existing ethical codes by conforming with their values while experiencing disgust that we are doing so. The struggle to find acceptance and security, along with our distaste for our need to do so, has a devastating effect on the desire freely to create one's authenticity.

The issue of authenticity as an ethical value is far from being adequately clarified or conclusively settled, and most of the thinkers on authenticity remain ambivalent about it. Kierkegaard requires some aspects of traditional Rationalism to cope with it, while the phenomenological ontologies of authenticity have recourse to an element quite incompatible with their subject-matter and their self-proclaimed break with philosophical tradition. Camus ends up speaking of the universal human essence, and Nietzsche voices his ambivalence by sending forth Zarathustra from the cave of subjectivity and personal pathos to an undisclosed destination. To society? To an objective ethic? It remains notably unclear. All the heroes of authenticity surveyed (including Kierkegaard's Abraham) were in fact fictional figures who remained in the twilight zone between objective ethic and subjective pathos.

In his study of authenticity, Charles Taylor warns against an unrestrained, egocentric individualism. His sympathetic attitude to the ideal of authenticity as countering the 'malaises of modernity'[1] is remarkable evidence that the issue is far from having been closed by Camus, or, for that matter, by the present study, which stresses the aesthetic model of authenticity.[2]

There is today a grave danger that we are facing the death of authenticity. Poststructuralist thought and the other currently fashionable streams of what is vaguely called 'postmodernism' attempt to dissolve the subjective pathos of authenticity which lies at the heart of existentialist concern. This study should be seen as an attempt to redress the postmodernistic devaluation of the authentic self by embarking on historical reconstruction.

Yet one thing is certain: the fact that this ideal demands serious consideration has already made many in this society more authentic. The clamour for authenticity on the part of prominent philosophers and writers of the last two centuries, and the thirst of readers for its pathos, surely indicate that in this ideal we have much more than empty 'jargon', as Adorno argued.[3] Despite the ratiocinations of Adorno and his followers, I firmly believe that the deepest longings and urges of individuals – to create their own individuality and remain what they are – cannot be suppressed.

As there is no proof of the impossibility of authenticity, the search for it will continue. And the impact of this search for authenticity is itself significant, despite the ontological or ethical difficulties involved. The search may not authenticate us, but it does make us human (as do attempts to establish an equal and just society). The very wish to live genuinely, the very attempt to become authentic, expresses courageous determination not to despair or to yield to the powerful processes of levelling, objectification and depersonalization. To be human is to search for one's true self and to yearn for authentic relations with others. While it is hard, almost impossible, to attain public authenticity within the prevailing social ethic, with its instrumental personal and economic relations, it is certainly feasible to attempt to do so – to take responsibility for one's actions and to foster true concern for others. Though the philosophers of authenticity had doubts about our ability to become authentic, they may well have been willing to settle for less – they may have simply hoped to arouse our thirst for our genuine selves and to encourage us to dare to satisfy it. Merely attempting to be what we are individualizes us from the anonymous inauthentic mass of everydayness that engulfs us. To use Heidegger's expression, we will fail 'proximally and for the most part', but we should still try, for in trying we are already succeeding.

Let me end with a personal vision expressed in terms of a musical analogy. I envisage a society of authentic individuals as analogous to an orchestra without a conductor, where each individual plays her own composition. Sometimes one member of the ensemble will be in tune with the others, but not always. There is only one proviso: no one composition can overcome the others, and no player can suppress another's self-expression. From the outside, the music produced by these individuals sounds like sheer cacophony, but for the participants each of their pieces has meaning, while the music played by the others functions as the inevitable background against which they struggle to perfect their original melodies.

How can such a scenario ever be realized? In former times, it was thought possible only if secured by Providence or the state. Could it be, however, that today we are mature enough to undertake this responsibility ourselves? That is, to work out arrangements allowing for self-creation and self-expression without impeding these processes in others? If not today, then perhaps this will someday be possible; in which case, in addition to the rarely implemented categorical imperative, a new imperative will emerge – the imperative to follow the regulative ideal of creating one's authentic self.

Finally, let us recall Kierkegaard's historical description of the emergence of the authentic ideal: 'With every turning point in history there are two movements to be observed. On the one hand, the new shall come forth; on the other, the old must be displaced.'[4] At these turning-points we will encounter the authentic individual. Just as the decline of the ethic of objectivity set in motion the appeal for authenticity, so the decline of the ethic of subjectivity in the postmodern era, and the suppression of individuality encouraged by the mass media and multinational markets, will invigorate the quest for authenticity as a personal, corrective ideal if not an objectively viable norm. Only the return to our authentic pathos can prevent the betrayal of what is dearest to each of us: our own selfhood.

Notes

1 To wit, lack of 'a higher purpose, of something worth dying for', 'lack of passion', 'the primacy of instrumental reason' and 'loss of freedom' (Charles Taylor, *The Ethics of Authenticity* (Cambridge, Mass., and London: Harvard University Press, 1991), pp. 2-10.

2 Another interpretation of authenticity stresses its origins in *auctoritas*, inherent authority. Recent American versions of existentialism, particularly those of David Carr, Robert Solomon, Merold Westphal and Bruce Wilshire, tend to adopt this interpretation: see Q. Smith, 'Bruce Wilshire

and the Dilemma of Nontheistic Existentialism', *Philosophy Today*, 33 (1989), 358–73.
3   T. W. Adorno, *The Jargon of Authenticity*, trans. K. Tarnowski and F. Will (London: Routledge & Kegan Paul, 1973).
4   *The Concept of Irony*, pp. 277–8.

Bibliography

A General surveys: authenticity and ethics

Adorno, T., *The Jargon of Authenticity*, trans. K. Tarnowski and F. Will, London: Routledge & Kegan Paul, 1986.

Berman, M., *The Politics of Authenticity*, New York: Atheneum, 1970.

Charmé, S. Z., *Vulgarity and Authenticity*, Amherst: University of Massachusetts Press, 1991.

Cooper, D. E., *Existentialism: A Reconstruction*, Oxford: Basil Blackwell, 1990.

Grene, M., 'Authenticity: An Existential Virtue', *Ethics* 62 (1952): 266-74.

Llewelyn, J., 'Value, Authenticity and the Death of God', in G. H. R. Parkinson (ed.), *An Encyclopedia of Philosophy*, London: Routledge, 1988, pp. 641-64.

MacIntyre, A., *After Virtue*, London: Duckworth, 1981.

Macquarrie, J., *Existentialism*, Harmondsworth: Penguin, 1972.

Olson, R. G., *An Introduction to Existentialism*, New York: Dover, 1962.

Olafson, F. A., *Principles and Persons: An Ethical Interpretation of Existentialism*, Baltimore, Md: The Johns Hopkins University Press, 1967.

Taylor, C., *The Ethics of Authenticity*, Cambridge, Mass.: Harvard University Press, 1991.

—— 'Responsibility for Self', in G. Watson (ed.), *Free Will*, London: Oxford University Press, 1982, pp. 111-26.

Trilling, L., 'Authenticity and the Modern Unconscious', *Commentary*, Sept. 1971, pp. 39-50.

Wahl, J., *Philosophies of Existence*, London: Routledge & Kegan Paul, 1969.

Warnock, M., *Existentialist Ethics*, New York: St Martin's Press, 1967.

Wild, J., 'Authentic Existence: A New Approach to "Value Theory"', *Ethics* 75 (1965): 227-39.

Williams, B., *Problems of the Self*, Cambridge: Cambridge University Press, 1973.

B   Authenticity, sincerity and honesty

Hampshire, S., 'Sincerity and Single-Mindedness', in his *Freedom of Mind*, Oxford: Clarendon Press, 1972, pp. 232–56.

Olson, R. G., 'Sincerity and the Moral Life', *Ethics* 68 (1957/8): 260–80.

Trilling, L., *Sincerity and Authenticity*, London: Oxford University Press, 1972.

Wood, D., 'Honesty', in A. Montefiore (ed.), *Philosophy and Personal Relations*, London: Routledge & Kegan Paul, 1973, pp. 191–223.

C   Authenticity and literature

Booth, W. C., *A Rhetoric of Irony*, Chicago, Ill.: University of Chicago Press, 1974.

Cohn, D., *Transparent Minds: Narrative Modes for Presenting Consciousness in Fiction*, Princeton, NJ: Princeton University Press, 1978.

Doležel, L., 'Truth and Authenticity in Narrative', *Poetics Today* 1 (1980): 7–25.

Jaspers, K., *Philosophy*, trans. E. B. Ashton, Chicago and London: University of Chicago Press, 1969–71, Vol. II.

Knee, P., 'Ironie et mauvaise foi', *Philosophiques* 11 (1984): 71–90.

Rimmon-Kenan, S., *Narrative Fiction: Contemporary Poetics*, London: Methuen, 1983.

Rorty, R., *Contingency, Irony and Solidarity*, Cambridge: Cambridge University Press, 1989.

D   Søren Kierkegaard

Collins, J., *The Mind of Kierkegaard*, London: Secker & Warburg, 1954.

Golomb, J., 'Kierkegaard's Ironic Ladder to Authentic Faith', *International Journal for Philosophy of Religion* 32 (1991): 65–81.

Taylor, M. C., *Kierkegaard's Pseudonymous Authorship*, Princeton, NJ: Princeton University Press, 1975.

Wahl, J., *Études Kierkegaardiennes*, Paris: Aubier, 1938.

E   Friedrich Nietzsche

Golomb, J., 'Nietzsche on Authenticity', *Philosophy Today* 34 (1990): 243–58.

—— *Nietzsche's Enticing Psychology of Power*, Ames: Iowa State University Press, 1989.

Kaufmann, K., *Nietzsche*, Princeton, NJ: Princeton University Press, 1968.

Nehamas, A., *Nietzsche: Life as Literature*, Cambridge, Mass.: Harvard University Press, 1985.

F   Martin Heidegger

Ciaffa, J. A., 'Towards an Understanding of Heidegger's Conception of the Inter-relation between Authentic and Inauthentic Existence', *Journal of the British Society for Phenomenology* 18 (1987): 49-59.

Farwell, P., 'Can Heidegger's Craftsman be Authentic?', *International Philosophical Quarterly* 29 (1989): 77-90.

Guignon, C. B., 'Heidegger's "Authenticity" Revisited', *Review of Metaphysics* 38 (1984): 321-39.

Harries, K., 'Heidegger as a Political Thinker', in M. Murray (ed.), *Heidegger and Modern Philosophy*, New Haven, Conn.: Yale University Press, 1978.

Levinas, E., *Ethics and Infinity*, trans. R. A. Cohen, Pittsburgh, Pa.: Duquesne University Press, 1985.

Richardson, J., *Existential Epistemology*, Oxford: Clarendon Press, 1986.

Stambaugh, J., 'An Inquiry into Authenticity and Inauthenticity in *Being and Time*', in J. Sallis (ed.), *Radical Phenomenology: Essays in Honor of Martin Heidegger*, Atlantic Highlands, NJ: Humanities Press, 1978.

Waterhouse, R., 'The Vacuity of Heidegger's Authenticity', in his *A Heidegger Critique*, Brighton: Harvester, 1981, pp. 179-92.

Zimmerman, M., *Eclipse of the Self: The Development of Heidegger's Concept of Authenticity*, Athens: Ohio University Press, 1981.

G   Jean-Paul Sartre

Anderson, T. C., 'Is a Sartrean Ethics Possible?', *Philosophy Today* 14 (1970): 116-40.

—— *The Foundation and Structure of Sartrean Ethics*, Lawrence: Regent's Press of Kansas, 1979.

—— *Sartre's Two Ethics: From Authenticity to Integral Humanity*, Chicago: Open Court, 1993.

Barnes, H., *An Existentialist Ethics*, New York: Knopf, 1967.

Bell, L. A., *Sartre's Ethics of Authenticity*, Tuscaloosa: University of Alabama Press, 1989.

Brinker, M. 'A Double Clearing of the Fog: Sartre's "The Childhood of a

Leader" and its Relation to His Philosophy', in L. Toker (ed.), *Commitment in Reflection*, New York: Garland, 1994, pp. 101-19.

Catalano, J., 'Authenticity: A Sartrean Perspective', *Philosophical Forum* 22 (1990): 99-119.

Fell, P. J., *Heidegger and Sartre*, New York: Columbia University Press, 1979.

Frondizi, R., 'Sartre's Early Ethics: A Critique', in P. A. Schilpp (ed.), *The Philosophy of Jean-Paul Sartre*, La Salle, Ill.: Open Court, 1981, pp. 371-91.

Glynn, S. (ed.), *Sartre: An Investigation of Some Major Themes*, Aldershot: Avebury, 1987.

Gorz, A., 'Jean-Paul Sartre: From Consciousness to Praxis', *Philosophy Today* 19 (1975): 287-92.

Jeanson, F., *Sartre and the Problem of Morality*, trans. R. V. Stone, Bloomington: Indiana University Press, 1980.

Lauder, R., 'Choose Freedom! Sartre's Search for Authenticity', *New Catholic World* 216 (1973): 269-72.

Manser, A., 'A New Look at Bad Faith', in S. Glynn (ed.), *Sartre: An Investigation of Some Major Themes*, Aldershot: Avebury, 1987, pp. 55-70.

Santoni, R. E., 'Morality, Authenticity and God', *Philosophy Today* 31 (1987): 242-52.

Smith, W., 'Authenticity in Sartre's Early Work', *Southwest Philosophical Studies* 11 (1989): 65-72.

Smoot, W., 'The Concept of Authenticity in Sartre', *Man and World* 7 (1974): 135-48.

Stone, R. V., 'Sartre on Bad Faith and Authenticity', in P. A. Schilpp (ed.), *The Philosophy of Jean-Paul Sartre*, La Salle, Ill.: Open Court, 1981, pp. 246-56.

Warnock, M., *The Philosophy of Sartre*, London: Hutchinson University Library, 1965.

H Albert Camus

Brée, G. (ed.), *Camus: A Collection of Critical Essays*, Englewood Cliffs, NJ: Prentice-Hall, 1962.

Cruickshank, J., *Albert Camus and the Literature of Revolt*, London: Oxford University Press, 1959.

Doubrovsky, S., 'The Ethics of Albert Camus', in B. L. Knapp (ed.), *Critical Essays on Albert Camus*, Boston, Mass.: G. K. Hall & Co., 1988, pp. 151-64.

Henry, P., ' "The Myth of Sisyphus" and "The Stranger" of Albert Camus', *Philosophy Today* 19 (1975): 358-68.

Schofer, P., 'The Rhetoric of the Text: Causality, Metaphor and Irony', in A.

King (ed.), *Camus's 'L'Etranger': Fifty Years On*, New York: St Martin's Press, 1992, pp. 139-51.

Solomon, R. C., 'Camus's *L'Etranger* and the Truth', in his *From Hegel to Existentialism*, New York and Oxford: Oxford University Press, 1987, pp. 246-60.

Sprintzen, D., *Camus: A Critical Examination*, Philadelphia, Pa.: Temple University Press, 1988.

Index